TELEVISION AND CONSUMER CULTURE

TELEVISION AND CONSUMER CULTURE

Britain and the Transformation of Modernity

Rob Turnock

I.B. TAURIS
LONDON · NEW YORK

Published in 2007 by I.B.Tauris & Co Ltd
6 Salem Road, London W2 4BU
175 Fifth Avenue, New York NY 10010
www.ibtauris.com

In the United States of America and Canada distributed by Palgrave Macmillan
a division of St Martin's Press 175 Fifth Avenue, New York NY 10010

ISBN: PB 978 1 84511 079 6
       HB 978 1 84511 078 9

A full CIP record for this book is available from the British Library
A full CIP record is available from the Library of Congress

Library of Congress Catalog Card Number: available

Printed and bound in Great Britain by TJ International Ltd, Padstow, Cornwall
From camera-ready copy typeset by Oxford Publishing Services, Oxford

For Veronica Taylor

CONTENTS

ACRONYMS AND ABBREVIATIONS

ABC	(ABC Television) Associated Broadcasting Corporation (Britain)
ABC	American Broadcasting Company (US network)
ABDC	Associated Broadcasting Development Company
ACTT	Association of Cinematograph Television and Allied Technicians
ACT	Association of Cinematograph and Allied Technicians
A-R	Associated-Rediffusion
ATV	Associated Television
CBS	Columbia Broadcasting System
CND	Campaign for Nuclear Disarmament
FBI	Federal Bureau of Investigation
HP	hire purchase
HTV	Harlech Television
IBA	Independent Broadcasting Authority
ITA	Independent Television Authority
ITC	Independent Television Corporation
ITN	Independent Television News
ITPC	Incorporated Television Programme Company
ITV	Independent Television
JP	Justice of the Peace
NBC	National Broadcasting Company

OB	outside broadcast
PMG	Postmaster General
RAF	Royal Air Force
STV	Scottish Television
TAM	Television Audience Measurement
TUC	Trades Union Congress
TWW	Television Wales and West
UHF	ultra high frequency
VE	victory in Europe
VERA	Vision Electronic Recording Apparatus
VHF	very high frequency
VTRs	videotape recorders
WWN	Wales (West and North)

ACKNOWLEDGEMENTS

This book could not have been written without the support of a number of institutions and individuals. I would first like to thank the Arts and Humanities Research Board (now Council) for funding the project 'Did ITV Revolutionize British Television?' out of which this book has developed. I would like to thank the staff of the former Independent Television Commission library, the British Film Institute library, the Viewing Services of the National Film and Television Archive, and Andy O'Dwyer at the BBC for all their help in supporting the research for this book.

I would like to thank friends and colleagues from Royal Holloway, University of London and from Bournemouth University for their help while I worked at these institutions. In particular I would like to mention Chris Hand, Matt Holland, Julia McCain, Jan Lewis, Marina Miltiadou and Sherryl Wilson. Other friends have provided practical and emotional support. They include Alison Preston, Ilja Gregory and Toby Pearce, and also Matt Bouch (who liked to argue about everything). I want to extend warm thanks to Dick Fiddy and Veronica Taylor at the National Film Theatre for their help, and for inspiring my interest in broadcasting history. Veronica has come to my rescue on more than one occasion, and I would like to dedicate this book to her.

I would like to thank Philippa Brewster and Susan Lawson at I.B.Tauris. In particular I would like to thank Susan for her editorial advice, which helped me bring the final manuscript to completion. I would like specially to mention Hugh Chignell at Bournemouth University for reading various chapter drafts and for discussing the ideas contained within them. This book would not have been undertaken if it had not been for John Ellis who not only gave me the opportunity to work on the ITV project, but who also has consistently offered me friendship and support in my academic career. Finally, but by no means least, I would like to thank Cathy Johnson for her advice on the book, for long debates about television, and for pretty much holding everything else together.

INTRODUCTION

This book is about the expansion of British television in the 1950s and 1960s and its relationship to society and culture. Television as a technology, cultural form and practice had existed in Britain since the 1930s, with a low-definition 'experimental' service being transmitted from BBC Broadcasting House from 1932, and the opening of the BBC's licence fee funded high-definition service from Alexandra Palace in north London on 2 November 1936.[1] Yet the passing of the Television Act of 1954 controversially broke the BBC's monopoly of broadcasting to establish commercial television in Britain. This new commercial service, which came to be known as ITV (Independent Television), was to be funded by advertising revenue and was to be made up of different regional broadcasting companies.

A regulatory body, the Independent Television Authority, was quickly set up to issue franchises to the new regional companies, and the first of these started broadcasting in the London area on 22 September 1955. The new commercial service reached the Midlands and north of England in different stages in 1956, parts of Scotland in 1957 and parts of Wales in 1958. Programme companies continued to open until 1962 when the fifteenth regional company was launched. From 1955, therefore, British television broadcasting was constituted by two services, the BBC and ITV. In the Television Act of 1963, a third television channel was awarded to the BBC, and BBC2 started transmission on 21 April 1964.[2] Just as importantly, during the same period, television changed from a minority interest watched by

1

a small percentage of the population to being a cultural activity of national interest. From 1954 to 1964 the number of television licences held in the United Kingdom, with one licence per household, rose from just over three million to almost 13 million, effectively a national audience.[3]

This expansion of television services and of the television audience also coincided with profound social and cultural changes taking place in Britain. Following a period of postwar austerity, characterized by rationing and meagre provisioning, there was a boom in the economy in the 1950s, with full employment, a house building programme, new technologies and the advent of a new consumer culture. Although consumerism had been evident in British society before this period,[4] the 1950s and 1960s were characterized by an economic affluence and social change that set it apart as a 'Golden Age'.[5]

Technological innovation and new manufacturing processes also meant that a range of new commodities was available and accessible to a mass public for the first time. They included domestic appliances such as refrigerators and washing machines, and items more associated with leisure such as transistorized radios, electric record players and vinyl records. There were developments in women's and men's fashions, an increase in the number of private cars, and an increase in the number of people taking holidays abroad. These developments led to improvements in living standards, to new forms of leisure pursuit for a larger public, and the development of new cultural forms such as rock and roll and skiffle. Importantly, these changes marked an apparent cultural shift from a Britain characterized by postwar austerity and consensus to a society marked by consumer culture, social fragmentation and individualism. So profound were the changes from the late 1950s onwards that Britain could be said to have experienced a 'cultural revolution'.[6]

In this book I shall explore the complex interrelationship between the expansion of television during this period and this social and cultural change. In particular, my analysis will be motivated by three important and interrelated questions. First, what was the impact of the expansion of television on television *itself*? This potentially raises definitional issues about what television *per se* is. As John Corner has suggested, television is a 'multifarious' object of study, made up of institutions (organizations), practices (programme making), programmes (forms, representations and aesthetics), technology and, in a wider sense, its diffuse connections with society and culture ranging from the world of politics to domestic audiences.[7] I shall consider all these aspects to show how television developed as a *whole*. It is thus necessary here to differentiate between television institutions and *the* television institution. One of the contentions of this book is that television emerges as an institution in this period – namely as a complex social and cultural set of practices and relationships that increasingly come to be defined by industrial and professional practices and by its programming. The television institutions that formed *the* television institution in the 1950s and 1960s are the BBC and ITV.

In this book I shall look at the connections and similarities between the BBC and ITV television services – both of which came to define the television duopoly until the arrival of Channel 4 in 1982 – as well as their differences. The arrival of commercial television in the mid-1950s was clearly a key moment in the expansion of television. An emphasis on the similarities between BBC and ITV is crucial here because it allows us to understand the workings of television from the late 1950s as a consolidated industrial and cultural form. To examine both television services together is also, in part, to make up for an absent history.

As Johnson and Turnock have argued, ITV has often been marginalized in British broadcasting histories because of a set of persistent prejudices.[8] This is because ITV has not been popularly or academically associated either with public service values or with the production of quality programming, both of which have been seen to be the domain of the BBC. Part of the problem, Johnson and Turnock conclude, is that there is an academic disdain for what is perceived to be commercial culture. This disdain is both intellectually and culturally inherited, and it stems in part from academic anxieties about studying 'serious' culture and from Frankfurt School type critiques of popular culture.[9] At the same time, it potentially stems from middle-class distaste for popular 'mass culture'. As a result, Creeber has argued that when academics have considered ITV they have often done so from the perspective of the impacts it has had on BBC television.[10] Such an approach, by situating changes in television as the dialectical interplay of two competing television services, however, misses some of the fundamental characteristics and complexities of television's organization, practices, technologies and programming. Here I shall therefore explore what it is that BBC television and ITV have in common, and look at the impact that their combined expansion has on television culture in Britain.

The second and third questions here are ones of context. What significance or impact did the social and cultural context have on the expansion of the television institution in Britain? And what impact did the expansion of television have on that social and cultural context? The first of these two questions clearly sets the scene in which the television institution expands in the 1950s and 1960s. As I shall explore in Chapters 1 and 2, for example, the government influenced the construction and operation of television by acts of parliament and committees of inquiry, and this raises important issues about concepts of national and public service broadcasting.

Cultural discourses about television as a communications technology since the 1930s were also to influence the development and deployment of recording technologies in the 1950s and 1960s, and this was to have an impact on television programme forms and aesthetics, as will be explored in Chapter 3. At the same time, as we shall see in Chapter 4, demographic change was also to have an impact on developments in television. The postwar baby boom, the expansion of suburbs and development of new towns, slum clearance and the development of new housing are important for thinking about the rise of television as a domestic phenomenon, and for thinking about the subject matter of much of television programming. Of course, the development of consumer culture, which will be looked at more closely in Chapters 5 and 6, is also a key constituent of the social and cultural context in which the television institution expands.

Examining the impact of television on the social and cultural context is, however, much more difficult. This is because television's 'multifarious' nature and diffused interconnections with other social and cultural activities make it potentially too big and too complex to make macro assessments that are both meaningful and academically sensible. Yet Janet Thumim has demonstrated, in her feminist analysis of the development of television culture in the 1950s and 1960s, that it *is* possible to assess the profound impact that television has made on society and culture.[11] For Thumim, a generation of young women who watched the multiple, competing and contradictory representations of women on television in this period went on to become feminist scholars in the 1970s. This means that the ability to *see* representations of women had long-term social, cultural and political impacts. Crucial to Thumim's analysis is John Ellis's theory of 'witness'.[12] For Ellis, the twentieth century was the century of 'witness' where, through the media of photography, film and television, mass audiences could see new places, people, objects and events from afar. These audiences, by becoming witnesses to events then became complicit in them. As Ellis suggests, '"I did not know" and "I did not realize" are no longer open to us as a defence.'[13] It is this seeing, knowing and realizing that politically motivated a generation of women in the 1970s. In exploring 'witness' and the representation of women, Thumim was able to understand and demonstrate how television was able not only to '*reflect* cultural change in the mid-twentieth century but also to *produce* it.'[14]

In this book, however, mainly because social and cultural changes were already taking place in the 1950s and 1960s, I shall be a little more cautious about television's role in such changes. Nonetheless, television was still to have an impact on those changes and it is important here to differentiate between the *promotion* of change and the *production* of change. In looking at the promotion of change in this book, I too shall recognize the significance of 'witness'.[15] As we shall explore, television in the 1950s and 1960s allowed viewers to see places, people, objects, events and ideas for the first time. To some extent, photography and cinema had already made this possible in the last half of the

5

nineteenth and first half of the twentieth centuries respectively. As I shall demonstrate, however, communication of these phenomena into the home on a daily basis via television was a profoundly novel experience. As television institutions expanded, with the arrival of more services and the expansion of television audiences at home, a whole nation of viewers was brought into contact with the outside world. As will be discussed, the novelty of this experience in the 1950s was felt in several ways.

Importantly, the acquisition of the television set was often a visible marker of a new found affluence, and its development was a marker of 'modernity', of entering into a new Elizabethan age characterized by the coronation, the jet aircraft and the atom bomb. While the austerity of the postwar period had been brightened by the new look in women's fashions,[16] television made a public act of looking in the 1950s a domestic phenomenon. It made the world newly visible to its audience at home. I would suggest, therefore, that while the new look characterized the late 1940s, a new visibility characterized the 1950s. This new visibility is central to our understanding of how television promoted social and cultural change.

I contend that the expansion of television institutions *promoted* social and cultural change through the development of production practices, technologies and programme forms that made culture increasingly visible in this new way; and this visibility promoted consumer culture and class conflict. At the same time, I will show that the phenomenological experience of television *per se*, as a cultural form with newly emerging practices of production and consumption, promoted, legitimized and embedded new forms of social and cultural activity. Yet there is also a sense in which television did *produce* social and cultural change. By drawing together discussion from across the chapters here, and by thinking about sociological theories of social change and media power, it will be possible to consider the profound impact that the expansion of the television institution had in the 1950s and 1960s. I conclude that the expansion of television *produced* social and cultural change because it established television, its institutions, practices, programmes, technologies and socio-cultural relations as an increasingly significant cultural form that had the *power to promote change and define social experience*. As a result, this will not only tell us about an important moment in the development of television, about a period of profound social and cultural change in Britain, but it will also help us understand the workings of media power today.

Approaching the histories

In recognition of television's multifarious nature, the approach I adopt in this book is multidisciplinary. As previously indicated, five different aspects of television can be studied – institutions, programme-making practice, programmes and genres, technologies, and the socio-cultural position of television.[17] Each of these approaches requires different methodologies and disciplinary paradigms. First, television institutions have often been the domain of institutional or political historians, involving document archives and, where possible, interviews. The main examples of this are Asa Briggs's five-volume histories of the BBC, and the different histories of ITV between 1946 and 1992 by Sendall; Potter; and Bonner (with Aston).[18] Second, to understand how television programmes are made, contemporary production studies can be conducted through a combination of interviews and participant observation, as in Silverstone,[19] but historically minded production studies would involve the analysis of archive papers and, again, where possible, interviews.

On the third approach, a number of studies in recent years have combined an analysis of programme making with programme forms and genres. Of the studies that fall within the period under discussion here these include James Chapman's analysis of action-adventure series,[20] Catherine Johnson's analysis of 'telefantasy'[21] and Susan Sydney-Smith's examination of early police dramas.[22] Programme and genre studies often focus on some aspects of their production or critical reception, but the programmes as such are subject to textual analysis.[23] As Corner suggests, however, one of the problems of conducting this kind of analysis in historical study is often an absence of programmes that make textual analysis possible.[24] One approach to this, which has much in common with archaeology, is to analyse the discourses surrounding a programme form and aesthetics, which exist in archived documents, as well as press and magazine publications from the period. This particular approach has been pioneered in Jason Jacobs's seminal study of early television drama, and has also recently been used in Su Holmes's investigation into cinema programmes in the 1950s.[25]

For the fourth approach, namely television as a technological form, Corner suggests that the work of Raymond Williams[26] and Brian Winston[27] may provide examples of how to understand television technologically while retaining cultural and media studies insights into our understanding of the phenomenon.

The fifth way to look at television is as a socio-cultural phenomenon. This, given its wide-ranging and diffuse connections, has meant it has been studied from a range of perspectives and disciplines. In the field of television studies, theories and methodologies from a range of disciplines such as sociology, social anthropology and social psychology are often adopted and appropriated. These have proved particularly influential in studying television audiences, using a range of social survey and ethnographic techniques. These disciplines have also been influential in some key works that have sought to theorize television. Most notable in the context of this book are Roger Silverstone's *Television and everyday life* and Paddy Scannell's *Radio, television and modern life*.[28]

In the light of these approaches to understanding television, it is important, as Corner says,[29] to try and understand the historical connections that operate between these five different aspects. Clearly, as Corner points out, studies that focus on a specific, single aspect of television have the benefit of depth and breadth. To negotiate the demands of a multidisciplinary approach with the advantages of more in-depth and wider ranging analyses, therefore, this book will be revisionist and theoretical. It will allow me to build on existing histories of the period that have explored their subjects in more detail and that have already looked at institutions, programme-making, programmes, technologies and wider social and cultural elements. I will look at other social and cultural histories of the period to understand better the changes that were already taking place in Britain. Crucially, I shall draw on sociological theory to understand television's relationship to social and cultural change. I will supplement this with original textual analysis of programme forms from the period by way of examples and case studies. With this combination of theory and textual analysis, it becomes possible to develop new theoretical propositions with which to make strategic links between different areas and themes.

This more theoretical approach is consistent with the idea that historical analysis is an interpretive process that has a complex relationship with facts. As the historian E. H. Carr has demonstrated, for example, facts are deployed in the service of history rather than constituting that history.[30] This is because the past (as is the here and now) is full of facts and events. The work of history is to decide what constitutes a relevant or meaningful fact. Relevance or meaning is therefore subject to hierarchies of historical values (that are subject to change), models of historical thinking (that are subject to change), and the individual historian's thesis.

The individual historian's thesis is also a theoretical construct because it makes a narrative of the past and puts it into a coherent structure. As Keith Jenkins has argued, drawing on the work of critical historiographer Hayden White,[31] 'people in the past *did not actually live stories* either individually ... or collectively'.[32] So the stories that historians tell, Jenkins holds, and the coherence and structure that historians give to the past, are effectively imagined or fictional. Events in the past were not experienced as stories or structures by the people alive at the time. For Jenkins, this means that historians need to be explicit about the interpretive framework they use to make sense of the past. In the context of television history, Corner has described such interpretive frameworks as 'normative schemes'.[33]

The interpretive framework, or 'normative scheme', here is organized mostly around a sociological rereading of historical studies of television in this period. There is a danger, of course, that by drawing on existing accounts I will potentially reproduce the preoccupations of scholars who have already studied the period, and this is a necessary evil. The historical turn in the study of television is still also a relatively recent phenomenon, and there are therefore a number of key texts that will recur here. These are, for example, Bernard Sendall's studies of ITV.[34] As discussed earlier, there is a dearth of writing on the history of ITV and its programmes compared with the BBC, so Sendall's work is particularly important here, as is that of Janet Thumim. While the latter covers much of the same period as I do, as we shall see, in this book, with its wider and more sociological and contextual underpinning, I take a different position from Thumim's more 'practical feminist approach'.[35]

For an understanding of Britain in the period, my account also draws significantly on the wide-ranging and multifaceted historical works of Hobsbawm, Marwick and Sandbrook.[36] Although in this book I shall draw on some sociological work and literature from the period, these historians have already brought together enough wealth of social and cultural detail to offer rich and vibrant histories. What will invigorate the historical analysis here, however, and this is the cornerstone of my interpretive framework, is the use of key media and sociological theorists. I include Paddy Scannell for his phenomenological understanding of broadcasting,[37] Pierre Bourdieu for his insights into taste and class conflict,[38] Georg Simmel for his analysis of the pathologies of 'modern' society,[39] Erving Goffman for his social psychology of everyday interaction,[40] and Nick Couldry for his compelling analysis of media rituals and power.[41] The significance of these theorists is that they provide the social and cultural theory by which to understand better the relationship between the expansion of television in Britain and its social and cultural context.

There is a final point here, and this relates to the period of history with which this book is concerned. Corner has alerted television historians to the 'problem of periodization'.[42] Grouping together a range of developments into a particular period can help establish relationships and patterns, but it can also place undue stress on certain relationships, or fail to notice developments over a longer term. As Corner suggests, 'The most obvious example of this is the treacherousness of decades as a way of classifying historical change.'[43] Yet, clearly, television went through significant changes in the 1950s and 1960s, and this is something on which the historical accounts concur. A lot of this change happened in a ten-year period between 1954 and 1964. In 1954 the Television Act was passed to legislate for the start-up of commercial television in Britain, the breaking of the BBC's monopoly and the beginning of a period of expansion of personnel, studios, broadcasting hours and programmes. Ten years later, in 1964, the arrival of BBC2 could be said to mark the end of this period of expansion and the consolidation of the television duopoly between the BBC and ITV, which lasted until the arrival of Channel 4 in 1982.

Janet Thumim deployed this kind of periodization, for example, in her feminist analysis of the development of television culture in Britain between 1955 and 1965. For her, this period begins with the opening night of ITV in September 1955 and ends broadly in 1965 as, effectively, the mid-1960s.[44] A similar approach was also adopted in Dominic Sandbrook's history of Britain, in which he covered the period between 1956 and 1963.

Sandbrook's rationale is that this was the period of Harold Macmillan's Conservative government and the rise of consumer society. The main title of Sandbrook's book, *Never had it so good*, is itself drawn from Macmillan's infamous phrase that seemed to sum up the new found affluence apparent in Britain.[45] Yet both Thumim and Sandbrook allude to the leakiness of these periodizations. Thumim refers to some earlier debates about broadcasting and to the significance of the period for television in the 1990s and 2000s. Sandbrook, on the other hand, sees elements that were seen to characterize the late 1950s and early 1960s in earlier periods, such as youth violence at the end of the nineteenth century and consumer culture in the 1920s and 1930s.

In this book I shall mainly focus on the period between 1954 and 1964, between the passing of the 1954 Television Act and the start of BBC2. However, I too will permit a certain leakiness with reference to developments in broadcasting in the 1930s and 1940s, as well as programme forms in the later 1960s.

The arrangement of this book

I have arranged the book in six chapters and a conclusion. In the first chapter I examine the developments that took place in the nascent television industry in the 1950s, partly spurred on by the arrival of ITV, and show how industrial and institutional practices emerged and the effect these had on discourses of professionalism, programme production and internal reflexivity about television broadcasting.

In Chapter 2 we see how television in this period negotiated between regional and national broadcasting, taking particular account of the regional principle legislated by the Television Act of 1954 and how it operated within an increasingly national structure constituted by the ITV network. We also see how discourses of nationalism were circulated in major 'media event' style programming. After examining issues of consensus and fragmentation, I go on to argue that the structuring of television via the duopoly and mixed-programme schedule offered a model of cultural centrality, but that this model should be treated with caution. I also look at issues of reflexivity and 'confidence' within the medium and its forms.

On examining the role of technological development in the expansion of television broadcasting in the 1950s and 1960s, in Chapter 3 I look at the use of film, telerecording and the development of videotape in a range of programming, including advertising, television comedy and drama. Having looked at the discourses that inhibited the deployment of recording technologies in the 1950s and before, I go on to suggest that the use of these technologies permitted an increasing range of styles and choices for producers in the 1950s and 1960s. This meant that producers were able to respond to changing preoccupations and concerns in the period. While the emphasis in these first three chapters is on the significance of the expansion of television institutions and the television institution, in the next three chapters this emphasis shifts towards the impact this expansion had on programme forms, and how programming intersected with the changes taking place in British culture and society.

In Chapter 4 we take a look at the relationship between television and major social and demographic changes taking place in Britain. A discussion on the nature of these changes, such as the development of new housing in suburbs and new towns, is followed by an exploration of how television sets became increasingly prevalent household items. I go on to assess how television depicted some of the concerns and anxieties about social change through television drama and end the chapter by examining how television negotiated distance from the local to the global by looking at ways in which the new medium brought the outside world into the home in a range of new programme forms, and the potential cultural consequences of this.

In Chapter 5 I examine how television circulated discourses of consumer culture. I explore advertising as a new form of television programming, and explore models of social aspiration in programmes such as action adventure series, women's and music programming. I then go on to explore class and 'taste' conflict in sitcoms, and then the kind of cultural judgements of taste and distaste made about programme forms such as quiz and game shows.

Chapter 6 is an exploration of the various ways in which television viewing promotes consumer culture. I examine quiz and game shows and issues of 'celebrity' in the 1950s and 1960s and the way in which some forms of television performance obscured the relationship between production and consumption of television programming. I show how television became a quotidian cultural form for the first time, and how its 'dailiness' promoted and naturalized the process of consumption. I go on to examine how television had the potential to legitimize and embed new social categories for the first time, categories that may have longer-term significance for shaping social experience. In the conclusions at the end of the book I draw together the discussion as a whole, and examine the implications of this for thinking about television and social and cultural change, and for thinking about theories of media, culture and society today.

Chapter 1
RATIONALIZATION

The growth of television in Britain in the 1950s and 1960s had four facets. First, there was the extension of television broadcasting to a national audience through a programme of transmitter construction. This was conducted initially by the BBC in the early and mid-1950s, and then complemented by a rival wave of transmitter construction in the second half of the decade with the advent of commercial television. Second, though not necessarily contemporaneous or directly commensurate with the extension of the broadcast signal(s), television came of age as a mass medium as more households adopted the new technology. Third, there was an extension of the number of hours of television broadcast each week. In 1936 the BBC broadcasted approximately 20 hours of television a week, whereas by 1950 the Postmaster General (PMG) was allowing it to transmit on average between 30 and 35 hours a week. From September 1955, after negotiation between the PMG and ITA, broadcasting hours for both ITV and BBC were extended to up to 50 hours a week each.[1] Fourth, the start-up of the new commercially funded companies radically expanded the production base of television, with new studios, personnel and equipment.

These new companies, funded by spot advertising revenue and licensed by a publicly appointed regulator, were placed around the UK to serve regional communities and to compensate for the BBC's metropolitan, predominantly London-centred bias. This expansion of television continued with the arrival of BBC2 in 1964. Across both the BBC and ITV, the emergence of a full-blown television industry meant *more* television production and *more* television programmes. This expansion had a profound impact on the range of programmes being made. Significantly, it also both reflected and constituted an important development in the relationship between cultural production, commerce and the state in Britain, and as such it marked an important stepping stone in the larger shifts said to take effect from the 1970s onwards.[2]

In broadcasting, the relationship between cultural production, commerce and the state was evident earlier in the century in 1923 when the BBC, in its genesis as the British Broadcasting *Company*, provided the rationale for the sale and purchase of radio sets. In the early 1920s radio manufacturers realized that no one would buy their sets if there was nothing to listen to. Then, in the 1930s, BBC radio had commercial competition from Radio Luxembourg and Radio Normandie, which transmitted programmes into Britain in English, with adverts.[3] In terms of programme content, from the start the BBC promoted events, stars, performers and performances that were already part of a wider entertainment economy. In television broadcasting in Britain, the BBC provided the only service (apart from some experiments by John Logie Baird in the 1920s and early 1930s) until the mid-1950s. An existing television service, too, was a rationale for the acquisition of a television set by which to receive sound and images. Nonetheless, by the early 1950s, manufacturers wanted an additional service to promote television sales and rentals further.

The relationship between the state and broadcasting in Britain in the 1950s had also been a longstanding one. Although the BBC had been free from direct editorial and institutional control from the government,[4] the Corporation had received its charter and finance by government legislation in the late 1920s. The arrival of commercial television did not substantially alter this relationship between the state and broadcasting in the 1950s. ITV, 'Independent' television, was less independent of government than it at first appears. Although commercially funded, the new programme companies were licensed and regulated by a public body, the Independent Television Authority (ITA), appointed by government and mandated by an act of parliament. The government also had the ability to change legislation to alter the shape of commercial television or even, as the Labour Party threatened to do in the 1950s, overturn legislation and take ITV off the air. As a result, the legislation of commercial television marked a degree of continuity with principles that had governed the early development of British broadcasting. These principles marked an ongoing commitment to the ethos of public service established by the BBC in the 1920s and 1930s.[5] As BBC historian Asa Briggs notes: 'As far as the constitution of the ITA was concerned, the language of the Act of Parliament of 1954 that created the new Authority was borrowed language that had related previously to the BBC. It obliged the Authority to "inform" and to "educate" as well as to "entertain".'[6]

Yet what is significant here is that the expansion of television in the 1950s and 1960s consolidated, on an industrial scale, the relationship between culture, commerce and the state. The advent of commercial television, in particular, explicitly contributed to this by placing commercial principles and imperatives within British broadcasting, and by making cultural productivity (programme making and cultural dissemination) an increasingly economic activity. Significantly, though, both BBC television and ITV stood within a triangular framework between state, commerce and culture. Occupying an increasingly strategic position in the articulation and dissemination of cultural forms, the expansion of television broadcasting in this period both required and promoted the expansion of bureaucratic and capitalist *rationality*. In the 1950s and 1960s this process in broadcasting marked a crucial step towards postmodernity where the expansion of capitalist markets was accompanied by an intertwining of state control, bureaucracy and industrial process in which culture became increasingly commoditized.[7]

It is this rationalization and its relationship with British television that is the focus of this chapter. In exploring the expansion of television, I place less emphasis on the difference between the two existing television channels, BBC and ITV (and then BBC2), than on the commonality the two broadcasters shared. I show that rationality was promoted both *in* and *through* television. First, rationalization *in* television brought about an increasingly streamlined, efficient and cost-effective mode of production. With the expansion of broadcasting, it led to both *professionalization* and *industrialization* of television broadcasting, and this had impacts on both production culture and the production of culture.

It will become clear that the expansion of television also involved a rationalization of culture *through* television, a sense of centralized cultural provision, and this will be the subject of Chapter 2. To summarize the direction I take over these two chapters, the expansion of the television institution in the 1950s and 1960s meant that the production of television programmes became increasingly complex and industrialized, and this led to an increasing diversity of broadcast outputs and genres. As a result, the evolving technological medium, organized on bureaucratized and industrial lines to service a mass audience, increasingly made visible disparate aspects of British society and culture and brought them together in a unified cultural form characterized especially by the mixed-programme schedule.

The political-economy of a new television service

According to John Ellis, three distinct eras have marked the historical development of television globally. The first was the 'era of scarcity', which lasted mostly until the 1970s and early 1980s, in which a very few channels broadcast for only part of the day. This is compared with the 'era of availability' in which television channels 'jostled' with each other for audience attention, and the 'era of plenty' in which the broadcasting industry predicts the accessibility of television via new technologies with 'interactive TV' and 'television on demand'.[8] British broadcasting in the period in question clearly falls within Ellis's 'era of scarcity'. From 1936 until 1955, with a break due to the war between 1939 and 1946, the BBC held the monopoly of high definition television broadcasting in Britain.[9] At the beginning of the 1950s, however, the BBC did not necessarily have a monopoly of television *production*.

Prior to the advent of the new programme companies that constituted the new commercial television service, independent film production for television (as opposed to in-house production for the BBC) was already evident in the early 1950s. There had, for example, been film production for television by ABDC, a company related to High Definition Films at a studio in Highbury, north London, since 1952. ABDC later became incorporated into Associated Television, one of the new television licencees based in the London area, and was in a position to show filmed programmes to members of the Independent Television Association as early as 16 September 1954.[10] This was only a matter of weeks after the 1954 Television Act of parliament had received royal assent to establish the new television channel, and just over a year before the actual launch. At the same time, as Susan Sydney-Smith has noted,[11] another film company, Trinity Productions, was making episodes of *Fabian of the Yard* (1954–57) for broadcast on the BBC and for sale abroad from 1954 onwards.

Nonetheless, until 22 September 1955 television broadcasting in Britain was effectively constituted by a single channel operated by the BBC from London. The acrimonious and bitter debates that surrounded the emergence of the second channel have been usefully described and summarized elsewhere,[12] but it is worth revisiting some key points. What becomes evident is the strong connection that emerges between state, commerce and broadcasting from the initial debates through to the setup of the new channel.

The issue of competition in broadcasting, which will be explored further below, was not entirely new, but the impetus for competition in television in the 1950s arose from a particular conjunction of factors. As Andrew Crisell argues in his book *An Introductory History of British Broadcasting*, there were three main reasons why competition became such a burning issue.[13] First, he argues that the debate surfaced because of deficiencies in the television service at the BBC. At the beginning of the 1950s there

was suspicion in the BBC hierarchy about the value of television, and more importance was attached to radio within the
Corporation. This led to some dissatisfaction among staff in the
BBC television service, and a leading advocate for a new
commercial service was an ex-BBC executive, Norman Collins.
Second, Crisell argues that there had been a change in the socio-
economic climate, a shift towards democratization, with a
backlash against what Briggs describes as the sense of managed
information and 'bureaucratic paternalism' which had characterized the BBC during the Second World War.[14]

This apparent backlash, however, might not have been so
widely felt or expressed. This was because the public was
largely absent from the debates surrounding the new channel.[15]
When the public was consulted its view of commercial television was not so favourable. In a Gallup poll held in June 1953,
only 36 per cent agreed with the idea of a commercial channel
competing against the BBC.[16] The reaction against the BBC may
therefore have been more prevalent among particular interested
parties in positions of authority or influence. This leads to
Crisell's third reason, 'perhaps the most powerful' challenge to
the monopoly, which was economic.[17]

After years of what has been known as 'postwar austerity',
Britain in the early 1950s was on the verge of economic prosperity. The end of austerity was most visibly signalled by the
end of rationing in 1954, but other economic indicators such as
rising incomes gave advance warning that the situation was
improving.[18] For this reason it is important to add here a
qualification to Ellis's characterization of the early period of
television as the 'era of scarcity'. This is because this era does
not necessarily coincide with a period of economic scarcity. In
this sense, in the 1950s, even though there were effectively only
two television channels (with the caveat that ITV was constituted by a number of programme companies), Britain experienced a major economic upturn. It was in July 1957 that the
Conservative prime minister Harold Macmillan publicly
declared that 'most of our people have never had it so good'.
This does not mean to say that there is no correlative effect
between television and the economy. It was around the same

time that Roy Thompson, chairman of Scottish Television (STV), announced that having a television station was like having a 'licence to print money'.[19]

As Crisell argues, the growth of the economy resulted in the growth in production of commodity items, which resulted in a corresponding demand for advertising space in newspapers and magazines. In 1954, for example, there was a three-month waiting list for advertising space in *Vogue* magazine.[20] Advertisers therefore saw potential in the relatively new medium of television. Indeed, as Sendall argues, a number of individuals from some of the larger advertising agencies were 'crucial' to the final success of the campaign for commercial television.[21] That said, the battle lines drawn between those in favour and those against breaking the BBC's monopoly were far from clear. As Sendall further argues, some advertisers were hostile to these new developments, and the Institute of Incorporated Practitioners in Advertising 'adopted a policy of more or less benevolent neutrality' with regards to competition because it had previously campaigned for advertising on the BBC.[22] The possibility of the appearance of advertising on the BBC in the 1950s was less unlikely than it might now seem looking back. In debates about the future of broadcasting, the BBC director general Sir Ian Jacob submitted a report to the BBC governors early in the decade outlining 'Possible Broadcasting Systems'.[23] Out of four plans discussed, three involved revenue from advertising, and one even included advertisements being carried by the BBC.

Significantly, those driving through legislation in parliament for a competitive television service were drawn from the backbenches of the Conservative Party, which had been elected to power with the slimmest of majorities in 1951. These backbenchers were comprised of a handful of individuals from the world of free enterprise and competition, and a semi-official association known as the 'One Nation Group' who were opposed to any form of monopoly and not just that of broadcasting.[24] As H. H. Wilson pointed out in his book *Pressure group: the campaign for commercial television*, the government's majority of 16 may have provided the small but cohesive band of backbench 'libertarians' with a disproportionate amount of influence over the government.[25]

Negotiations took place in the back rooms of government between Lord Woolton, the Tory party chairman, and the 'One Nation Group' to focus on breaking the BBC's monopoly in television.[26] As Sendall argues, the party leadership saw television as less important than radio, and had also felt that it had been in radio that the BBC had made its reputation. What is clear is that a deal was done allowing the Tory agitators to have commercial television as long as they left radio alone.[27] Such a move may have been seen as a matter of political expediency and would not necessarily have conflicted directly with views held at the BBC's headquarters in Broadcasting House where many in senior positions were still suspicious of the relatively new medium of television.

Of importance here, as Curran and Seaton suggest,[28] is that powerful entertainment industries, including Pye Radio, West End theatre management, as well as some advertising agencies supported the campaign for commercial television. Inevitably, as proved to be the case, the new commercial television service proved highly lucrative to its financial backers. In *Pressure Group*, Wilson went on to argue that the campaign for commercial television in parliament more or less constituted a capitalist conspiracy. These claims were followed by those of Clive Jenkins, who listed the company interests of the television franchise holders in his book *Power Behind the Screen*.[29] The official ITV historian Bernard Sendall denied such claims, suggesting (perhaps in a somewhat woolly manner) that the list of influential political figures who supported the campaign for commercial television should prove that it was not motivated by profit.[30] The Lord Chancellor, in response to such claims in 1962, also denied that the campaign for commercial competition was motivated by financial gain.[31]

It is not the purpose here to prove or reject such claims, but what is evident is that commercial enterprises *did* have much to gain from backing the new television channel. Such enterprises, in a capitalist economy, are rarely run for altruistic reasons. The point here, simply, is that with the Television Act of 1954 and the establishment of the new commercial television service, big business had a significant investment in cultural production in a major way.

Nonetheless, the new television channel was subject to strict controls. Marking a degree of continuity between the BBC and the new channel, and being under a regulatory framework legislated by government, the new channel was still subject to a level of state control. Not least, it was still in the government's gift to repeal the Act. In fear of the potentially degrading excesses of commercialism, the Independent Television Authority was established to provide a regulatory framework for the new competing programme companies. What is important is that the new channel still had to conform to a 'public service' remit in much the same way as the BBC, with a duty to educate and to inform as well as to entertain. In this way ITV had to provide a news service, as well as religious programmes, be closed for the same periods, for example the 'toddler's truce', and conform to specific rules about Sunday broadcasting. Furthermore, as a consequence of the Beveridge Report (published in 1951), which had criticized the metropolitan bias of the BBC, the new channel was to be comprised of programme companies representing regional interests. These regional services will be discussed in the next chapter and, as will be seen, a certain metropolitan bias continued to prevail.

There was also another way in which the new television channel *could* have had stronger links with government. Indeed, as Sendall has argued, had misjudgement on the part of the programme companies not interfered with negotiations, the ITA could have set a precedent for the commercial service to be partly funded by licence fee.[32] In the initial act of parliament, the ITA was to appoint commercial companies to make programmes – this programme-making function was separate from the ITA's regulatory work. However, the Postmaster General (PMG) promised that a sum of £750,000 should be made available to the ITA from the television licence fee in the event that it felt programmes should be 'made up' to maintain a proper balance of programmes. This balance was to ensure that public service, minority and 'high brow' programming that failed to attract advertising revenue should be produced as well as popular and commercially successful programmes. This money was to be especially important should the regional companies find themselves in financial difficulties.

As it turned out, the PMG was far from forthcoming in providing this money as the government did not want to be seen to be giving money away to a commercial venture in the wake of the Suez crisis in 1956. This was a political fiasco caused when the British and French governments sent troops to seize the Suez Canal after it had been nationalized by Egypt. This produced an international outcry, however, and the British and French governments were forced to back down. Not only was the military adventure a diplomatic blunder, but it was financially costly. As a result, the British government felt the need at least to be seen to be tightening its belt. Nonetheless, after much wrangling between the ITA and the government, the PMG agreed in November 1956 to allocate £100,000 to the authority for the financial year 1957/8. The payment was to be made to the ITA as, 'a purely temporary device ... for the purpose of procuring the inclusion in the programmes of items which in its opinion are necessary for improving the balance of the subject matter of the programmes'.[33] The types of programming the ITA had in mind at that time were religious services, news and related programming, educational and minority programmes. Yet the statement was made in government at a moment when the chairman of the ITA was abroad, and in his absence the four biggest programme companies (the 'big four') issued a joint statement suggesting, politely if unreasonably, that the PMG could keep his insulting sum of money. With such a public rebuff the offer of money was withdrawn. Unfortunately, the affair had been completely mishandled because the money had been offered to the ITA and not the programme companies.[34]

Bernard Sendall concedes that the PMG had probably been right to prevaricate over the money in the first instance as the larger programme companies were soon posting large profits, and were well able to afford to maintain balance within the television schedules. He goes on to argue that the larger programme companies had behaved inappropriately and exceeded

their authority because the loss of money potentially disad-
vantaged the smaller ITV companies that had been tied into
unequal networking arrangements (which I shall discuss further
in the next chapter). A short while after this incident, the
managing director of Television Wales and West (TWW) wrote
to the ITA lamenting that some of this money would have been
useful to help pay for Welsh language programming.[35] As will
be seen in Chapter 2, another Welsh programme company had
difficulty meeting its original commitments to Welsh language
programming and went out of business. In any event, what was
lost to the ITA was not so much the small amount of money
involved but the principle that commercial television could
claim a proportion of the BBC's licence fee money in the future.

Television and competition

It has often been popularly suggested that the arrival of competition in the form of ITV shook up BBC television in the 1950s.
Yet this is to misunderstand long-term developments in British
broadcasting more generally and television in particular. In the
first instance there *was* already competition in British broadcasting in the 1950s. This was between the three BBC radio
services (the Light Programme, the Home Service and the Third
Programme), the commercial Radio Luxembourg being
transmitted from abroad, and BBC television itself. Secondly,
part of the BBC's philosophy, as evidenced by the three radio
services, was based on choice. As the director general, Sir Ian
Jacob, wrote in *The Listener* in 1954:

> A public-service broadcasting service must set as its aim the
> best available in every field. ... It means that in covering the
> whole range of broadcasting the opportunity should be
> given to each individual to choose freely between the best
> of one kind of programme with which he is familiar and the
> best of another kind which may be less familiar.[36]

Indeed, television in the 1950s could have been extended to a
second BBC television service rather than a commercial

competitor. In the early 1950s, according to Jacob's article, the BBC was very keen to expand and develop, but it was under intense strain through a lack of resources, with government keeping a firm control of capital expenditure, which inhibited the development of the Corporation. Certainly one of the biggest challenges the BBC faced early in that decade was the extension of the service to a national audience through a wave of expensive transmitter construction insufficiently funded by the limited number of television licences then held. The initial capital investment had to be spent before audience members invested in television sets and licences. Yet the ambition to expand was still there, and it was publicly suggested as early as 1955 that the BBC was intending to run a second television service.[37] So the BBC was developing the television service, according to Jacob, but was inhibited by a lack of resources during the period.

The third point to make here is that when ITV did arrive in 1955, it did not look that different from the BBC. Grace Wyndham Goldie has observed that the new television service was constituted in the mirror image of the BBC, set up by statute and operated, like the BBC, via licence from the PMG.[38] It was regulated by a public body, and the members of this body, who came to be known as 'Members of the Authority', effectively had a similar function as the BBC governors. The Authority members, like the BBC's governors, were appointed from the same pool of the 'great and the good'. Indeed, the two men at the top of the ITA had been steeped in public service and arts cultures.

The first director general of the ITA was Sir Robert Frazer who had been director general of the Central Office of Information. The first chairman was Sir Kenneth Clark, who had been chairman of the Arts Council, and prior to that director of the National Gallery.[39] In organizational terms the BBC and ITV separated out editorial control from their main funding sources. The BBC received a licence fee and the ITV companies received funding from the sale of spot advertisements, but in both cases the role of day-to-day programme-making was conducted by specific production teams separated from the business of administration and management.[40] As will be seen, many of the people who worked at the ITV companies had originated from the BBC anyway, and took with them BBC ideas and ways of doing things.

One of the big debates at the time concerned the competition for audiences between BBC television and ITV. A popular and recurring view is that ITV 'stole' the BBC's audience. The durability of this view stems partly from the fact that ITV programme companies were constantly shouting about their apparent successes from the rooftops, no doubt in a bid to inspire confidence among advertisers. The hyperbole of ITV claims was, however, transparent when viewed from the ground. Writing in *Sight and Sound* in the spring of 1956, the critic David Robinson wrote: 'After the publication of the ITA's first Annual report began the battle of the statistics, which eventually destroyed all faith in figures, and culminated in the publication by ARTV [Associated-Rediffusion Television] of a triumphant half-page advertisement in *The Times* proclaiming, as it appeared, the utter rejection of the BBC's claims upon any audience.'[41]

Warming to the theme, Robinson went on to add, 'In the opinion of some statisticians who have practical concern with the measurement of television audiences, an unqualified acceptance of all the figures Sir Robert [Frazer] quotes is not recommended.' What emerges, however, is a discrepancy in the way in which the figures were calculated. The restricted number of people who could receive ITV was far outstripped by those who watched BBC. Right up until the early 1960s, the BBC had the majority audience, yet the figures published were based on those who *could* receive ITV.[42] This might suggest that where audiences had a choice, they preferred the new service. This is, however, complicated by two related factors. To be able to receive the new service viewers had either to purchase a new television set or modify their existing aerial. People who had gone to the effort or expense to access the new channel may therefore have been more predisposed to watching it. The corollary to this was that those who did not go to the effort to make modifications or to purchase new sets may have been less interested in watching ITV. The moment when the BBC was credited as maintaining a 50 per cent audience with ITV in 1962 was exactly the moment that ITV had national reach.

This is further complicated by the continuing growth of television ownership, and another supposition is that the popular appeal of ITV drove up the number of people purchasing or renting television sets for the first time. The economist Chris Hand has asserted that in the 1950s, 'It would not be correct to attribute all of the increase in the level of television ownership to the appeal of the new commercial television channels.'[43] Hand argues that the introduction of a second channel would have meant, effectively, a price cut for consumers who were buying the new ('multi-channel') television sets: they would be receiving two channels for the price of one. The significance of this is that consumers were adopting a new cultural experience in general, television, rather than this necessarily being due to the supposed appeal of ITV in particular.

What also seems evident, in the early days at least, is that both critics and audiences alike had some difficulty differentiating between the two channels. Writing in *The Listener* on 6 October 1955, the drama critic Philip Hope-Wallace stated optimistically, 'So the *TV Times* and *Radio Times* are spread out, red and blue pencils are sharpened, and presently ticks and whorls and crosses disfigure those fair pages. Kierkegaard with his "either or" could not be more tormented.'[44] Three weeks later, in *The Listener* of 27 October, however, he was writing, 'The best parlour game today is trying to decide which of two almost exactly similar programmes you wish to watch. Hesitate long enough and with luck you may miss them both.'[45]

As for the audiences, in a Gallup poll from October 1955, an unsurprising 66 per cent did not know whether ITV programming was better than the BBC. What is unclear is whether or not this 66 per cent had actually seen ITV.[46] Of the rest, 11 per cent said that ITV was better, 11 per cent said that BBC was better, and a further 12 per cent saw no difference at all. In a Gallup poll from December 1957, 29 per cent saw ITV as better compared with 19 per cent who said that the BBC was better. Meanwhile, 20 per cent said they saw no difference and a further 32 per cent did not know. Of those who did have an opinion, 39 per cent clearly did not see ITV as the better channel. This is also confirmed by a question in the same poll asking respondents to name their favourite television programme. Only one ITV show, *Sunday Night at the London Palladium* appeared in the top five. The other programmes, all BBC, were *Panorama*, *What's My Line?*, *This is Your Life* and *Hancock's Half Hour*.

It is commonly held that ITV 'stole' the BBC's audience through its variety and light entertainment shows. This might be confirmed to a certain extent by a poll that asked respondents which programme types they thought ITV or the BBC did better. For variety, 41 per cent felt that ITV did better compared with 8 per cent for the BBC. This might seem conclusive, but the majority of respondents, 51 per cent, stated that there was no difference. As another example, it has often been suggested that ITN popularized and democratized news provision. Yet the same poll has 31 per cent claiming that they thought BBC news better compared with 15 per cent in favour of ITN. Again, however, the majority, 54 per cent, saw no difference. These figures raise questions about the validity of claims that the 'mass' audience preferred ITV. What is also clear is that there was a large audience who saw no tangible distinction, or at least saw no distinction in terms of preference, between BBC and ITV in the early days. Yet even Bernard Sendall, the first official ITV historian, saw little difference in the programming between the two services, suggesting, 'the general ITV programmes were not complete innovations; with the possible exceptions of *Sunday Night at the London Palladium* and the "giveaway" shows, they might have been made, albeit in a different style, by the BBC.'[47]

This seeming lack of differentiation between the two channels is important for understanding the expansion of television in the 1950s and 1960s. The commercial and BBC television services constituted a 'duopoly' with a unity and commonality that transcended any perceived differences between them. As Bernard Sendall concedes, in institutional terms, the competition between BBC and ITV television became increasingly subordinated to a 'planned co-existence'.[48] Significantly, the expansion of this duopolistic broadcasting system had an impact on the culture of production, as discussed below, by making it internally competitive, self-reflexive, professional and industrial.

Expansion, industrialization and professionalism

Probably the biggest change in television in the 1950s and 1960s was its enormous rate of expansion, which in the BBC was in many respects under way at the beginning of the 1950s. In the 1940s the shortage of studio space was acute, and while the BBC moved into film studios at Lime Grove in 1950, plans were afoot in 1949 for a completely new, purpose-built television studio at White City in west London to be opened in the late 1950s. There was also an increase in the number of personnel at the BBC. In 1956, for example, the BBC had around 880 staff working exclusively in television, but by 1964 it had 9640 – including some technical and ancillary staff.[49] The arrival of commercial television also significantly expanded the numbers of personnel working in television. In doing so, it also helped consolidate hierarchical structures while at the same time increasing fluidity of movement within the industry.

In the first instance, the setting up of the new service, comprised of a number of regional licencees, was to provide a range of staffing and technical problems.[50] The Television Act, which heralded the launch of the new commercial service, received royal assent on 30 July 1954, and only a matter of days later, on 4 August, the ITA held its first meeting in London. The ITA envisaged a federal structure to fulfil the requirements of the act and, on 24 August, advertised the first round of licences for three areas, London, the Midlands and the north of England, with franchises split between weekday and weekends to accommodate four companies. The ITA received 27 applications and announced its decision on 26 October 1954. The London weekday contract was awarded to a company that came to be known as Associated-Rediffusion (A-R). The London weekend and Midlands weekday contract was awarded to the Associated Broadcasting Development Company (ABDC), which came to be known as Associated Television, and the north of England weekday contract was offered to Granada. The Midlands and north of England weekend contracts were later offered to the company that operated as ABC Television. These four companies came to be known as the 'big four'.

Independent Television formally began transmission in the London area on 22 September 1955, which meant that the London franchise holder, Associated-Rediffusion, had less than a year in which to start a programme company from scratch. This meant moving into a building on Kingsway in the centre of London, recently vacated by the Air Ministry, which became 'Television House', with newly equipped offices and studios, and further studios at Wembley and other London locations. More than 1000 staff were recruited to Associated-Rediffusion in this period, with many of them having to endure the dust and rubble of the frantic building work going on around them. Associated Television (ATV), being formed out of the Associated Broadcasting Development Company and the Incorporated Television Programme Company, already had access to film production studio space in Highbury, north London. It also had access to a number of theatre spaces, including the Theatre Royal, Drury Lane, the London Coliseum, the London Hippodrome and the London Palladium. By September 1955 the company had a television control centre in central London and its own theatre in Wood Green, north London. Significantly, ATV also had two outside broadcast (OB) units that were able to transmit the first *Sunday Night at the London Palladium* with the popular comedian Tommy Trinder and singer Gracie Fields during its opening weekend on 25 September. With administration, production and engineering, it is estimated that ATV recruited around 200 staff for its weekend London operation.

With the engineering challenge of building new transmitters across the country, the non-London contracts had a slightly longer period in which to get organized. The Midlands service began on 17 February 1956 and a crude partnership was formed between ATV, which owned the weekday franchise, and ABC, which was to operate at weekends. Between them they formed a joint company, Alpha Television, to set up joint studios in a nineteenth-century theatre that had been converted into a cinema. The partnership between the two companies was never easy because they were in competition for advertising revenue. Furthermore, as Sendall noted,[51] both companies had interests elsewhere (ATV in London and ABC in Manchester) and, since they used the Alpha Television studio as a kind of temporary halfway house in which to stage productions when required, neither company fully settled in the Midlands region. This was only finally resolved in 1968 when ATV lost its London contract and became the seven-day-a-week franchise holder in the Midlands.

In the north of England, the technical difficulties of transmitting a television signal across the high ground of the Pennines meant that commercial television reached the region in two separate stages. Granada television finally began broadcasting to Lancashire on 3 May 1956 and to Yorkshire on 3 November of the same year. Preparation for transmission included the construction of a purpose built television studio, including workshops and offices, in Manchester. The Granada operation also included two 'travelling eye' units, which were specially designed 'studios on wheels, capable of being serviced by mobile power generators and with sound and vision links direct to the transmitter'.[52]

The roll-out of ITV companies continued over several years. These included Scottish Television, which opened on 31 August 1957, Television Wales and West on 14 January 1958 (for South Wales and the west of England), Southern Television in the south on 30 August 1958 and Tyne Tees in the northeast of England on 15 January 1959. Further stations opened with Anglia Television for the east of England on 27 October 1959 and Ulster television on 31 October 1959. The full service was not complete until 14 September 1962 when Wales (West and North) went on air. By this time, there were 15 programme contractors in operation for 14 franchise areas.[53] This expansion in programme companies was also complemented by the Independent Television News company (ITN), which had started up in 1955 to provide an independent news bulletin service nationally across the commercial network.

The expansion of broadcasting in commercial television was also complemented by the launch of BBC2 on 20 April 1964. The opening night of BBC2 was an inauspicious beginning. A fire at Battersea power station in southwest London caused a major blackout across the capital, affecting transport, lighting and the first night of the new service. A makeshift service, with a man providing intermittent news updates from behind a desk at the ageing television studios at Alexandra Palace, replaced the raft of programmes that was supposed to have been broadcast from Lime Grove. The following night the BBC2 service began properly with a candle being blown out and the studio lights coming on.

The setting up of BBC2 marked an uneasy conjunction of broadcasting policy, political debate, technological change and the rapid expansion of the television industry. For many years the BBC had been considering a distinct and separate second television service. Indeed, the idea of 'healthy competition' between BBC broadcasting services had been openly discussed in BBC radio during the Second World War. Following the end of the war BBC radio was divided into three services, the Light Programme, the Home Service and the Third Programme, with the Reithian mission to 'inform, educate and entertain' broadly spread across services aimed at lowbrow, middlebrow and highbrow tastes respectively. As we have seen, in the early 1950s consideration was already being given at high levels in BBC management for expansion of the television service, although at that stage the immediate concern was the expensive wave of transmitter construction to extend television broadcasting nationally.

Despite these financial constraints, the BBC was already admitting publicly that it was interested in opening a second television service to extend the range of programming to appeal to more educational and 'minority' interests. Following the breaking of the BBC's monopoly of television in 1955 and the expansion of the ITV network, the government convened a committee of inquiry under Sir Harry Pilkington in 1960 to review the new commercial service and report on the future of British broadcasting. The report of the Pilkington Committee, published in 1962, was highly critical of the ITV companies for a lack of adequate 'balance' in programming. The committee recommended that there should be an entire overhaul of the commercial system and that the ITA should take control of programme planning and sale of advertising. It claimed that the ITV companies were intransigent to the power and effects of broadcasting, and ruled that a future television service should be awarded to what they deemed to be the more publicly responsible and quality conscious BBC.

It also considered technological developments taking place within European broadcasting and ruled that British television should move from the 405-line VHF system to the higher-definition 625 UHF system. The proposed overhaul of ITV was rejected, but the government did award the new television service to the BBC on the 625-line system, and this was legislated in the Television Act of 1963. The award of the new service to the BBC seemed to validate a rigorously public service mission to provide an extended range of educational and minority programming. However, the new 625-line system, to which BBC1 and ITV would later have to adapt, imposed programming restraints on BBC2. This was because viewers had to buy new television sets or modify their existing sets to be able to receive the new UHF service, and there might be little incentive to do this for solely educational or minority programming. To attract viewers to switch over to the new system, and to appease the demands of television set manufacturers and retailers, the new television service had to appeal to a much broader audience.

Yet the radical expansion of the television broadcasting infrastructure from its small beginnings at the BBC was perhaps never quite as big as the intense period around 1955 and 1956 with the start-up of the first three franchise regions. The start-up of these big companies in the mid-1950s required new personnel, and one ready source of trained and experienced television practitioners was, of course, the BBC. With such a short period of time to start up the new television companies in London, Associated-Rediffusion and Associated Television lured BBC staff away with lucrative new contracts.

The ITA's chairman, Sir Kenneth Clark, jokingly alluded to this in his speech at the inaugural ceremony of ITV at the Guildhall in London, transmitted live on the opening night on 22 September 1955. Commending the hard work of the personnel behind the launch of the new service, he said, to laughter, 'the programme companies have discovered and equipped their studios, collected – or should I say *kidnapped* – their staff.' So large was the exodus from the BBC to the ITV programme companies that Sir George Barnes, director of television broadcasting at the BBC estimated in 1956 that during a six-month period he had lost a quarter of his staff to ITV.[54] A large proportion of these were technicians. As the respected documentary film maker Harry Watt at Granada was to observe at the time, in the *Daily Express* on 8 March 1955, 'I have to get hold of men who are with the BBC. They have the monopoly of technicians'.[55]

According to Tom Burns, who conducted extensive interviews with BBC staff members in the 1960s and 1970s, the Corporation certainly did not do itself any favours by placing its own staff on short-term contracts in the run-up to the launch of ITV.[56] As Sir George Barnes at the BBC concluded, it was effectively the development of BBC training schemes that trained up existing and replacement personnel, that helped the Corporation sustain the haemorrhage of staff. The BBC was later to complain to the Pilkington Committee that ITV did not institute enough training schemes, leaving the senior broadcaster to bear the brunt of most training needs for the industry.[57]

It is evident that the emergence of the new commercial service brought an increasing degree of career mobility and fluidity to television, with television practitioners enjoying a wider range of employment opportunities. Yet, because the expansion of television broadcasting entailed an increasing degree of bureaucratic organization, hierarchical structuring and an increasingly specialized division of labour, that mobility was still regulated. This had a lot to do with the shift in the television 'institution', which increasingly saw itself as an industry and which placed more and more emphasis on professionalism. One reflection of this was the increased involvement in television during the very early days of ITV of a variety of trade unions that represented the interests of a range of staff with particular work experience and specialized skills.

Until 1956 the BBC Staff Association represented the interests of personnel at the BBC. This was the only union the BBC recognized for workers in radio and television, but it was a union that lacked any significant bite. In 1949 only 46 per cent of the BBC's staff belonged to it;[58] it had not applied for affiliation to the Trades Union Congress (TUC) and was not held to be particularly popular with any of the other unions. Part of the reason for this was that it was not particularly militant. In 1950, the association's general secretary Leslie Littlewood wrote in the association's bulletin, 'Staff of the Corporation, whether or not they are members of this Association, regard the broadcasting service as one which, above all, should be free from interruption by disputes.'[59] As a result, the other unions treated the Staff Association with some suspicion for being 'dominated by establishment orientated middle-class individuals who had no notion of "real" unionism'.[60] With the advent of commercial television, the association, as the only *de facto* union representing radio and television workers, sought to make some headway with the new companies and in 1956 changed its name to the Association of Broadcasting Staff.

Although the association had some initial success in recruiting members from the new companies, it ultimately lost out to the Association of Cinematograph and Allied Technicians (ACT) whose members were engaged in film work for the new programme companies. The power of ACT was demonstrated as early as April 1955, even before the official launch of ITV, in a dispute with Associated-Rediffusion over the recording of a television play at the Shepperton film studios. A-R fell foul of ACT by failing to recognize the rights of the union to represent its members directly in the negotiation of employment terms and conditions. ACT promptly advised its members not to work on the production, and A-R quickly acquiesced, also promising to advise the other programme contractors to enter into negotiations directly with ACT.

Shortly afterwards, to reflect its increasing interests in

television, the union became the Association of Cinematograph, Television and Allied Technicians (ACTT). The roll call of other unions involved in negotiating with commercial companies demonstrates the wide range of professions and trades, often from film and theatre, increasingly finding employment in television. In the 1950s these included Equity, the National Association of Theatrical and Kine Employees, Film Artistes Association, Electrical Trades Union, Concert Artistes Association and the Musicians Union.

Yet, the BBC had also been undergoing a period of job specialization in the 1950s. This was evident, for example, in the BBC's drama department, and it had led to new functions and job titles. One development was the inauguration of a script unit and a play library in 1949. This was to help organize the various scripts the BBC had at its disposal and to build up a raft of new works especially designed for television rather than for stage or film. This in turn helped evolve a more organized planning and scheduling policy, rather than the last-minute nature of drama programming up until that point.[61] This was also complemented two years later when Nigel Kneale and Philip Mackie were hired as the BBC drama's first television staff writers.

At the same time there were other changes. The BBC's move to the Lime Grove Studios in 1950, bought from the Rank film company, brought about a rationalization of production and planning. It signalled a strict division of labour with new ancillary departments, including make-up, costume and tele-recording.[62] This included a rationalization of administrative and communications systems with colour-coded paperwork for departmental requests. So, white forms were available for make-up and costuming, orange for captions and pink for film.[63]

The increasingly routine nature of programme production, evolving as it was into a more industrialized mode of production, also required staff who were experienced and competent in specific areas. This was reflected in the establishment of a proper training arm at the BBC in 1951. In BBC drama increasing specialization also involved, at a relatively early stage, the separation of the functions of director and producer. Until the early 1950s, the drama producer was effectively assigned to manage and 'put on' a drama production, but during this decade the technical aspects came to be increasingly designated to a 'director'. This partly emerged, as Jason Jacobs has noted, out of nurturing less experienced staff in programme production. Citing an article by Michael Barry, head of BBC television drama in the 1950s, from the *Radio Times*, Jacobs notes, 'The distinction between drama "producer" and "director" was also established during the 1950s, as part of a training process where the "director is responsible for the casting, rehearsal and transmission of the piece under the overall responsibility of the producer whose hand, probably more experienced in television practice, may be seen helping in the background".'[64]

The shift towards more serialization taking place at the BBC in the early 1950s, which will be explored further, was also responsible for bringing about a separation in the role of producer and director.[65] The development of 'striking it weekly' meant that the producer had overall responsibility for the long run of script and budget, but individual directors would be responsible for particular editions or episodes.[66] Another new function to emerge from the rationalization of television drama in the 1950s was the role of story editor. This was first pioneered under Sidney Newman at ITV in ABC's *Armchair Theatre*.[67] Comprised of single plays, this was not serialization in the sense of a long running format with the same characters, settings and casts. Yet it did involve the production of weekly live broadcast outputs using the same crews and production personnel.

One of the story editors Newman appointed was Irene Shubik who has written about the intimacy and camaraderie of working under such conditions, 'We always worked with the same excellent camera crew. Everyone concerned with the productions on a week-to-week basis knew the talents and temperaments of everyone else.'[68] When the BBC poached Newman and he started there in January 1963, he divided the drama departments into separate sections for series, serials and plays, and also established the story editor function at the BBC.[69] This helped rationalize production further with stable teams of personnel. Newman subsequently enticed Shubik to the BBC, but was to complain that working for the BBC meant having to deal with new personnel and crews. Given the further expansion of the industry with the advent of BBC2, many of the staff with whom she had to deal – directors, designers, wardrobe, make-up and camera crews – were often new at their jobs.

What is crucial here, and this is intricately bound up with issues of industrialization, is that the hierarchy and division of labour evident through routine production, staff training and the consolidation of new posts were all part of an increasing discourse about 'professionalism' in television. John Caughie has argued that the BBC's postwar television service was characterized by amateurish qualities. He claims that the arrival of competition in 1955 and developments in technology brought about increasing professionalization and the beginning of the process of institutionalization of the TV mode of production.[70] This is echoed by Susan Sydney-Smith who refers to the period 1955–65 as the 'era of Professional Television'.[71] This sense of professionalism infused a whole range of programme-making. It included, for example, news and current affairs. During the 1950s, ex-members of parliament like Christopher Mayhew and Aiden Cawley appeared on television as commentators and interviewers. Grace Wyndham Goldie, head of BBC Talks and Current Affairs, characterized this as 'the era of the MP as television commentator',[72] but as the decade wore on the 'era of the full-time professional television journalist' superseded it.[73] As we shall see in a short while, professionalism in current affairs programming facilitated staff movement between companies.

The emergence of professionalism also raises important issues about competition and about reflexivity within television production. In a very clear sense, many have argued that ITV woke the BBC from its complacent monopoly to improve broadcasting standards and to compete directly in programming and scheduling. Yet, competition was much more complicated than a straightforward battle between two broadcasting institutions might at first suggest. As I discussed earlier, the BBC as an institution was no stranger to competition. Not only had the BBC faced competition from English language radio services from abroad since the 1930s, but radio and television producers faced competition from each other *within* the BBC. Producers working in television had been competing with the BBC radio for audiences since the start of the high-definition television service in 1936. On ITV's opening night in 1955, for example, BBC television did not just face competition from the new commercial service but also with BBC radio, which killed off the character of Grace Archer in the long running soap *The Archers*. It is estimated that nearly nine and a half million peopled tuned in to this episode.[74]

There were also institutional struggles within the BBC between television personnel and a radio friendly management that was suspicious of the new upstart medium. This meant that senior television staff at the end of the 1940s and beginning of the 1950s was often in conflict with BBC management over organization and administration, resources, personnel and facilities.[75] Competition within the BBC was not just restricted to senior managers, but was also between programme-makers on the ground. While senior television personnel lobbied for additional funds, staff and equipment, producers at the hard end of programme making also had to compete with each other for resources and access to airtime for their programmes.

Janet Thumim has described, for example, how production personnel in the Women's Programme Unit of the BBC Talks Department in the early 1950s had to compete with other sections for access to resources, including trained staff.[76] Yet, despite the problem of access to resources and staff, BBC producers still had to, according to an internal BBC written report by H. Rooney Pelletier in 1951, 'develop new forms of television' and give 'professional presentation to almost any subject'.[77] A long-term spur to professionalism may have been the starvation of funds and management support, which meant that television programme-makers had to become efficient at working to tight constraints, deadlines and budgets. The pressure for programme-making resources is likely to have impelled professional competence because the television practitioner must use, and must be *seen* to be using, his or her resources competently and effectively.

This impetus towards professionalism is also likely to have meant that individual programme-makers and production personnel sought the approbation of their peers. This is because the social psychologist Erving Goffman has argued that social groups, especially occupational and professional groups, conform to what he describes as 'team behaviour'.[78] Groups such as doctors, lawyers or teachers tend to have standardized codes of behaviour and will adopt a uniform professional demeanour to other groups or teams, especially client groups. Thus doctors will all tend to behave in the same way towards patients, and teachers all in the same way towards pupils. Members of different teams, such as patients, pupils or clients, do not tend to belong to that professional world, and are therefore not qualified to cast professional judgement on good practice or professional service. Only members of the same team, one's professional peers, or those of a higher hierarchical status in the same occupation have the right to question, criticize or commend individual practice. The more 'professionalized' and rigid the nature of that occupation, such as through lengthy training or experience (often both), the less authority an alternative 'team' has in making judgements or statements. Such team behaviour is equally applicable to the broadcasting context.[79]

Individual creative practice, in a range of programme-making roles, effectively becomes more professional by the scrutiny and approbation of one's peers, not necessarily by one's audience. In his classic study of the BBC in the early 1960s and 1970s, Tom Burns observed this phenomenon when he saw that television programme makers were perhaps less bothered about what the audience thought of their programming than what their fellow colleagues or superiors thought.[80] In the 1950s and 1960s this kind of reflection was taking place in meeting rooms, corridors, staff canteens and bars. With the development of recording technology this also became increasingly formalized as staff reviewed programmes on film and videotape for training and feedback purposes, such as at BBC sport.[81]

Significantly, this was further emphasized by the expansion of broadcasting in the 1950s and increased mobility of staff. As the sociologist Georg Simmel has written, when any social group expands there tends to emerge an increasingly complex social organization.[82] As a result, within social groups marked by complex hierarchical social structures individuals in any one group may tend to have more in common with a person of similar status in another group than people of higher or lower status within their own social group. This is an appealing model in connection with the hierarchical structures of television broadcasting here, not least evident in the union activity taking place in the commercial television companies, but also among those engaged at the hard end of television producing and directing.

This was especially evident where ex-BBC staff had moved to the commercial companies. Not only did they effectively import BBC values and practices into the new companies, but they also left behind old friends and colleagues at the BBC. It is perhaps no surprise that Goldie was to write, 'there was a camaraderie at the lower levels between the television staff of the BBC and those of commercial television, however cut-throat the competition became at the top.'[83] As a result, ITV workers might have been friends with workers at the BBC and tried to impress them, and vice versa.

Within the commercial context, television workers from different ITV companies were in competition with each other for the sale of programmes to the network, and this too would have engendered friendly (and perhaps at times not so friendly) rivalries. This professional competition was particularly evident, for example, in the newly developing area of current affairs television in programmes such as *Panorama* (BBC 1953–), *This Week* (Associated-Rediffusion 1956–68) and *World in Action* (Granada 1963–98).[84] Among these programmes, and overlapping with the area of news, there was often an exchange of staff. In 1959, for example, two high profile reporters Robin Day and Ludovic Kennedy were lured to *Panorama* after they had been presenting for ITN and *This Week* respectively.

A compelling example of the emerging professional *esprit de corps* in current affairs occurred in 1963 when the ITA refused to transmit a particularly contentious edition of Granada's *World in Action* because it was deemed to lack journalistic balance.[85]

After collusion between the respective production teams, an extract of the *World in Action* programme, 'Down the drain' – about Britain's wasteful spending on defence, appeared on the next edition of the BBC's *Panorama*. This led to a senior figure at Granada and *World in Action*, Denis Forman, referring to 'the freemasonry amongst television producers' that transcended individual companies or programme series.[86] This sense of peer review, reflexivity and mutual professional respect was highly important for the development of existing and new forms of television programming.

Intricately linked with all these processes, expansion, emergent divisions of labour, a sense of professionalism and rationalization, was the increasing industrialization of the television mode of production and institution. This was particularly evident with the emergence of what has often been described as 'the programme factory'. This referred to the mass-production of programmes that can be explicitly associated with the rise of serialization, and then facilitated and consolidated by emergent recording technologies.

Serialization at the BBC can perhaps be traced back as early as 1951 to a weekly half-hour crime story documentary programme called *I Made News*.[87] This experimental programme, which emerged from the BBC's Documentary Unit, looked each week at the exploits of crime investigators in the news and included the work of, for example, the Dutch police and the United States Federal Bureau of Investigation (FBI). The actual detective in question would introduce the programme; there would be a dramatized re-enactment of events and the programme would close again with the same detective. It was significant because it was conducted as an experimental case study to see whether the BBC could handle serial production on a 'weekly strike'.[88] This had been instigated by Cecil McGivern, the controller of television programmes at the BBC, who, though not initially interested in the series form, saw the practicality of efficient practices and had been impressed by methods in the United States for weekly production.[89] The series also experimented with the separation of producer and director roles, with the producer imposing a continuous style over a series and directors being responsible for individual programmes. This constituted a more efficient division of labour and what it established, according to Sydney-Smith, 'was a more collaborative process, taking away the authority of the writer and delegating it to a team'.[90] As Sydney-Smith goes on to state:

> Series as such could not happen in 'live' television until the weekly strike had been perfected. *I Made News* introduced a new unit scheme with a single producer and two directors, each working on two separate, overlapping productions. This system of production worked on the lines of film practice, having a producer in charge of all productions, but with the newly appointed directors, responsible for rehearsal and studio presentation. The system was to remain in place from 1952 onwards and formed the basis of series television production as we know it today.[91]

The development of the series form had other advantages. As well as helping institute an efficient division of labour within a collaborative team enterprise, it was cost-effective. As the 1950s developed, there was an increase of serialization in forms ranging from cop shows like *Dixon of Dock Green* and soap operas such as *The Grove Family*, to the filmed adventure series associated with the new ITV companies like *The Adventures of Robin Hood*. These provided a way of making programmes on the basis of an 'economy of scale', where production costs could be offset on a weekly basis by the repeat use of sets and costumes. Each week the same police station set, suburban living room or wardrobe of green tights could be wheeled out without any great additional expenditure.

The cost-efficiency could also be applied, initially, to cast members, with actors hired at a job lot rate across a series rather than paid perhaps a slightly higher amount for a single play. Although individual actors might earn less for a single programme hour, they would certainly benefit from having continuous employment and a regular, stable wage. The advent of serialization certainly had a number of advantages, yet this was particularly consolidated by the increased use of recording

technology. The development of recording television programmes will be explored in more depth in Chapter 3, but it is
worth noting here that recording helped facilitate a mode of
production that was more efficient in its use of staff, crew, cast,
studio space and equipment as and when they were available.
This in turn had an impact on programme aesthetics.

Programmes and criticism

The expansion and rationalization of television broadcasting in
the 1950s and early 1960s clearly led to an expanded range of
television outputs, both quantitatively and qualitatively. The
quantitative increase in the number of television channels, from
one to three, with an increase also in broadcasting hours in the
day, entailed the production of *more* television programmes. The
qualitative expansion of broadcasting, on the other hand, can be
considered in two interrelated ways. First, it can be understood
as the dramatic expansion of the range of programmes being
made, of different tone, style, format and genre at the end of the
1950s and early 1960s. These included new kinds of quiz and
game shows. In drama it meant new kinds of series and serials,
including soap operas, cop shows and filmed adventure series
ranging from the costumed swashbuckler to the modern action-
spy hero. It also included new kinds of news and current affairs
programme, from which the satire boom on television found its
antecedents, new forms of sitcom, and new forms of music
programme. Yet, as I have discussed, these new changes were
not *simply* propelled by the advent of commercial television, but
were part of a more diffuse form of reflexivity brought about by
rationalization, professionalization and industrialization.

The second qualitative expansion in broadcasting relates to
the kinds of quality assessments to which this expanded range
of programming was subjected. As we have seen, increasing
professionalism and competence in programme production
required the scrutiny and approbation of one's television peers.
These issues became explored in a range of different media as
television increasingly became the subject of interest. Janet
Thumin argues that over this period there was a dearth of

serious television criticism in the press, with only short reviews appearing regularly in some of the broadsheets and tabloid newspapers. Thumim argues that this presented a potential problem for programme makers looking for useful critical feedback, such as in the area of television drama.[92]

Nonetheless, it should be noted that what limited press criticism there was complemented other print media, in magazines and books, which generated and catered for a broader public interest in television. This included the *TV Mirror*, *The Listener*, the yearly roundup in the *Television Annual*, and weekly listings magazines such as the *Radio Times* and *TV Times*. More specifically, however, space for industry discussion and reflection was provided in a range of trade magazines and trade union newsletters. These included, for example, *Ariel* (1936–) the weekly staff newspaper of the BBC, *Television Mail* (1959–73), which later became *Broadcast* (1973–), and *Admap* (1964–), a monthly magazine for the media, advertising and marketing industries.

Print media discourses surrounding television were also accompanied by self-referentiality in television. This is discussed further in the next chapter, but a useful example here would include the BBC's *Points of View*, which has run since 1961 and was initially presented by Robert Robinson, a programme allowing viewers to write in and complain, or praise, the BBC's television outputs. Other programmes, like the ATV documentary *The Dream Machine*, broadcast on ITV on 11 November 1964, explored the production of a television variety show, and the show's producer, Francis Essex, is seen in the staff bar explaining his philosophy of programme production. In these and other programmes, implicit value judgements were made about broadcast outputs in the period. It has been argued that a preoccupation with the workings of television on television can potentially indicate a lack of confidence and maturity within the medium. Su Holmes has suggested, for example, that the depiction of the workings of television (and film) in the early 1950s in the cinema programme *Current Release* (BBC 1952–53) indicates a self-consciousness about television as a new technology.[93] In a different context, writing about radio in the

1930s, Paddy Scannell and David Cardiff argue that the lampooning of serious radio outputs in light entertainment programmes in the 1930s also reflected self-consciousness and lack of maturity in the radio medium.[94] What I argue, and shall explore further in the next chapter, is that by the 1960s some of the programme forms that are reflexive about television and that show its workings demonstrate a self-assuredness and professional confidence.

Moral judgements were also made about broadcasting in public and political debates. Concern was being expressed about the power of television over its audience, and in 1958 the Nuffield Foundation published its results of a study of television and children, and this was followed by joint research conducted by the BBC and ITV. The schoolteacher Mary Whitehouse launched a campaign to 'clean up' television, and the first convention of the National Viewers and Listeners Association was held in 1967. Politically, a clear articulation of the kinds of moral questions relating to broadcasting were found in the Pilkington Report, which accused ITV of trivialization and pandering to 'populist' tastes out of commercial interest. As we shall discuss in the next chapter, such accusations reflected a clear middle-class bias, replicating values derived from a Victorian culture predicated on paternalism and philanthropy. The so-called working classes, in whose interests these Victorianist descendants were claiming to speak, may have felt differently.[95] These political debates impacted on the television industry through legislation and its onward impact on BBC charter renewal and ITV franchise rounds. The kinds of moral judgements made in these political debates also had aesthetic consequences. In the mid-1960s, for example, the serious intent and disorientating narrative and style of the ITV drama series *The Prisoner* (ATV 1967–68) could be seen as a response to some of the criticisms of 'trivialization' made by the Pilkington Committee.[96]

To sum up briefly, the arrival of ITV in 1955 marked a continuity with the public service values and state sanction that had previously characterized BBC radio and television services. While the BBC had not existed in a commerce-free vacuum, for radio and television services provided a rationale for marketing radio and television receivers, the arrival of ITV brought the triangular relationship between state, commerce and culture into sharper focus. Furthermore, the arrival of ITV companies (and the subsequent arrival of BBC2) characterized a radical expansion of the television institution.

As I have argued, this expansion helped accelerate the emerging tendency towards a more rational, industrialized mode of production within television, and new discourses of professionalism and organizational structures started to institutionalize programme-making practices. This expansion, coupled with the development of new broadcasting technologies, as I shall argue in Chapter 3, was to have a significant impact on the number, sophistication and diversity of programmes being made. Yet, significantly, this rationalization of the emerging television industry coincided with the extension of television to a national audience. As a consequence, not only did expansion of the television institution lead to a rationalization of the emergent television industry itself, but it also entailed an increasingly centralized form of cultural provision. This will be explored in the next chapter.

Chapter 2
CENTRALIZATION

In the period immediately following the Second World War, it has been popularly suggested that Britain was marked by a degree of cultural and social consensus. Britain had, after all, emerged triumphant from seven years of gruelling war. This was a war in which national conscription forced young men from around the country, from different social strata, to fight common enemies together. On the home front, a civilian population not only rallied round to support the 'war effort' but also had to endure rationing and the blackout. Parts of the civilian population were effectively placed in the frontline as British cities and industrial centres faced intense aerial bombardment. The sense of collective spirit was ideologically emphasized in UK wartime propaganda films like *In Which We Serve* (directed by Noel Coward and David Lean in 1942) and *Fires Were Started* (directed by Humphrey Jennings in 1943), and found daily iteration in the collective experience of listening to BBC radio broadcasts.[1]

Yet, despite the collective rhetoric of cultural forms during the war, the sense of unity and shared purpose may not have been evenly felt or experienced. Angus Calder, for example, in his book *The myth of the blitz*,[2] argues that there was a gap between reality and the 'myth' about the home front during the Second World War. Despite the myth of the 'blitz spirit', of everyone pulling together, parts of British life were still characterized by a range of social ills as they had been during peacetime, from adultery and illegitimate children on the one hand to looting, crime and black marketeering on the other. There were also different experiences following the war. One marker of this was the wide political division about the future of Britain manifested in the results of the 1945 general election.[3] Another was the different geographical experiences of war and its aftermath across Britain.[4] 'The tangible effects of the war … were distributed unevenly as if by some ferocious, but casual, wizardry. Tracts of London, Merseyside, the Midlands, Plymouth, Clydeside, and many historic towns besides, lay desolate; in other areas, new factories, new roads, new bridges, gave an air of bustle and prosperity which had been lacking for a generation.'[5]

One way in which a *sense* of consensus was sustained following the war was through centralized cultural provision. During this period, culture was perceived to be the 'high modernist' arts, in architecture, sculpture, painting, music and literature, often sponsored by the state and promoted by the establishment. This reflected what has been described as an 'Arnoldian consensus' after the Victorian philanthropist Matthew Arnold.[6] In his influential book, *Culture and anarchy*, first published in 1869,[7] Arnold argued that intellectuals and artists should take an important lead in social and cultural affairs. Echoes of this thinking were clearly found in an establishment consensus in the 1940s and 1950s that cultural institutions such as the Arts Council, National Trust and BBC should play an important role in the country's intellectual and cultural life. This consensus was clearly articulated in the relationship between the Arts Council and the BBC because, as the historian Richard Weight has argued, 'the success of the Council's work "on the ground" depended to a large extent on the BBC's ability to prepare a mass audience for it.'[8]

This cultural promotion was effectively fulfilled by the BBC's Third Programme on radio, and its constituency was a new cultural establishment of artists, composers, writers and intellectuals. This establishment was fiercely *for* the promotion of 'high culture' and fearful of American mass consumer culture. As Weight suggests, 'As a result, the canteens of the Arts

Council and BBC became as fierce a battleground to prevent American supremacy as the committee rooms of the Foreign and Colonial Office in the 1940s and early 1950s.'[9]

The debates about high and low culture over this period were, of course, to find their acrimonious articulation over the advent of commercial television, undermining any notion of an easy cultural or political consensus. Weight has argued that the arrival of ITV signalled the end of the 'Arnoldian consensus' and marked an apparent shift towards a more fragmented and individualized society.[10] It was the explicit promotion of the arts at an elite level, however, that led the Cambridge academic Raymond Williams to argue that Britain up to the 1950s had been characterized by two cultures – an establishment arts culture and a working-class popular culture that was hardly visible.[11] In most intellectual and academic discourses at the time working-class culture was barely 'culture' at all (a view that still finds expression today, in some quarters, as an antipathy towards the academic study of television, the media and popular culture).

In the postwar period, Krishan Kumar has suggested that the process of centralization and homogenization of British culture was promoted from a 'golden triangle' between London, Oxford and Cambridge.[12] However, the historian Richard Weight has argued that (up to the time he was writing) there was more arts legislation passed by the Labour government in the postwar years than in any other period of British history, and the aim of this legislation was to *decentralize* British culture. This was due to the belief by government and the intelligentsia that a regional pluralism lay at the heart of British life. It was also believed that the way to democratize British culture was to encourage participation in the arts at a local level.

This view was consistent with arts policy during the war, which had sought to promote the arts in the provinces. It was also a response to Scottish and Welsh nationalism. Following the 1945 general election, both the BBC and the Arts Council announced their regional policies. The BBC restored its six regional home service departments, and the Arts Council established 12 regional offices to help distribute funds more efficiently. This decentralizing tendency was evident in the Beveridge Report, which called for increased regional broadcasting, especially from Scotland, Wales and Northern Ireland. Although the report's findings against competition were overturned with the passing of the Television Act in 1954, the principle of regionality was retained to countervail the mainly London-centric, metropolitan bias of the BBC's television service.

According to Briggs, regional broadcasting in radio, however, had been very strong.[13] Scotland, Wales and Northern Ireland were described as national regions, and each was represented on the board of governors. In 1958 there was a substantial amount of radio programme output from the regions, which employed one-seventh of the BBC's staff. As well as the three 'national regions', there were three English regions. There was the North region (located in Manchester), the Midland region (based in Birmingham) and the West region (based in Bristol but extending as far east as Brighton). London and the southeast, which had never had a regional frequency assigned to it, relied on national programmes transmitted from London.[14] While radio remained the dominant medium, between 1945 and 1955, the regions enjoyed considerable autonomy. 'BBC Television, however, was organized from the start on a national basis,' according to Briggs, and where regional activity spread, it 'was grafted on to a national system. It could not develop "from below".'[15]

One of the organizing principles of ITV, however, was the development of regional television companies. This was effectively an extension of the decentralizing arts policies of the 1940s and early 1950s. Yet it was also an attempt to encourage powerful and resourceful companies in the provinces.[16] Economically speaking, why should London monopolize the jobs in the nascent television industry? The success of this regional principle in commercial television is, however, on several levels, debatable.

As we saw in Chapter 1, the initial round of franchise appointments was located in three main regions, London, the Midlands and the North. The 'big four' companies that serviced these regions, as we have seen, were Associated-Rediffusion (A-R), Associated Television (ATV), Associated Broadcasting Corporation (ABC) and Granada. Yet the structuring of four companies across three regions probably inhibited a fully developed sense of regional output. In the case of Associated-Rediffusion, the company was completely London based. On its opening night on 22 September 1955, transmission started with a stiff voice-over eulogizing London's long history with shots of the Houses of Parliament, Westminster Abbey and the Tower of London. Before moving to live transmission of the inaugural dinner and speeches held at the Guildhall, the voice-over continued firmly to locate the birth of commercial television, as a 'miraculous' feat of organization and engineering, both geographically and historically within the nation's capital:

> In January this year, the contractors charged with the execution of this new Elizabethan enterprise had nothing more than paper letterheads and hope. Now, nine months later, something approaching a miracle of organization and design has been accomplished: studios, staff and technical equipment have all been assembled. A new public service is about to be launched over the rooftops of London.

With studios and a range of entertainment interests in London, the new contracting companies effectively endorsed rather than provided an alternative to the BBC's London-centric and metropolitan bias. As we have seen, the practicalities and cost efficiencies of a regional service in the Midlands being run by two companies across the week and the weekend meant sharing local resources. Alpha Television, the joint company owned by ATV and ABC, was set up as a temporary measure, with neither company being fully established in the Midlands until franchise reallocations in 1968. The exception to a lack of clear regional focus at this early stage was Granada, which had constructed purpose-built television studios in Manchester, and which made a range of distinctive programmes, the most popularly known, surviving today, being the soap opera *Coronation Street* (1960–).

Yet, before we examine the roll-out of regional contractors in other areas, it is worth noting that programme outputs from the companies often overlapped in terms of regional interest or bias.

A-R (based in London) made a documentary, for example, called *Beat City*, which was transmitted on Christmas Eve in 1964 about the burgeoning pop music scene in Liverpool. On the other hand, Granada made a documentary, *Sunday in September*, about a CND rally in London on 17 September 1961 and transmitted it the following day.

Providing a snapshot of a day in London, it starts with the chimes of Big Ben at 7 a.m., with road cleaners working their way down rain-swept streets, and pigeons playing in puddles in Trafalgar Square. As the day progresses, a Royal Air Force parade marches down Whitehall, past the names of the dead on the Cenotaph, for a memorial service at St Clement Dane's church in the Strand. Crowds of young people start to amass in Trafalgar Square and, in the late, damp afternoon, they start to stage a mass sit-down. Scuffles ensue with police, resulting in arrests and people being dragged away. The documentary closes with an empty Parliament Square, a night-time Piccadilly Circus, and shots of demonstrators in London pubs relaxing with drinks or examining police bail papers. On one hand this documentary could be read as critical of a political event taking place in London. On the other hand, though, made by a northern television company, it could be argued that this documentary celebrated the lived experience and public spaces of London streets, and located them as the site of struggle between national institutions of authority and popular revolt. The programme, however, was not networked or shown in the London area because Granada had been unable to plan ahead and secure a place for it in the schedule.[17]

After the initial round of contracts in the mid-1950s came the roll-out of ITV franchise companies with regional ties explicitly announced by their company names, such as Scottish Television (1957), Southern (1958), Television Wales and West (1958), Tyne Tees (1959) and Ulster Television (1959). The emergence of these new companies did add a number of programmes with specific regional themes. It also marked a trend, in some cases, towards explicit nationalism. Jamie Medhurst has argued, for example, that broadcasting has played an important role in the cultural life of the Welsh nation.[18]

In 1937 BBC Radio Wales was granted autonomy as a national region. BBC Television arrived in Wales in 1952, and commercial television in 1958 with Television Wales and West (which also served the west of England area). When the ITA cast about for its last licence contractor for the west and north Wales region, there were many who felt the company should be in Welsh hands, due to an anxiety about creeping Anglicization. The contract was given to Teledu Cymru (Wales West and North) a home-grown company with high aims and ideals headed by the director of education for Flintshire, Dr Haydn Williams. The view was held that ITV could be the saviour of Welsh language and culture, with a plan to broadcast Welsh language programmes during peak hours. Within ten months the company had folded.

Part of the problem was a delay in transmitter construction, with only one out of the three promised ready for transmission in September 1962. Had all three been ready, WWN would have had an audience of one million. Medhurst suggests that the problem may also have fallen at the door of the ITA because parts of Wales were already being serviced by two companies. Granada (north) had been broadcasting since 1956 and had included a miscellany programme called *Dewch I Mewn*, as well as taking Welsh language programmes from TWW. As a result, it was deemed that any company in the area could only make marginal profits. Consequently, the company had had to bow to commercial pressure not to show Welsh language programmes during peak hours, signalling a clear clash between culture and commerce. WNN might well have both survived financially *and* provided a peak-time service in Welsh had money been available from the licence fee in the form discussed in the last chapter. In the end, when WNN closed down, the ITA reduced the rent for the three transmitters and ABC, Granada and ATV provided programming free of charge until TWW was able to take over the franchise.

The complex relationship between regional programming, nationalist discourses and a *de facto* national network can be seen in a number of programme examples from the period. For the opening night of Television Wales and West on 14 January

1958, for instance, there was a 20-minute programme presenting well-known local stars to the audience, *Stars Rise in the West*. In this programme national and international performers from Wales, such as Stanley Baker (film)[19] and Harry Secombe (radio), were introduced to the audience and invited to say some words. The actor Donald Houston said 'hello' to his grandmother on camera, and the performer Tessie O'Shea, one of only two women to top the bill at the London Palladium, who was both Welsh and still resided in Wales, said 'hello' to her relatives and her old school headmistress.

In retrospect, the programme appears excruciatingly gauche and self-conscious, but in fairness, part of the problem of course was that the newly emerging industry was still finding its professional form. Yet parochialism was perhaps something of which the industry and its performers were aware. On the fifth anniversary of its launch, STV staged a celebratory programme in 1962 with music and dancing. The programme included live pieces from other shows from the period, including *Lucky Diamond*, an STV local talent show, and a music programme called *Jig Time*. Introducing the *Jig Time* segment, the anniversary programme's presenter, Bill Tennant, alluded to either a genuine sense of cultural conflict, or a sense of twee chocolate box parochialism:

> They called it *Jig Time* and they put it out tentatively wondering if the previous association of English television hadn't perhaps weaned the Scots off their traditional obsession for the ceilidh. ... Yes, dressed as he may in his bowler hat and English cut suit, the Scot is still, in imagination at least, a claymore swinging highlander who likes to invade the dance floor with a blood curdling shriek and swing some bonnie partner into breathless dance.

Before the programme finished with prayers and a discussion between clergymen, an award was made for the best (presumably Scottish) television presenter of the year, which went to Bill Tennant. Perhaps out of modesty, but perhaps also out of recognition of the small pool of talent eligible for the award, or the inward-looking and partisan nature of the local television audience, Tennant accepted the award with a groan, and said 'it just shows how parochial we are.'

Nonetheless, the principle of regional broadcasting was fundamentally undermined in two significant ways. First, there was still the continued centralization of production from London, which remained the economic and talent capital.[20] This was mainly pragmatic because television (both BBC and ITV) had started in London, and this was where the initial production facilities were concentrated. Also, the larger entertainment industry located in London, including theatre, film and radio, which employs performers and a larger supporting infrastructure like agents, administration and management, complements television. As Sendall says, 'The Authority's policy had always been to moderate this metropolitan tendency and that was why it had appointed companies not for the whole network of London, Midlands and the North, but for individual areas.'[21] Yet he goes on to note, 'It had to be admitted that there was a "pull" in programme production towards London, and a good many programmes produced by ATV, Granada and ABC Television were, in fact, produced there.'[22]

For example, the ABC studio, a former cinema in Didsbury in Manchester, was the location for the live performance of *Armchair Theatre* from July 1956. Performances were rehearsed in London and then transmitted from Manchester with just one rehearsal day in the studio.[23] In another example, on the closing night of Television Wales and West on 3 March 1968, the poet John Betjeman paid tribute to the regional programming of 'Tellwelly' coming out of Bristol and Cardiff, and claimed its loss was 'like the death of an old friend'. He alluded, however, to a centralization of talent and culture. 'It [TWW] realized the importance of London … at times you have to be there. … If you are in the world of entertainment and journalism, and television is both, you have to come to London for artistes and ideas, otherwise there's the risk of getting too narrow.'

Medhurst notes that although TWW had proved relatively successful and its annual income had risen to £5m, one of the reasons it lost its franchise in 1967 was the charge that the company was too 'London based'.[24] Part of the problem was that TWW had its head office in London, and a rival applicant for the local franchise (the successful HTV) had made a lot of this fact.[25] Significantly, however, the ITA (then the IBA) was based in London. This was to cause particular problems for Granada and its current affairs series *World in Action*, when potentially controversial programmes produced in Manchester had to be approved in the last few days before transmission by the London based regulator.[26]

While TWW had opened with the programme *The Stars Rise in the West*, which featured national and international stars who had come from Wales, the opening night special *The Big Show* on Tyne Tees television on 15 January 1959 featured performers who had originated from outside the region. The programme was a curious mix of skits and segments to illustrate forthcoming programming. There was certainly a sense that there would be something of interest for locals, with a local talent show, and a segment where members of the audience were shown film clips from members of their family on active duty in Cyprus. Yet the segments were linked by presenters with a certain 'received punctuation' with little in common with the more local vernacular. It also included a segment featuring Surrey-born southerner Bill Maynard with locals telling their favourite short stories or jokes, the film star Bill Travers playing out a sitcom scene with Virginia McKenna, and various dance routines including an interpretation of 'Begin la Beguine'.

The second way in which ITV regionalism was undermined was through programming arrangements between the companies, and these had arisen out of practical and economic necessity.[27] As Sendall states:

> Not only was it cheaper and more convenient to produce television programmes where the primary pool of talent existed, but it was just not possible, given the costs of television production, for there to be a number of independent major centres of production, each providing all the programmes for the local area. ITV, however profitable it had turned out to be, could not operate economically if

each programme company was responsible for all its own output.[28]

Networking therefore provided a means of programme sharing to allow each company to reduce or cover its costs. Yet the system that emerged in the late 1950s may well have served some companies better than others, and this raises an issue about the nature of television competition. Under the terms of the Television Act of 1954, the ITA was instructed 'to secure that there is adequate competition to supply programmes between a number of programme contractors'.[29] In the spirit of monopoly breaking and free enterprise, the ITA originally had a different vision for how the commercial service would look. This vision included companies competing with each other in a given region. In the ITA's first annual report it was stated that competition 'can be obtained fully only when viewers have at all times a choice of two or more programmes, or in other words when there are at least two stations covering each area. This the Authority hopes ultimately to bring about.'[30]

The ITA had been unable to do this in the first instance due to the lack of frequencies allocated to it. Having just broken the monopoly, the ITA seemed confident that future frequency allocations would allow them to expand the commercial service to allow for more than one station in any area. As Sendall states:

Monopoly had at last been broken: they can hardly be blamed, in view of all that had been said, for assuming that it was to be succeeded by genuine plurality and not by mere duopoly. They were not to know that in later years the notion of competition, except in terms of competition between BBC and ITV, would lose favour; and that even between these two organizations competition, as distinct from planned co-existence, would come to be increasingly deprecated.[31]

In the event, the ITA had awarded the initial round of franchises to the 'big four'. As the system expanded, newer, smaller regional companies set up affiliation agreements with one or other of the larger companies, which effectively acted as a parent to supply the majority of programming material. The small affiliated company would pay a fixed programme charge, and a percentage of its net advertising revenue calculated on the basis of population coverage, to the parent for the widest range of programming. Yet, although the arrangement had been made only with the parent company, the other three big companies also agreed to make their programmes available to the smaller company. The smaller companies were at first happy to enter into this arrangement because it guaranteed a regular and dependable supply of programme material to fill airtime, but as this temporary solution to programme production and supply became more permanent problems were later to emerge.

In the first instance, in a process Sendall describes as the 'network carve up', the smaller regional companies had to take programmes they did not want. Effectively, the big four divided up between them regular patterns of programme provision and supply.[32] Tied by affiliation agreements, the smaller companies were obliged to take programme material provided by the big four, and were resentful at being excluded from programming decisions. The smaller companies also felt particularly resentful because they were not always happy with the quality of programming coming from their parent companies, feeling that they themselves could do better. Indeed, a further cause for resentment was that they had difficulty selling their own programmes to the network. According to Sendall, there was a feeling that the big companies had made a deliberate policy to exclude the programme output of the smaller companies. Sendall, however, prevaricates on the issue, saying that it was only natural that the big companies, which had taken big risks in undertaking the commercial television enterprise, were justified in seeking to spread their costs in programme sharing and sales to affiliated companies.

The bigger companies also saw the newer ones as ungrateful because the success of the new stations was predicated on their earlier risk-taking, and on the established popularity of shows that the big companies had either produced in Britain or bought in. At the same time, Sendall also argues that the newer companies had *not* been contracted to provide programming to the network. The newer companies had been contracted to provide programming for their local areas, and franchise applications with grand plans had been discouraged. This had been the case with the southern, northeast England and East Anglian franchises where return lines to London had not been included as part of their contracts. As Sendall states, 'The producing of programmes for the network by the smaller companies could ... be regarded as in a sense a diversion of their efforts from their proper job of serving their local area.'[33]

The bias towards the centralized provision of national and established programmes was evidenced on the opening night of Anglia Television on 27 October 1959. Starting with aerial footage of the region, and then local scenes from Essex, Norfolk, Suffolk and Cambridge, it moves inside the studio at Anglia House in Norwich. The show promotes its new local programming, including local news and programmes such as *All About Anglia*, *Farming Diary* and *Town and Gown* (a programme about Cambridge). Yet the show also goes on to promote programmes that had already proved popular on the network, including *Sunday Night at the London Palladium, Educating Archie, Emergency Ward 10, What the Papers Say, This Week* and ITN headlines four times a day. It also included in its list pop programmes such as *Boy Meets Girl* and *Cool for Cats*, quiz shows such as *Take Your Pick* and *Double Your Money*, and a raft of popular American Westerns such as *Maverick, Rawhide* and *Gunlaw*. So, even though Anglia was a regional franchise, it was still heavily dependent on nationally networked programming.

Furthermore, locally produced programming within the franchise areas covered by the smaller companies, such as Anglia, tended to be restricted to those areas. The network did not offer up a fully competitive system between companies and it did not allow for a plurality or diversity across the areas. So the small companies were unable to exchange or buy and sell programmes between themselves. What programme provision there was came from the big four companies that still reflected a metropolitan bias (Manchester, Birmingham and London), with

Manchester and Birmingham still predominantly deferring to London's talent capital.

Media events

During the 1950s and 1960s, there were other programme forms and outputs that conflicted with a sense of regional diversity to offer a more collective sense of 'Britishness'. These sought explicitly to establish a rhetoric of national reach and interest. One example was television news – as constituted by both the BBC and ITN. Yet perhaps a more useful example would be the television coverage of major media events. Such events included the coronation in 1953, the state opening of parliament in 1958, the general election in 1959, Winston Churchill's funeral in 1965 and the World Cup final in 1966. The basic model of media events as formulated by Dayan and Katz is that they are planned live events that interrupt and dominate the schedules and attract large audiences.[34] They can cover major state events such as the Queen's coronation, or the funerals of John F. Kennedy and Churchill, they can cover major sporting events such as the World Cup, or groundbreaking events such as the first landing on the moon. They are organized outside the media establishment, but uphold the definitions of the event as posited by the event's organizers.

Provided with access to the whole event (or most of it), with cameras in multiple, prearranged locations, and with voice-over commentary and exposition, the audience at home is often drawn more into the symbolic meaning of the event than the people in the actual attendance. When the state or the establishment organize the event, audience size becomes a marker of its significance, and the ratings are read 'as a confirmation of loyalty, as a reiteration of the social contract between citizens and their leaders'.[35]

In many respects, Dayan and Katz's arguments are compelling and they have proved influential. This is not least because they conform to the BBC's own claims of providing a central focus for the British nation-state. As Scannell suggests in his discussion of early public service broadcasting, the early

BBC philosophy was that, 'By providing a common access for all to a wide range of public events and ceremonies – a royal wedding, the FA Cup Final, the last night of the Proms, for example – broadcasting would act as a kind of social cement binding people together in the shared idioms of public, corporate, national life.'[36]

Reflecting on the first address made by a monarch on radio, King George V at the British Empire Exhibition on 23 April 1924, John (later Lord) Reith described the effect as 'making the nation as one man'.[37] Indeed, the Queen's coronation on 2 June 1953 seems like an apposite model for both Dayan and Katz's thesis and for BBC claims because it has been exemplified as an indication of national unity and solidarity. It has also been popularly heralded as one of the defining moments in British television. Yet, while the coronation stood alongside the Festival of Britain as one of the two major state festivals to sponsor national unity in the early 1950s, it proved to be the site of much debate and negotiation.[38] There were many arguments over the meaning and purpose of the coronation, and they did not strictly fall into debates between left-wing and right-wing factions, but between traditionalists and populists.

Such debates were often centred on television, and Winston Churchill was among those vehemently opposed to televising the service for fear it would demystify the workings of authority and make profane an otherwise sacred event. There were also complaints about exploitation of the event by the government and private companies. As Weight suggests, 'The arguments were based on traditionalist fears that a sacred religious event was being turned into a mere entertainment for the masses.'[39] Yet the Anglican *Church Times* supported televising the event, and it was also reported that even the Queen wanted the cameras to be there. The issue was forced through a House of Commons debate and the populizers won.

It took the BBC a whole year to organize,[40] and it proved it capable of embarking on an event of national scale. For Scannell, the coronation marked a singular transformation of the monarchy from being the symbolic head of the aristocracy to being the symbolic head of a whole nation, the whole of British society. This was achieved, he argues, by virtue of the media.[41] Yet this had previously been predicated on the evolution of a new kind of public that was commensurate with the whole of society. This was achieved prior to the war with the BBC offering a new kind of democracy to its listeners.[42] As Scannell and Cardiff argue, 'Broadcasting equalized public life through the principle of common access for all.'[43] As a result of this equalization, 'If the culture of radio depended on a shared public life brought into being by broadcasting itself, a central aspect of this process was the creation of a sense of participation in corporate national life.'[44]

In just the same way as the BBC had provided a ready audience for the work of the Arts Council, so too had it paved the way for a 'corporate national life' symbolized by the monarchy. On the day of the coronation, the BBC's live television coverage lasted 11 hours, with 56 per cent of the adult population watching the service on television and a further 32 per cent listening to it on radio.[45] In Dayan and Katz's terms, the enormous audience signified an act of national solidarity and a legitimation of the monarchy. Later in the decade, sociologists Edward Shils and Michael Young were to write that the coronation constituted an act of national communion where people from the periphery of society were reconnected to its centre and rededicated to its values.[46] In one of their examples, two feuding neighbours were reconciled so that one could invite the other in to watch the event on television.[47]

Yet, just as we have had to question the notion of consensus at the end of the Second World War and at the beginning of the 1950s, this perception of community and consensus should perhaps be treated with a degree of caution. Support for the monarchy and its symbolic role as head of a national community is perhaps the first thing that should be queried. In his classic quasi-ethnographic analysis of the British working classes (first published in 1958), Richard Hoggart argued in *The uses of literacy* that the working classes were distinctly indifferent to royalty. As he suggests, the working classes were 'not royalists by principle. Nor do they harbour resentment against it; they have little heat. They either ignore it or, if they are interested, the interest is for what can be translated into the personal.'[48]

Hoggart argued that some adolescent girls may have been interested in royalty for its glamour, in much the same way as they would be interested in film stars, and that others more likely to be interested in royalty were women over 25 years of age. However, he argued, men were on the whole uninterested or even 'vaguely hostile', remembering the unwelcome discipline and rigours of military parades during national service.

Aside from attitudes to royalty, there is also the question of how people responded to the coronation and its coverage as an event, and whether or not they were genuinely interested. In one sense, a radio and television audience had been created for the coronation coverage because people had been given the day off work. Nonetheless, there were organized street parties on the day and community activities, so listening and viewing would in many cases have been conducted alongside a range of other activities. At the same time, the potential indifference or ambivalence of part of the audience towards the monarchy complicates this further. As such, viewership of the coronation may have been distracted, disrupted and, in some situations, boisterous. Actual audience behaviour in front of the screen, or in private, can often be dismissive of any of the core texts or values being presented on television (or radio).

Scannell and Cardiff record, for example, that during the radio coverage of the coronation of King George VI and Queen Elizabeth in 1937 there were those in the country who were not entirely deferential or attentive.[49] Of course such lack of apparent respect among an audience is not just the preserve of those watching on television or listening to radio.[50] As Richard Dimbleby,[51] the BBC commentator for the day, was ruefully to notice when he returned to Westminster Abbey in the evening for a postscript to the event, 'Tiers and tiers of stalls on which the peers had been sitting were covered with sandwich wrappings, sandwiches, morning newspapers, fruit peel, sweets and even a few empty miniature bottles.'[52]

For Weight, a popular appeal of the coronation may have been a reminder of previous times of togetherness, with images in the popular press of people sleeping in the rain-swept Mall at night being reminiscent of the blitz. Indeed, empirical social research from the time seems to confirm this point. As Philip Ziegler notes, 'Mass Observation returns revealed that people felt uplifted not so much by a bright display of pageantry amidst the continuing gloom of austerity Britain, but by the return of wartime camaraderie which they felt had been absent since the euphoria of VE Day.'[53]

The popular appeal of the television coverage, with such high viewing figures, may well also have been the novelty of television itself. As Chris Hand has observed, for most people to have seen the coronation on television they had to have watched it somewhere other than their own home.[54] What this suggests is that viewership might have been predicated on the combination of social setting and the novelty of watching television itself rather than any clear legitimation of the national values being represented and celebrated on the television screen. This clearly undermines some of the sense of Dayan and Katz's description, explanation and expectation of what media events are and what they are about.

A myth of centrality

It is worth briefly summarizing the key points so far in this discussion of regional and national culture and consensus. First of all, the claim that the arrival of ITV signalled an end of consensus culture is problematic. This is because consensus itself may have been mythical, with different regional situations and contexts, not to mention class contexts, defining a variety of different British experiences. The advent of regional programming with the arrival of ITV was an innovation in television, but as we saw, this may have had varying degrees of success. In many cases, such programme provision was still predicated on talent and cultural institutions based in metropolitan centres, most significantly London. At the same time, the construction of collective, British television experiences through media events is also problematic, mainly because a large audience does not necessarily guarantee consensus of attitude, experience or behaviour.

Can, for example, the viewership of the general election on television in 1959 really have had a united audience? It may have united an audience in interest, potentially, but it would probably not have been politically united. Furthermore, what kind of collective unity would have been experienced following England's win of the World Cup in 1966, which Briggs has argued broke all records for viewership of a sporting event?[55] Did viewers (if they were watching) in Scotland, Wales or Northern Ireland necessarily share in the ecstatic jubilation? So in negotiating between regional and national culture, the regional programming and media event genres may not have been entirely successful in their institutional (ITA and BBC) aims. Yet there did appear to be a tendency towards cultural rationalization and centralization in television that appeared at odds with an increasing sense of fragmentation in British society and culture.

As we have seen, Scannell argues that Reith saw the role of the BBC as a kind of 'social cement'.[56] The result was a common form of culture for all social groups (who listened), by bringing together things that had previously been discrete and separate within the mixed-programme schedule on radio. In one sense, this implied commonality had to be constructed, and it was constructed on the basis of what was familiar to all, or with what its listeners would be familiar. As Scannell and Cardiff note, 'One resource that could always be relied on as a shared point of reference available to all listeners was the culture of radio itself.'[57] As a result, a sense of collectivity and common audience-hood was constructed from broadcasting techniques such as catch-phrases and signature tunes, as well as recurring topics and subject matter.

One example Scannell and Cardiff cite is the composer Stravinsky. 'It is notable', they argue, 'that Stravinsky is presumed to be a familiar topical reference – familiar, that is, only through the widely accessible cultural resource that radio itself constituted.'[58] This was also evident in a degree of self-reflexivity and lampooning of some of the more serious programme forms by other artists in variety and comedy acts. Scannell and Cardiff suggest that this was because BBC radio was like one of Erving Goffman's 'total institutions', which effectively allow 'inmates' the chance to let off steam, or as they put it – a way of 'laughing off the BBC's most acute embarrassments'.[59] Scannell and Cardiff imply that this was because BBC radio in the 1930s was still an immature form and that it still had to find its own mode of being.

Developments in television in the 1950s had some parallels with the earlier development of radio. In the first instance, both BBC television and ITV had mixed-programme schedules. For the BBC, the public service broadcasting ethos of open access to a range of entertainments previously accessible to small audiences changed the nature of public participation in Britain's social life. 'Particular publics were replaced by the *general* public constituted in and by the general nature of the mixed programme service and its general, unrestricted availability'.[60] With the arrival of ITV, this ethos continued, and the ITA was eager to ensure a balance of programme provision from the ITV companies. Yet, for the programme companies the mixed-programme schedule was also a matter of practicality and showmanship. When Lew Grade, deputy managing director at ATV, was asked in a documentary about how he put together a successful schedule, his answer was 'varied entertainment'. Comparing scheduling with running a variety bill at the theatre, Grade went on, 'Because when you put a variety bill together, you cannot please the whole audience with the whole programme. Therefore you need to have sufficient elements so that at least half the programme appeals to all the audience. I used the same tactics on television.'[61]

As Janet Thumim argues, the mixed-programme schedule, by offering a variety of programmes of mixed appeal and interest, was the way to attract the widest possible audience. The magazine programme, characterized by short segments on different topics in different tones, and used to build an audience and develop a television culture in the 1950s and early 1960s, is, she claims, paradigmatic of television itself.[62] Yet what this mixed programme strategy effectively established, in the cases of both the BBC *and* ITV, was a unified cultural form that placed discrete and separate cultural activities in a direct relationship with each other. News programmes could now coexist alongside sitcoms, opera alongside variety, drama alongside music, and with the advent of ITV they could also coexist alongside advertisements for beer, cigarettes, toothpaste or washing power.

A typical example of an evening's mixed programming on ITV might be the Palm Sunday schedule, 22 March 1964. It included a specially produced programme *The Rise and Fall of a Hero*, which consisted of a simple darkened stage and a number of performers, including Keith Barron and Jane Asher, singing songs, reading poems and narrating sections from the Bible. The evening included a US adventure series about private investigators in California, from Warner Brothers Studios, *77 Sunset Strip*. There was variety in the form of *Val Parnell's Sunday Night at the London Palladium*, and a comedy with Millicent Martin and Roy Kinnear, *Happy Moorings*. The evening also included two bulletins from ITN, one a brief summary of the headlines, and the second a longer edition with some filmed footage and analysis. Items included details of a power strike due to take place the next day, negotiations about the release of US aircrew shot down over East Germany, and the funeral in Dublin of Irish playwright Brendan Behan. There were adverts for Dutch panatella cigars, Cannon cookers, Michelin tyres, Courage beer, and Atrixo hand cream.

The relationship of these programmes to each other was a temporal arrangement as part of the television flow. Irrespective of whether an individual was watching BBC or ITV on a particular evening, different programmes, themes, issues, ideologies and values were conjoined in relation to each other in a new way by being part of the television broadcasting experience. This temporal arrangement was the significant way in which fragmentation was negotiated within a unifying cultural form. It was in this way that television addressed itself as being central to the social and cultural life of Britain. As already observed, the BBC in radio had manufactured a sense of total British experience. This had been consolidated during wartime, but was also potently articulated, Scannell and Cardiff observe, through the calendrical arrangements of broadcasting, 'Nothing so well illustrates the noiseless manner in which the BBC became perhaps *the* central agent of the national culture as its calendar; the cyclical reproduction, year in year out, of an orderly and regular progression of festivities, rituals and celebrations – major and minor, civil and sacred – that marked the unfolding of the broadcast year.'[63]

This too was replicated in television with the annual round of sporting events, memorial and religious festivals. On the week of the launch of ITV, for example, the BBC held a special event to commemorate the anniversary of the Battle of Arnhem in the Second World War. Scannell and Cardiff argue that one of the major events of the broadcasting year was Christmas, marking a conjunction between state, religion and the home.[64] On radio this was also marked by the 'invented tradition'[65] of the monarch's address to the nation, and this was instituted on television on Christmas day on BBC and ITV in 1957. It was also supplemented by the kind of major events referred to above such as the Queen's coronation, which *appear* to have a unifying 'function' in Dayan and Katz's terms. Such events were also broadcast by ITV, as will be discussed below.

As I have already noted, however, such media events can prove problematic in assessing consensus or unity. Yet, although people may be watching for different reasons or with different feelings and thoughts, the temporal act of viewing – a simultaneous moment of spectatorship – can articulate a powerful sense of the nation, of what the historian Benedict Anderson has described as an 'imagined community'.[66] For Anderson, because it is impossible for the members of a nation to know all its other members, a sense of nationhood, or community, is very much an imagined experience. The imagining process is facilitated by mass media such as newspapers, which both promote issues of common interest and, by publishing daily in morning or evening editions, imply a shared moment of readership. This sense of shared moment is enhanced in the broadcasting experience by the transmission of any single programme to a mass audience that may potentially number millions of viewers.

The ostensibly centralizing tendency of television as a cultural form was reinforced by the increasingly reflexive nature of the medium. As we saw in the case of early radio, Scannell and Cardiff saw self-reflexivity as a BBC response to constructing an audience that had something in common, even if that something was radio itself. At the same time, they argue, reflexivity in terms of humour was a sign of an immature self-consciousness – with one part of the radio's address embarrassed by the other.[67] Certainly, self-reflexivity was apparent in television in the 1950s. One example of this is the celebrity slot on the BBC panel game *What's My Line?* Every week panellists would be blind-folded and have to guess the identity of the celebrity guest by asking them 'yes–no' questions. One edition featured the big band leader Victor Sylvester, who at that stage had the longest running television show in the world. At that time, Sylvester would only have been known to most of the audience, or his work at least, through television or radio. Similarly, there were other BBC shows that celebrated or interviewed well-known people, including *This is Your Life* and *Face-to-Face*.

The first ever *This is Your Life* (transmitted on 29 September 1955) was hosted by Ralph Edwards, the host of the version aired in the USA where the show originated. The unwitting victim was Eamonn Andrews, the *What's My Line?* presenter who went on to host *This is Your Life*. A particularly notorious edition of *Face-to-Face*, an intimate one-to-one interview pro-gramme hosted by former MP John Freeman, featured perhaps the best-known television celebrity of the 1950s, Gilbert Harding. The interview (transmitted on 18 September 1960) was deeply probing and exposed Harding's profound sense of unhappiness and disappointment. It touched a raw nerve on the subject of bereavement, with Freeman unaware that Harding's mother had died only a short while earlier. Not long afterwards, Harding too was dead.[68] The point is that, like the early days of radio, tele-vision had to address an audience that shared the same common denominators. However, at this time, when the television audience was still expanding, such self-reflexivity was a means by which television could validate its own personalities while simultaneously making them known to new viewers.

Yet, as we have discussed, Scannell and Cardiff see the early days of radio-reflexivity as a sign of potential immaturity.[69] By contrast, I want to argue that self-reflexivity in television at the end of the 1950s and 1960s was a sign of increasing sophistication and maturity. Certainly by the early 1960s, the satire in programmes such as *That Was the Week That Was* demonstrated a confidence that audiences *would* know the names, faces and voices of people in the public domain. People would have found Willie Rushton's impersonation of Harold Macmillan funny only if they knew what Macmillan looked like, what he sounded like and what he stood for. This self-reflexivity was dependent on other areas of output within the mixed-programme schedule, and also on the output of the 'other' channel. Reflexivity was self-supporting and mutually comfortable.

A useful indicator here (again) is the realm of media events and politics, which, as we have seen, also *seemed* to uphold the claim that television *was* something central to British life. This claim was reinforced by the arrival of ITV, especially when both channels covered or reported on major events. This is because television is seen to depict what is important. One example of this is the live televised state opening of parliament in 1958, broadcast on both BBC and ITV. As Scannell observes, there were two very different 'demeanours' towards the event by each channel's commentator. At the closing stages of the event, Scannell compares the two commentaries.

RICHARD DIMBLEBY (BBC): The Throne remains, rich and shining, near and yet remote, the symbol of this rare meeting of the Queen, the Lords and the Commons – the Three Estates of Parliament. And so begins, with ceremony that springs from the very roots of our democratic history, the fourth session of the three hundredth Parliament of the Realm.

ROBIN DAY (ITV): Everyone is wondering at Westminster what Government will write the next speech from this Throne. Before Her Majesty sits on it again there may be a General Election. That is when we have our say. And what Her Majesty reads from this Throne depends on what we put in the ballot box.[70]

These 'demeanours' demonstrate the different approaches of the two broadcasters, but despite this both services validated the same occasion as an important event. The BBC achieved it through positioning the Queen as symbolic head of the nation, legitimized by the weight of tradition and history. ITV achieved it through positioning the audience as participants in the democratic process. Although the commentaries are different, each channel shores up the legitimacy of the other channel's coverage.

The construction of events on television as important shared national experiences was 'worked through', in John Ellis's sense,[71] in some of the political satire on television in the early 1960s. In *That Was the Week That Was*, transmitted on 28 December 1963, David Frost performed a spoof commentary of the Queen joining a barge in the Pool of London to sail out to the Royal Yacht *Britannia*. In a reverent tone, with received pronunciation, Frost delivered a commentary in a slow, solemn style familiar to viewers well versed in royal events.

> And as the barge moves slowly away from the quayside it is becoming clear that something has gone wrong. The Royal Barge is, as it were, sinking. The sleek royal blue hull of the barge is sliding gracefully, almost regally, beneath the waters of the Pool of London. Perhaps the lip-readers amongst you will be able to make out what Prince Philip has just said to the Captain of the Barge ... and now the Queen, smiling radiantly, is swimming for her life. Her Majesty is wearing a silk ensemble in canary yellow.[72]

Such a sketch does not reflect an embarrassment with other forms of BBC output *per se*, but an embarrassment with certain forms of television generally. Alternatively, it could be read as critical of other establishment institutions (such as the monarchy), or, more likely, the establishment itself. In an almost philosophical sleight of hand, the satire too (on television) established itself as having unparalleled access to a sense of how things really are, or being at the centre of events. Not only was this constructed in *That Was the Week That Was* through reference to political events in the national news, it was also signalled by the visibility in-camera of other cameras, lighting rigs, other studio equipment and the studio audience.

Su Holmes has argued that the fascination with the workings of television in cinema programmes of television in the early 1950s demonstrated a self-consciousness about the development of the new medium.[73] With *That Was the Week That Was*, however, there was a bullish confidence about breaking the conventions of television, about deliberately having the mechanics of television's operation in vision. The jazz musician and critic George Melly later described this as 'the new television brutalism', a reference to the modish 'brutal' architecture of public buildings and council estates in the period.[74] The impression was one of being up to the minute, of seeing 'behind the scenes', witnessing the workings of broadcasting, and having less 'mediated' access to the issues of the day (or week) that were central to national public life.

There is, however, a problem here, namely the idea that television (or radio) *can* act as a social cement, or allow an audience access to the central concerns of society or public life. Nick Couldry has been critical of the way certain academics have suggested that the media can either connect people to the central values of society or, as is increasingly the case with theories of postmodernism, that the media *as such* constitute that centre.[75] As seen here, Dayan and Katz[76] subscribe to the view, following Shils and Young,[77] that media events connect people at the peripheries of society to its core, central values. Yet Couldry, drawing on classical sociology, argues that because society is an abstract entity, it cannot exist in a concrete form, it cannot be touched or tasted, and it therefore cannot have a centre.[78] As a result, the media can neither offer access to the central concerns of society nor constitute such a centre.

Couldry's argument can help us understand the relationship between cultural fragmentation and centralization implicit in BBC and ITV television structures and schedules in the 1950s and 1960s. By providing a mixed-programme schedule aimed at developing a television culture among a diverse audience,[79] and with an increasing range of programming that addressed issues of class and difference (which we will explore in the following chapters), ITV and BBC could discursively claim to offer a range of perspectives on the British situation. Yet, while it is tempting to see ITV and its regional companies as exposing the geographical (and hence cultural) fragmentation that had hitherto been concealed by a dominant ideology of cultural consensus, perpetuated from London, this too would be to succumb to the idea of a social or cultural centre. It would imply that the television duopoly, constituted by BBC and ITV, positioned television as a centralized site of culture where it was possible to view and measure cultural fragmentation. Instead, I want to argue that television did not constitute direct access to the central concerns of British society, or act as a central cultural site through which the absence of consensus was measured, but rather that through its mixed-programme schedules it *looked* as if it did.

This development was a consequence of the expansion of television in the 1950s and 1960s, and it has implications for thinking about the construction of media power. Television, as a visual medium, constructed and made visible these cultural propositions for the first time. I shall return to this issue in Chapter 6 and in the conclusions. In Chapters 4 and 5, I shall look at the relationship between programme forms and social and cultural change. Before that, in the next chapter, it will be necessary to examine the impact that the expansion of the television institution has on recording technologies. This is important because it connects with processes of industrialization and the development of the programme factory in the period. It also connects with the increasing commodification of television, with recorded programmes being exported and imported, allowing audiences in different regions or countries to watch programming at different times. The development of recording technology also has important aesthetic impacts, and it allows television to respond and reflect ongoing social and cultural change, and to extend the range of programme forms in the mixed-programme schedule.

Chapter 3
TECHNOLOGIES

One of the reasons that it is often difficult today to study old television programmes is that they simply no longer exist. Until the late 1950s and 1960s most (though not all) programmes were broadcast live and were not recorded. One of the major changes in television broadcasting in the 1950s and 1960s, both in Britain and abroad, was the increased use of recording technologies. These were film[1] and video. The development and use of these technologies had profound impacts on the mode of production, programme aesthetics, broadcasting economics and cultural politics of television. Yet the development of film and video in television broadcasting is not a simple tale of chronological progress, advance or improvement. When television began being broadcast in high-definition services in Europe in the mid-1930s, film had effectively been around for 40 years.

A range of factors, however, constrained its use in television in Britain, including debates about what television actually *was*, and about what television should *look* like. With video, development was necessarily predicated on research in plastics and sound recording technologies in the 1940s, yet a range of practical and economic considerations inhibited its use at the end of the 1950s. These included the development of different types of videotape, broadcasting economics, international broadcasting policy, and also the increased use of film. In many respects, the arrival of ITV facilitated the use of these technologies.

Yet developments in and discourses surrounding television recording technologies found their roots prior to the 1950s and, complemented by a range of institutional, economic and cultural factors, these continued into the 1960s and beyond. In this chapter I first explore the highly visible ways in which commercial television made use of film before going on to look at how the BBC pioneered developments in recording both before and after the arrival of commercial competition. I conclude the chapter by looking at how recording technologies helped extend new forms of visibility over space and in space in relation to television drama, at how this permitted a new range of drama styles and aesthetics, and at how it made them accessible to a diverse television audience. This links directly to the discussion in the following chapters about how television can represent and promote social and cultural change.

Film and ITV

Perhaps the three most immediately visible programme innovations ITV introduced in the middle of the 1950s were all film related – namely advertising, the import of programmes from the USA, and action-adventure series. Indeed, a striking but often overlooked feature of the new ITV channel was the advent of advertisements, which were all produced on film. This deployment of advertising on television, which had, after all, been one of the motivating factors behind the campaign for commercial television (see Chapter 1), caused a major upheaval in the advertising and film industries.[2] Prior to 1955, apart from some advertising in cinema and on Radio Luxembourg, most advertising forms took place in print, in newspapers, magazines and on billboards. The presentation of television advertisements was not only a challenge for the advertising industry, but also a novelty for the television audience. On the opening weekend of ITV in London, the comedian Tommy Trinder announced to the audience at home, 'Now, you lucky people, what you've all been waiting for, THE COMMERCIALS!'[3] The first advert on the opening night of ITV was for Gibbs S-R toothpaste, and further advertisements promoted other products still known today, such as Kraft Cheese and Guinness.

Looking back on the early days of television advertising for ITV's twenty-first anniversary in 1976, advertising consultant David Meyrick argued that 'Many got it wrong at the beginning.'[4] He offers a number of reasons why, but what becomes clear is that the attitude towards television advertising at its outset was similar to the attitude that had characterized early definitions of television – and that was its hybridity. Rather than simply existing as a medium in its own right, television in its early forms, in the 1930s, was perceived as a mixture of film, radio, theatre and newspapers.[5] With television advertising in 1955, a similar attitude emerged in an advertising industry uninitiated to the new medium. Print and cinema were the dominating influences in this new hybrid television advertising form.

In the first instance, until 1955 advertising was predominantly a print-based medium, and the vogue for print-based copy at the time was a whimsical style,[6] using slightly fanciful or florid writing. An advertisement for Nestlé's cream on page 2 of the first edition of the *TV Times*, dated 20 September 1955, gives a slight impression of this type of style.

> Going... Going... Gone!
> If a mother leaves two growing boys, not to mention a husband alone in the house with Nestlé's Cream, what can she expect? Nestlé's Cream keeps fresh and ready to use indefinitely – but only as long as the family will let it.
> Nestlé's Cream is real cream, pure cream and nothing else. Ask any strawberry! Ask any peach!

As Meyrick argues, advertising agencies and copywriters did not necessarily know how to adapt to the new medium. On the opening night of ITV, for example, an advert for Guinness consisted of an attempt to bring one of its existing advertising billboards to life with a zoo keeper chasing a sea lion with a bottle balanced on its nose. A small-print advertisement on page

37 of the same *TV Times* had trailed the advert with the caption, 'Guinness posters come to life on commercial TV.'

The second medium that dominated the new advertising form was film (both as a technological form and as an industry). Yet this was to prove highly problematic at the outset of television advertising. Part of the problem was that film studio techniques had changed little since the war.[7] Cameras were large and lighting was numerous and bulky. Most film lighting, at this stage, was still created for cinema, and most lighting crew and cameramen were unable to meet the demands of the poor definition television screen.[8] The traditional cinematographer also lacked experience in product shots. Up until that time, product imagery had been the domain of still photography. Many agencies brought stills photographers onto the film studio floor, creating an uneasy alliance. As Meyrick notes:

> On ITV's first night, Kraft demonstrated that they had the right idea with a Cheese Slices spot, but the technical know-how was missing. The slices looked even more like floppy rubber than they usually do, and instead of showing one really appetizing sandwich, the camera settled on five, which the lack of technique and the low definition managed to reduce to a rather limp mass.[9]

It quickly became clear that putting stills photographers and cinematographers together was not working. Over time, however, equipment became lighter and more versatile, advertising agencies started developing their own television departments, and through experience experts began to emerge.[10] As a result, a number of successful production companies appeared, and they adopted a more industrial, factory style approach to producing adverts. As Meyrick suggests, 'Top directors and cinematographers were signed to exclusive contracts and they could script, produce, shoot, edit, record, print and distribute your commercial.'[11] Interestingly, many people working in advertising defected to the mainstream commercial cinema industry, though, as Meyrick argues, the skills and experience that were increasingly being required meant that television advertising soon ceased to be a temporary stopgap for production personnel between film or television contracts. As in the main television industry, those working in advertising also adopted rationalized industrial practices amid discourses of professionalism.

One of the major aesthetic developments to occur in the first few years of television advertising resulted from the time pressure that each advert faced on transmission. Until 1955, advertising had occupied space on the page of a newspaper, magazine or billboard. It could be measured in inches, often literally in column inches. With television, advertising occupied time, airtime, and in the very early days advertisements ran for as long as 60 seconds. A minute's airtime afforded many producers the luxury of including a range of standard film techniques. An advertisement might therefore include an establishing shot, a series of medium close-ups, ending in a long or pack shot. Running times were, however, soon reduced to 30 seconds. Indeed, by 1964, some advertisements on the Palm Sunday ATV evening were running for as little as 15 seconds.

This meant that the advertising agency producer was forced to condense material into a severely restricted timeslot. 'Given that situation', argues Meyrick, especially in instances where film shooting ran over by a number of seconds, 'it's hard not to see how the jump cut was born'.[12] In the mainstream film industry, continuity editing had been the dominant style, with narrative action being linked by connecting scenes. Increasing time pressure in television advertising, however, required more elliptical editing, which meant that extraneous connecting narrative sequences were omitted. As a result, 'a commercial could really start to move. The photographic techniques were joined by an equally fluid system of editing.'[13]

The second highly visible programme form that arrived with ITV was a large number of filmed series imported from the USA. Most of the initial raft of imports tended to be comedies, Westerns or, slightly later, police or detective shows. The very first to hit ITV screens, however, was *I Love Lucy*, a sitcom starring Lucille Ball who appeared on the first cover of *TV Times*. This sitcom had been running in the USA since 1951 and its novelty was that it was recorded with three cameras using film. During production, the performance was made in front of a studio audience, and then edited together in the cutting room with footage from the three cameras. The result was a tight and fast paced comedy, and with one camera trained on Ball at all times, scenes could be intercut with close-up reaction shots.[14]

Although it was filmed in front of an audience, a programme could be shot discontinuously, with scenes being restaged if necessary. As well as the fast pace and polished delivery, *I Love Lucy* also had popular appeal in America because the on-screen husband-and-wife relationship between Lucy and Ricky Ricardo was mirrored by their real-life marriage as Lucille Ball and Desi Arnaz.[15] The advantages of recording were demonstrated in 1952 when Lucy's on-screen pregnancy imitated that of Ball's real pregnancy. In an episode filmed on 3 October 1952, and broadcast on 8 December 1952, Lucy tells Ricky for the first time that she is pregnant, but circumstances conspire against her delivering the fateful news. The final scene is played out in Ricky's nightclub, and in the first take both Ball and Arnaz became intensely emotional. The scene was reshot as originally scripted with a more upbeat ending, but it was decided to keep the original, emotional take. The synopsis for the scene ('roll clip') therefore came to read:

> Ricky gets an anonymous note that a woman wants to tell her husband they are expecting a 'blessed event' and Ricky goes from table to table looking for the couple as he sings 'Rockabye Baby'. He comes to Lucy, realizes it is her, and after an emotional moment of realization, sings 'We're Having a Baby' as he walks around the stage with a tearful Lucy. The episode ends with a close-up of the couple, crying and laughing.[16]

The climax of the pregnancy narrative came when the filmed episode of Lucy giving birth to a baby boy was transmitted on the same day that Ball had been booked to have her baby delivered by Caesarean section, 19 January 1953. Ball and Arnaz's own baby also turned out to be a boy, and the next day the news headlines in the *New York Daily Mirror* read 'Lucy Sticks to Script: A Boy it Is!' Though recorded, *I Love Lucy* was able to blur, in America at least, 'the line between reality and artifice with the synchronic "real-life" and "fictional" births.'[17]

According to Goddard, a prefilmed *Amos 'N' Andy* had been shown on the BBC prior to the arrival of ITV in 1955. Following the success of *I Love Lucy*, however, by the end of 1956 no fewer than 12 US comedies had been shown on British television, more or less evenly divided between BBC and ITV.[18]

The other highly visible development, which emerged subsequent to the arrival of ITV in 1955, was the profusion of filmed series involving some kind of action or adventure. They included both American and British fare. The main imports from the USA fell within two genres, the Western and the cop/detective show. The use of film as a recording technology and the emergence of these two distinct genres was very much a product of the increasing involvement of the US film industry in American television. This signalled an increasing shift from New York as a site of production, traditionally associated with Broadway and the theatre, and away from the live televised play. Instead, Hollywood emerged as a leading player within the television industry, with rationalized serial production minimizing overheads, and with a ready supply of scenery and props from its film production of then popular genres such as the Western and film noir.

Not least, these filmed programmes could be transmitted across the USA in different time zones. Being recorded, as opposed to live transmission, they had repeat value and could be sold on abroad. The advantage was that domestic sales could recoup costs of production, whereas foreign sales were a way of making a profit. As such, these programmes could be sold relatively cheaply, and were very attractive to foreign television companies looking for an affordable way to fill their schedules. In the latter half of the 1950s, therefore, a number of well-known American television series graced the British television screen. In the Western genre they included *Gunsmoke* (first televised on ITV as *Gun Law*) first shown in 1956, *The Lone Ranger* (BBC 1957), *Cheyenne* (ITV 1958), *Maverick* (ITV 1959), *Rawhide* (ITV

1959) and *Bonanza* (ITV 1960). In the cop or detective genre there was *Dragnet* (ITV 1955), *Highway Patrol* (ITV 1956) and *77 Sunset Strip* (ITV 1960).[19]

Serial production on film also expanded in Britain. While imported serial programming was a very cost-effective way of filling the schedules, and while popular foreign series provided a relatively stable, known entity for television advertisers, there were quota restrictions on how much foreign material British broadcasters could use. With the opening up of the commercial sector in television, foreign quota agreements had been made with British trade unions to ensure that their members, engaged in a range of television production capacities (acting, writing, music, cameras, sets and lighting for example), did not lose their jobs. At ITV, an agreement had been made that foreign-filmed programmes should not exceed, on average, seven hours a week, of which not more than four on average could be shown in the evening. This worked out as a quota of 14 per cent a week.[20] Production of British filmed serials was therefore one way of ensuring work for British employees.

At the same time, there are three other reasons why there was a significant expansion of filmed serial production in Britain in the second half of the 1950s, which then went through a further resurgence in the 1960s. The first, as we have already seen, is that serialization is a useful way of reducing costs. Cast, crew and equipment can be operated on an economy of scale. With film technology, a piecemeal production line – known as the 'programme factory'[21] – can also rationalize the programme-making process even further, with the cost effective use and time allocation of resources.

Second, some of the interests of the new programme companies already included film production facilities, such as ABDC and ITPC, which had film studios in north London. This coincided with a general decline in British film industry revenues at the time.[22] The use of the film industry within British television production was a further rational use of available resources.

Third, television entrepreneurs such as Lew Grade shrewdly saw that recorded programming could provide a major revenue earning export commodity – though, as we shall see later, the BBC was starting to see similar potential.[23] Certainly, several figures were alert to the international potential of filmed serial production, and many of the players in the field were of a transnational hue. Two of the pioneers of filmed serial production in Britain in the late 1950s were, in fact American. The brothers Harry and Edward Danziger made a number of crime and thriller series cheaply for ITV, including *Mark Saber* and *Man from Interpol*. Other international productions included *African Patrol* (South Africa) and *Hawkeye* (Australia). Such imports or international cooperation were, however, not solely the preserve of the new commercial television channel. The BBC was involved with international co-finance and production with, for example, *The Third Man*.[24]

Audiences in Britain perhaps best remember the filmed swashbucklers from the end of the 1950s, particularly *The Adventures of Robin Hood* (1955–59) made by ITC in conjunction with Sapphire Films for Associated Television (ATV), with Richard Greene in the title role.[25] It was successfully sold in the US market at the end of 1955 for a reported million and a quarter dollars, or half a million pounds.[26] A number of other swashbuckling adventure series about costumed adventurers, knights and seafarers followed suit.

The big company success story in this respect was ITC, which became a full subsidiary of ATV in 1958 and acted effectively to provide its own international distribution. Three years later it acquired, re-equipped and refurbished the British National Studios, which, renamed the Elstree Studios, became the centre of ITC's production for its most successful programmes in the 1960s and 1970s.[27] For a brief moment, in 1960, however, *Kine Weekly* reported that filmed serial production was slowing up, with only ITC producing one series (*Danger Man*) and a number of pilots.[28] One reason was that British television companies had become interested in the new technology of videotape or (as is still the case with later series like *Z Cars* at the BBC) in producing live drama. This was complemented by the fact that film production was still very expensive. In the first series of *The Avengers* in 1961, for example, when episodes were transmitted live or recorded on videotape, the average cost per episode was £3500. By 1965, however, with the use of colour film, an average episode was costing between £35,000 and £40,000.[29]

The filmed serial at ITC seemed to go through a renewed phase of vigour in the 1960s. Moving from the costumed swash-bucklers of the late 1950s, there now emerged in British television new types of action and adventure programming of which *The Avengers* was a prime example.[30] Probably the first, however, was the only series in production by ITC in 1960, *Danger Man*. This announced a vogue for modish spy thrillers, and was in some ways modelled on the novels and cartoon strips that eventually spawned the James Bond franchise in the early 1960s.[31] *Danger Man* ran in two incarnations, a 39 half-hour episode series that ran from 1960 to 1961, and 45 hour-long episodes that were transmitted over a three-year period between 1964 and 1967. It was the second incarnation, called *Secret Agent* in the USA, that broke through to the American market and that sported Edwin Anstey's famous 'High Wire' theme tune, which had been changed to give it more of a Bond feel.[32]

With the rise of other action adventure heroes, such as Simon Templar in *The Saint*, and with the success of sales abroad, Lew Grade's ITC was the most profitable company in this area. Its foreign earnings amounted to $10.5 million in 1965 and $15 million in 1966, Grade was knighted and ATV won two Queen's Awards to Industry for its export success. So successful was Grade that he was able to pre-sell *The Persuaders* to ABC in the USA in 1971, even before its stars, Roger Moore and Tony Curtis, had even agreed to appear.[33] The most successful individual programme, however, was *The Avengers*. Starting life very differently, first transmitted live and then recorded on video, it featured two male leads in a dowdy quasi-realist detective style drama, with a dour jazz soundtrack and claustro-phobic interior settings. *The Avengers* morphed over a period of years into a glossy adventure series, archly parodying the form, yet at the same time providing a glamorous and ludic edge to a stylish British modernity – perhaps prefiguring an aesthetic shift to postmodernism.[34] As Chapman has argued: '*The Avengers* was the first British series screened on primetime network television in the USA (the other series had been bought primarily as schedule fillers) and, pound for pound, was probably the most profitable television export of the decade.'[35]

Film technology and the BBC

Despite the high-profile visibility of filmed programming on ITV, the BBC had pioneered film as a recording technology on British television. At the outset, however, what defined the television medium was its 'liveness'. This was because television was philosophically perceived as a communications technology. From its first beginnings with John Logie Baird's test transmissions of 'Stooky Bill' (the head of a ventriloquist's dummy) in the mid-1920s, television was effectively an exercise in transmitting an image from one space to another in real time. In perhaps a similar vein to the way radio broadcasting had emerged in the early 1920s, out of technology used for (military) communication purposes, television had not necessarily been conceived in aesthetic terms. When the BBC started to transmit low-frequency television signals in the early 1930s, they were mainly talking heads or scenes of dancers. Yet this seemed to be more a matter of extending the range and vision of a particular performance to a wider audience situated elsewhere. When the high-definition television service started on 2 November 1936, this apparent function of communications 'relay' persisted.

The relay function was also perceived as being the *modus operandi* in televised drama. A dominant discourse in circulation at the BBC during the 1930s was that television was a medium characterized by its live immediacy, its intimacy and its hybridity,[36] and that this profoundly influenced the presentation of dramatic material. Before the Second World War, much drama transmission centred on scenes from West End stage plays, either transmitted via outside broadcasting equipment or re-enacted in the television studio. The prevailing ideology of being 'live' meant that transmission was concerned initially with the theatrical mode of production, and that the close up, on the multi-camera set (variable lenses were not developed and deployed until the 1950s) provided a way of seeing better into the actor's performance. That is not to say, however, that all early television drama should be dismissed as 'stagey'. Although theatrical discourses and tropes persisted in television well into the 1950s and 1960s, this was due neither to technological limitation nor lack of aesthetic ambition. As Jason Jacobs eloquently and convincingly argued, there were producers who thought about the aesthetics of the new medium, and who sought to explore ways of presenting drama with camera movement and cutting.[37]

It would be wrong to assume that the *only* form of television in the early years was 'live', for television often transmitted filmed programmes such as cartoons, documentaries and newsreels.[38] When the BBC television service closed down on 1 September 1939, prior to the imminent outbreak of war, it infamously did so halfway through a Disney Mickey Mouse cartoon. Nonetheless, these were films that had been made for cinematic exhibition and had not been specifically produced *for* television. When television did produce its own films in these early days, it was for demonstration purposes. Charles Barr notes that these films tended to 'simulate' live transmission, but were produced for transmission outside ordinary television hours to help television salesmen demonstrate their product to potential buyers.[39] Film was also used over this period as inserts in live televised drama. This tended to be stock film footage culled from cinematic features (such as battle scenes), and it was not until the late 1940s that film was produced in-house for this purpose.

As Jacobs notes, however, competing discourses surrounded the use of specially filmed sequences in live drama. One issue centred on how to stage drama taking place out of doors. Only the film insert, telecined into live action, could provide the large contrast in scale between interiors and exteriors. This, however, was seen as adding 'impurities' to the aesthetic of live drama because – both temporally and spatially – it interfered with television's intimacy. According to Jacobs this was because the inserts 'vitiated the live co-temporality between performer, audience and producer, and expanded the production beyond the smaller spaces of the studio.'[40] Some at the BBC felt that the use of film within live television drama denigrated the quality of dramatic presentation. There was also the technical difficulty of matching the filmed material to the lighting and tempo of the studio scenes, and the difference in visual textures was perceived as 'unprofessional'.

In early televised dramas, film inserts had three particular uses – to provide special effects, such as rain, fog and fire, by being superimposed over one or more of the camera channels; to provide location or exterior shots that would have been difficult to do in the studio, such as establishing shots or battle scenes; and to provide a practical breathing space for scenery and costume changes. Following the Second World War there was a shortage of filmed material at the BBC, so the Corporation established a Film Unit that produced newsreels, travelogues and documentaries. The Film Unit also made inserts for live dramas using actors from the plays, but the problem of matching studio aesthetics with the film aesthetic remained. As a result, in the early 1950s studio producers and directors became increasingly engaged in producing external sequences. There were, however, still unhappy consequences, difficulties and arguments because the television producers often had little experience of using film equipment. When they did use it, they tended to favour the replication of the visual style of the studio (tempo, lighting and composition) rather than working in more cinematic tropes. This was further complicated when the producers had little contact with the film editors who cut and spliced the images together.[41]

This was to change because, while some had seen inserts as problematic, others saw them as a way of extending television drama's visual range. Although inserts had been used in the early days of television drama, their impact was perhaps more popularly felt in the early 1950s with the work of people such as the producer Rudolph Cartier. Cartier has been much credited with pioneering ways of overcoming the spatial limitations of live studio drama with a combination of filmed inserts and camera mobility. Interestingly, Cartier had come from a film background before the war and, with his experience of studio work at the BBC, he was well able to bridge the gap between the hitherto distinct and separate filmed and live sequences. Cartier also specifically wanted to push the aesthetics of the television medium outwards, in contradiction to discourses that placed, and wanted to keep, television within an intimate mode of address.[42]

As Sydney-Smith has argued, the use of filmed inserts could expand the screen story world by introducing 'extra-diegetic space'.[43] In Cartier's work, therefore, the film insert did not merely constitute an establishing or linking shot, or offer brief respite for harried cast and crew; it particularly provided a way of furthering the action and drama. Perhaps the best two examples of Cartier's *œuvre* here, both in collaboration with the writer Nigel Kneale, are his six-part series *The Quatermass Experiment* in 1953, and his version of George Orwell's *Nineteen-Eighty-Four*, first transmitted live on 12 December 1954.[44] I will return to the work of Cartier and Kneale later in this chapter.

Telerecording, as it was known in Britain, was a new technology that emerged after the war following developments by the US Navy and Air Force. Called *kinescope* in the USA, it recorded a programme output at the moment of transmission onto 16mm or 35mm film. It could not, however, be prepared in advance prior to transmission, but once a programme had been recorded it could be repeated. With the advent of this recording technology, producers, production teams and executives could now review programmes to reflect on techniques and representation styles. Maurice Gorham, who had for a short while been head of the BBC's television service, had predicted this development in the late 1940s.[45] His argument, written in 1949, has been neatly summarized by Jacobs. Telerecording would mean that 'producers would be able to see and evaluate their own productions after transmission (during transmission the producer would see both preview and transmission monitors). Telerecordings could also be used as training material for new producers.'[46]

Although this probably became a more commonplace practice once the use of film and videotape had become more widely established, telerecordings still provided a useful tool for analysis at a relatively early stage, especially of sporting or other such occasions. This was because events could be recorded and repeated at convenient times for viewers. An early example of this was the 1949 Oxford–Cambridge boat race, which was shown live in the afternoon but repeated in the evening. Such telerecordings were closely scrutinized at yearly meetings at the BBC to review sports commentary and presentation.[47] The use of telerecording, however, still perpetuated the ideology that television was a 'relay' technology. Events were still transmitted live, but now the primary event being relayed by the camera (for example a sporting event) could be shown again for an audience at a later time or date.

Primary events did not just have to be sporting occasions or special broadcasts, they could also be live studio drama performances. By the early 1950s, the BBC had restaged several dramas. For Jacobs, this meant that producers had the opportunity to experiment with the television form, trying out different ways of executing the production.[48] One example of this was Patrick Hamilton's 1929 stage play *Rope*, which was first adapted for television in 1939, and then revised in 1947 and 1950. However, the BBC also produced straightforward repeats of a live drama production within a short while of original transmission, using the same cast, principal crew, scripts and technical specifications. Such repeat performances were a useful way of filling airtime. In 1949 Gorham recognized that telerecording a live performance could provide valuable savings in resources. Effectively, it would save studio space and time because cast and crew would not need to reoccupy a studio to restage the live performance. As Gorham stated, 'At Alexandra Palace, for instance, it [telerecording] will be the equivalent of one new fully equipped studio, if not more.'[49] This was not fully realized until 1954, but agreements with Equity, the actor's union, had to be struck because performers did not want to lose fees from repeat performances. The potential financial benefits of recording drama productions were undermined, however, when the compromise deal dictated that recordings could only be made of the *second* live performance.[50]

The production of plays was to cause other problems for the BBC. When it wanted to produce a live version of *Clive of India* in 1938, for example, the BBC had to obtain permission from Twentieth Century Fox, which had made a film version four years previously.[51] Rights clearances became even more problematic with recording, and there were cases of recorded material being destroyed or recording prohibited, as for example in 1951 when Warner Brothers banned the recording of Robert E. Sherwood's play *The Petrified Forest*, which had been made into a film in 1936.[52] One way in which the BBC sought to overcome this problem was to commission its own drama writers, and it did this with the appointment of its own staff writers Nigel Kneale and Philip Mackie in the early 1950s. As Jacobs notes, this constituted an attempt by the BBC to generate new material, which it owned and could record by itself: 'This would not have been an issue before telerecording when television programmes could not be thought of as *material* commodities.'[53] In 1949 Maurice Gorham had predicted that telerecorded programmes could become commodities for potential export and, in 1952, the BBC established a transcription unit to distribute telerecordings and purpose made BBC films abroad, especially to Canada and Australia. In 1953 a recording of the coronation was rapidly processed and flown to the North American continent by Royal Air Force jet bombers for next day transmission.[54]

Developments prior to the arrival of ITV, however, also suggest that the BBC was interested in promoting or importing programme material that was shot directly on film. In July 1954, the BBC showed a 12-part filmed serial from the USA, *I Am the Law*, an early example of the US 'cop show' genre. Several months later, in November 1954, the BBC transmitted the first British filmed police series, *Fabian of the Yard*, which ran from November 1954 to March 1957. The series followed the exploits of real-life Scotland Yard detective Bob Fabian, who was played by the actor Bruce Sefton. The programme was shot in a mixture of studio settings and on location, with much of the footage using asynchronous sound and voice-over. Each episode would also end with the real Bob Fabian directly addressing the camera. While attempting to signal the show's authenticity, this led instead to a conflation of styles and registers. 'Such a confusion of the "codes" of representation', Susan Sydney-Smith suggests, resulted 'in an identificatory problem in which both the real-life detective, "Bob" Fabian himself, and the actor Bruce Sefton, lost out, each proving the other false.'[55]

Although based on a British character, and depicting a particular vision of a consensus postwar Britain, *Fabian of the Yard* was also made as an export commodity. Produced by a British film company external to the BBC, Trinity Productions, the programme was made with an eye firmly on the American market. This is explicitly marked by the snippets of introductory London history offered by the voice-over commentary in many of the external scenes shot on location. Such scraps of information assume an interested yet uninitiated audience. In 'Bombs in Piccadilly', a 1955 episode about a series of terrorist attacks in London, the voice-over introduces a number of historical curiosities. These include the Tower of London, the building of which was 'started by William the Conqueror in 1078', and also the hundred year-old Stock Exchange. Action also takes place in a bombed-out house, 'a victim of Hitler's air raids', and a chase on foot through Chelsea passes 'near the studios of James Whistler, famous American painter'. Such trivia might possibly have been neither new nor interesting to a domestic audience. In any event, what this demonstrates is that the BBC was taking a new interest in film as a recording technology (and serialization) prior to the arrival of ITV.

Although, in many respects, videotape was to become a dominant medium of recording at the BBC in the early 1960s, and was, in drama, confined to the studio, film was to play an important part in the emergence of the so-called 'Golden Age' of drama.[56] This included Peter Watkins's documentary dramas *Culloden* (1964) and *The War Game* (1965), and standards from the drama canon such as Ken Loach's *Up the Junction* (1965) and Tony Garnett's *Cathy Come Home* (1966).[57] This was in part facilitated by developments in lightweight 16mm synchronized film camera equipment, which could more easily be carried into the field by a camera person and accompanying sound person. This meant an increased use of *actual locations* in dramatic works, thereby opening up screen space into new outside spaces. This new equipment was to prove particularly useful to programme makers such as Ken Russell and Peter Watkins who had learnt their film craft in the amateur film movement of the 1950s.[58]

Videotape

Despite the widespread use of film, it is generally agreed that one of the most important technological developments in British television in the 1950s and 1960s was the advent of videotape. The impact of videotape was, however, slowly felt for a number of reasons. First, it did not simply arrive overnight, but was the result of several years of research and development. Second, it was not immediately adopted by television practitioners. It was also very expensive, which meant that it was not very popular with managers in television. Third, videotape editing was pioneered very slowly. This meant that in the early days programmes were recorded 'as live' – in chronological sequence in the same way as if they had been performed live in front of an audience. Fourth, videotape was predominantly confined to the studio.[59]

In the first instance, videotape emerged over a number of years and technical developments were still ongoing when broadcasters adopted it.[60] The developments that made videotape possible occurred in plastics and in sound-recording technologies. These had first been developed in sound tape, which had been used in radio in the United States, at the end of the 1940s. Pressure from performers who had to repeat radio performances across different US time zones had impelled the use of this new format. At that time disc recordings produced a much poorer sound quality than live transmission. In 1947 the American singer Bing Crosby had been particularly impressed by Ampex sound recordings, which used a reel-to-reel tape recorder, and radio broadcasters in the USA caught on to the development. Ampex continued its own research and development into video forms, and met with success in 1956.

In February that year, Ampex held a successful demonstration to 30 of its employees, showing a programme recorded an hour previously and then playing back a two-minute sequence recorded during the meeting itself. In the weeks that followed, Ampex showed in secret its new four-head Quadruplex system to representatives from the major broadcasters in the USA – CBS, ABC and NBC. It also showed the new technology to representatives of the BBC. The equipment was publicly demonstrated in Chicago in April 1956, and by the end of the year Ampex had orders for 84 video tape recorders (VTRs). Importantly, this included two for Associated-Rediffusion in London.

Videotape went on air for the first time in the USA on 30 November 1956 from CBS Television City in Los Angeles. It was in use with NBC at the beginning of 1957, and with ABC in April 1957. At this time it was claimed that tape was saving the networks $10,000 a week in film and processing.[61] The large number of orders meant that distribution was relatively slow and it did not arrive with Associated-Rediffusion until summer 1958. This was partly because the Quadruplex system had to be converted for UK transmission. At the time, the machine cost £20,000 and a 12½-inch reel of tape cost £100, but the economic saving was that this reel could be used 100 times.

In the meantime, the BBC had been conducting its own research into videotape technology from as early as 1952. According to Peter Axon, head of the recording section of the BBC's engineering research department from 1953 to 1958, the BBC had always maintained a continuous and active interest in engineering developments. This included recording and quality in sound and vision. The fruits of this labour, Vision Electronic Recording Apparatus (VERA), were formally unveiled to the public in an April 1958 edition of the current affairs programme *Panorama*. Within this live programme, the veteran television presenter Richard Dimbleby asked the audience at home to note the time on the studio clock. He then talked through pictures of the BBC's new technology as it was recording before asking technicians to stop the machinery and rewind to the moment when he had asked the audience to note the time on the clock. After showing the recorded sequence, he explains to camera, 'That was VERA. This is me again here, now, really.'

The BBC's new system offered the television producer a range of benefits and advantages over film. In the first place, unlike film, it offered instant playback of recorded material without any further processing. Furthermore, the picture quality from the camera could be monitored *as* material was being recorded. The videotape could be reused (recorded on) again and again. It offered very good picture quality on the 405-line system then in use in British broadcasting and, as well as high-quality sound it was able to use the half-inch sound tape currently available. These features VERA shared in common with Ampex. However, more impressive than Ampex at the time, which had not developed a successful means for videotape editing, Peter Axon claimed that producers could cut, join and edit using VERA without disturbing picture quality in subsequent reproduction. Yet, despite this significant advantage, the BBC's VERA system was short-lived. This was not due to any intrinsic fault of the system, but was very much a matter of timing, with the US Ampex system being adopted at the BBC for several reasons.

First, while VERA tapes could accommodate 15 minutes of programme time, Ampex could record material for as long as one hour. Second, although it had yet to be formally agreed, planning was under way in the UK, and most of Europe (except France), for a shift to a 625-line television high-definition service. Although VERA had the bandwidth to accommodate the 405-line service, it would have been unable to accommodate the higher-definition picture. Ampex had the technical advantage that it *could* accommodate the new system. The third reason, related to this, was both operational and economic. As Ampex and the new system were likely to be adopted round Europe, the BBC believed that standardizing its own system in line with the rest of Europe would facilitate simpler and more convenient programme exchange. Not only would the exchange of programmes be easier, but it would also be cost-effective. This is what perhaps sealed VERA's fate. Axon believed that improvements could have been made to the BBC's VERA system, but at the time Ampex simply represented an off-the-peg alternative, 'a manufactured machine in the first stages of adoption as a world broadcasting standard.'[62]

The BBC acquired Ampex in October 1958, and it was put to use in four editions of *Hancock's Half Hour* in November and December that year. It was testament to the prestige of Tony Hancock's show that he was allowed to use such expensive equipment so early on.[63] At that time, the pressure of live performance had been exerting an intolerable strain on Hancock. The show had also been changing direction from its earlier incarnation as a radio show programme in the early 1950s.[64] Writers Ray Galton and Alan Simpson had begun to introduce a note of increased realism, with fewer farcical situations, simpler and more believable plot lines, and greater reliance on characterization than on jokes and gags. Characters started to behave in ways the audience found more believable. There was also an increasing interest in using close-ups and reaction shots, which had heightened characterization and comedy moments in *I Love Lucy*. As we saw in Lucille Ball's show, there were usually three studio cameras, with one permanently trained on Ball to capture her reactions to events around her. With recording and editing on film, *I Love Lucy* had caused an impact with its fast pace and punchiness when it appeared on ITV screens in 1955.

Although the BBC had used the new Ampex technology on Hancock in 1958, it was not immediately able to adopt the fast paced cutting and editing of *I Love Lucy*. This was simply because of the technical limitations of the new recording technology. As I previously indicated, one way in which Ampex could not compete with film in this early stage of its development was in editing. It was not possible to edit on the Ampex videotape system. As a result, programmes that were recorded on the new technology were produced 'as live'. In one sense, it was possible to shoot in a discontinuous manner because a scene could be restaged and recorded *over* the previous take. But recording still had to follow the chronology of the script because it was not possible to intercut scenes or remove errors or fluffs at a later stage. Each production only had one (chronological) chance to get it right. Those programmes shot on early video that still survive in the archives today, such as some of the first episodes of *The Avengers*, can sometimes be seen to contain 'fluffs' and moments of ad-libbing.

In 1958 Ampex engineers had still not solved the problem of editing, but instead came up with a splicing block, and it was left to the individual engineers of the different broadcasting companies to find ways to cut and join the tapes. At the BBC, Hancock's producer Duncan Wood experimented and discovered that tapes could be cut and spliced together without loss of picture quality. Wood's technique, though effective, was still relatively crude and was not cost friendly because it meant that the cut tapes could not be recorded over again. At £100 a reel, the BBC considered this to be prohibitively expensive.[65] Hancock, however, forced the BBC's hand by refusing to sign a contract for another series unless his programmes were recorded on videotape. With Wood's splicing technique, *Hancock's Half-Hour* could now be shot discontinuously, in a stop–start manner, with cast and crew able to prepare better for the next shot, and scenes could potentially be shot out of sequence. The consequence was that the show became increasingly faster paced. Time did not now need to be spent on superfluous bridging dialogue while characters changed costumes, sets were rearranged or camera positions moved. It also eliminated some of the mistakes and gaffs. As Goddard has noted, it meant that the principal characters could spend more time on screen.[66] This was because cameras could spend more time on each character and not have to be constantly moving and ready for the next live shot. This meant more time on reactions and close-ups.[67]

With videotape expensive, and different companies forced to experiment with video-editing techniques, the roll-out of video was necessarily piecemeal. Whereas a third of BBC programmes were being recorded on videotape by 1961, as late as 1963 some ITV companies were still officially denying that videotape could be edited.[68] When an editing technique that did not destroy the reuse value and subsequent reproduction quality of the tape was discovered at Granada, however, Denis Forman, a senior Granada figure, hailed the development as 'rather more important than the invention of sliced bread'.[69] Nonetheless, despite the benefits of discontinuous recording and the 'programme factory', the problem of cost remained. As Forman points out, some managements were still reluctant to embrace the new technology because it was very expensive to install and use. Yet, once the technology took hold, management policy became increasingly relaxed. As Forman notes:

> Rules were set down – shows must be recorded in real time, edits must be authorized by a member of the board, there may only be two edits in a show, three edits, six edits, and as the months went by, a show may take no more than 50 per cent more time than it did when it was being transmitted live.[70]

Pros and cons characterized the use of Ampex at the BBC. As Briggs notes, its technical and operational advantages gave the television producer a degree of flexibility hitherto only known to the film producer. As a result, 'by 1963 the practice had spread to music production, religious broadcasting, and school and adult education broadcasting.'[71] Experimentation with colour television on the new 625-line system at the BBC was also to feed back into the development of videotape in the USA. In 1964 Ampex developed the VR-2000 Hi Band Colour Videotape based on requests from the BBC.[72] However, the use of video-tape was to cause some anxiety. Citing from the minutes of an operations' meeting on 22 October 1964, Briggs goes on to state that 'there were complaints that very few directors had "any experience at all of handling live productions".'[73] Briggs also cites a range of complaints about how crews and casts became increasingly 'fatalistic' about making mistakes. By 1967 it was estimated that studio time ran for three times the length of the final production and as much as two-thirds of tape ended up on the cutting room floor.

Yet while some recordings were seen as having commodity or reuse value, others were still deemed ephemeral and disposable. This was the view, for example, of the Light Entertainment producer Francis Essex who worked for the BBC and then ATV. In an ATV documentary called *The Dream Machine*, transmitted on 11 November 1964, about the staging and recording of a one-off variety show, *Six Wonderful Girls*, with appearances by Millicent Martin and Honor Blackman, Essex stated his credo:

Television is a transient medium, and I am a person who becomes bored with long runs in the theatre or any other form. I like the thought that I work to a deadline, and the ideas have to be thought of by such and such a time. And when the show happens it's finished, and I'm the next day onto the next show.

This ephemerality was foregrounded at the beginning of the documentary. Introductory shots focus on a number of clocks, and then on a man with an open-reel videotape working on a machine while the voice-over, in a staccato manner – in rhythm with the ticking clocks – explains what is happening.

> Clocks everywhere,
> Time king,
> Time precious,
> Time passing,
> Nothing permanent.
> A videotape,
> On it, a recording of a play,
> Sound and vision,
> Costing thousands to produce.
> And now wiped,
> Gone forever,
> Lost.

It was the high cost factor of tapes, and an enduring attitude that saw some television as a transient and ephemeral form, which led to many potentially 'classic' programmes being lost to the archives and to newer generations of viewers and researchers.[74]

Recording technology and the new visibility

The significance of the development of recording technologies was that television could now expand its range of stylistic choices for the presentation of different kinds of themes and issues in different kinds of programmes and genres. In so doing, it made new cultural forms (television *per se*), and forms of culture (the subject and themes of television) visible to the newly expanding audience. One way of apprehending how radical an impact recording technology had is to think, phenomenologically, about how it changed how television operated in 'space' and 'time'.

In the first instance, film and video meant that television forms could be extended *over* space in new ways. This was because the new technologies facilitated the movement of programmes as solid artefacts (film reels or videotapes) between different places. As we have seen here, programme material began to be viewed increasingly as a commodity export (and import) in the 1950s, and it meant that people in Britain could see American programming, and vice versa. Recording technology also extended television programming over time, and it did this here in two ways. In audience terms, an event that had taken place at a particular time or on a particular day could now be played back at a more suitable time for a mass audience. This proved to be the case initially with sports and ceremonial events in Britain, but had been an important technological driver in the USA where different time zones created scheduling difficulties. From the perspective of production it also meant, as we have seen, that a programme could be made over a period of time, as opposed to the instantaneous live transmission of an event taking place in front of the cameras. With the use of film (on location) and videotape (in the studio – once editing techniques had been developed) recording could be discontinuous and conducted piecemeal on an industrialized scale. Such developments were allied with the expansion of the television industry and increasing discourses of professionalism.

Significantly, the use of recording technology meant that television production could be extended *in* space, it could now enter *into* and articulate dramatic space in a different way. It has been argued that in early live studio drama there had been limitations in the ways in which screen, or dramatic space, could be used. One reason for this is that television cameras could not effectively enter screen space, meaning that they could not enter into and occupy the same physical and narrative space as the characters on set. This was because studio cameras in the USA, for example, were arranged in a line during the live transmission of drama.[75] Cameras could not enter into three-dimensional screen space for fear of catching another camera, a microphone or another part of the television apparatus in vision.[76] 'As a result, the television image was frontal and oriented toward the viewer in much the same way as a performance on a proscenium stage would be. This was reflected in the actors' playing, which Burger describes as "aimed ... at the fourth wall" in front of the cameras "much as it is on the stage".'[77] So, in this view, live television drama was effectively 'stagey', and this was an aesthetic restriction imposed by the technological limitations of the cameras.

Jason Jacobs, drawing on archive papers, complicates the view that the aesthetics of early television drama in Britain were determined solely by technology. Dismissing easy, and potentially lazy, assumptions that early dramas were 'stagey', he argues that drama producers at the BBC had aesthetic ambitions and had experimented with forms of dramatic representation on television. This, he asserts, could be demonstrated by transitions of sound and image sources, such as mixing live studio drama with filmed inserts.[78] This allowed for transitions in narrative spaces, such as the movement from inside to outside. There was also scene dissection: before and immediately after the Second World War it was technologically impossible to cut directly and quickly between cameras during transmission, but cutting *could* be achieved by dissolves between cameras.[79] There was also camera movement when out of vision, as when shots were being transmitted from another camera, or filmed inserts were being telecined, and camera movement on-air with live transmission of tracking shots.

What significantly prohibited development of drama forms in the 1930s, 1940s and early 1950s, Jacobs argues, were conventions and discourses surrounding 'liveness' and 'intimacy'. In drama, television's liveness assured immediacy. This was an enduring perception based on the premise that television was an instrument of communications relay. After all, it was possible to make filmed programmes and then telecine them on transmission. But in live television dramas the work of the television camera was seen to be to capture the pre-camera event and, as a result, co-temporality (the sense of shared moment) in drama was perceived as signifying authenticity and realism. The performance taking place in front of the camera in real time was, as in the theatre, *really* taking place. With television perceived as an ephemeral medium, recording technology initially seemed anathema to the televisual experience. At the same time moves towards recording programmes were inhibited by copyright and talent union agreements to ensure actors repeat live performances.

Liveness was also related to intimacy. According to Jacobs, critics and producers understood intimacy in terms of reception, the 'intimate sphere' of the home. Some critics believed that drama broadcast into the domestic sphere required a softer visual register, a restrained performance style and should be conversational in tone, rather than 'declarative'. In this view, television plays were expected to tackle emotional and psychological issues, and were based in intimate interior settings. Thus, characters' inner feelings and emotions were rendered through a *close-up* style of the television camera. This intimacy was provided by nearness of observation. This was significant for performance styles because the nearness of the camera, within a confined studio space, required concentrated work and use of facial expression by the actor. Television critics at the time therefore argued that television could see better into the performance. The actor on television had to use facial expression with more subtlety than on the theatre stage.

For Jacobs, however, the close-up style of the television camera was not used to visualize the 'motives and emotions' of character, but to monitor closely the performance and interpretations by the actor. As Jacobs suggests:

Such a close observation of performance details required a responsive production technique that privileges the close up style. The responsive production technique meant that the producer functioned as a 'stand-in' live audience, mediating performance through his creative and responsive consciousness, and choice of camera style. Live drama production had to be sensitive to – intimate with – the rhythm and tempo of the performance itself. This meant an intimate response to an intimate style.[80]

As a result, in discourses of early television drama, the use of film was seen to disrupt both the temporal and physical sense of intimacy. Yet, by 1953 there was already an alternative school of drama style. This coincided in the early 1950s with the expansion of the BBC television service and its production base. BBC television personnel had moved into larger studios at Lime Grove, with plans for a purpose built studio at White City. The move to Lime Grove brought with it new equipment, such as the arrival in March 1952 of new cameras with variable lenses that broke through the shallow field of focus. It also coincided with the appointment of a new head of television drama, Michael Barry, who particularly advocated that drama should rely more on the power of the image.[81]

The new expansive style, what Jacobs refers to as the 'expanding screen', was heralded by the arrival of Kneale and Cartier who, as we saw above, challenged intimate drama directly. Cartier, who had been a scriptwriter and director in the German film industry in the 1920s and early 1930s, was aware of the discourses surrounding the intimate domestic sphere of the home, but felt that television did not demand any singular style of address. Cartier is now recognized as a major influence on the visual development of British television drama. Indeed, Catherine Johnson demonstrates how Cartier combined both filmed inserts and live television for shock effect as early as 1953 with *The Quatermass Experiment*.[82] In one sequence an astronaut faints and falls directly towards the camera (suddenly filling the viewer's screen at home) and, in another, television's own workings are shown as an outside broadcast team capture an alien monster on camera, climbing up the inside of Westminster Abbey. The film inserts were not simply used as linkages, but expanded the drama outwards and moved the narrative forward.

Jacobs has also shown that Cartier used filmed sequences to

transcend the spatial limitations of *Nineteen-Eighty-Four* to similar effect a year later.[83] For Cartier, film extended the range of stylistic choices available, and these complemented the continued use of close-ups for reaction shots, emotional expression and shock scenes. The increased use of recording technology in the 1950s and 1960s, rationalized and institutionalized within industry practises, allowed television drama producers a much wider range of aesthetic and stylistic choices.

In the USA it has been argued that the use of film made television drama more cinematic. This is because the use of film in the USA occurs more explicitly in the early 1950s when the geography of television production shifted from New York, with its thriving theatre and radio scenes, to Hollywood, the centre for film making in North America.[84] It marked a shift from live single dramas to filmed television series. One consequence was that the 'syntax of televisual discourse became that of cinematic discourse'.[85]

The increased range of stylistic choices that were opening up to drama producers and directors certainly complicated the situation in Britain. In the early 1960s, for example, some television dramas were still being performed live, including early episodes of *Z Cars* and *The Avengers*. Nonetheless, filmed series such as *The Adventures of Robin Hood*, *The Saint* and *Danger Man*, clearly did have something in common with the more cinematic discourses of US television made in Hollywood, partly because they were produced with an eye for export to the American market. In such television, the drama moved away from a sense of relay of live theatrical performance where, as John Caughie describes, narrative was subordinate to performance.[86]

Instead, it moved towards a style of drama where the organization of space and time, through discontinuous recording and editing (and, I would suggest, performance), was subordinate to narrative in the sense of the 'classic' Hollywood cinema described by Bordwell, Staiger and Thompson (1985).[87] This shift of emphasis towards narrative and action, especially in series drama where cast reiterated their roles on a weekly basis, would have been a significant development at a time when television was newly expanding to a mass audience. It would have

marked a shift from the overtly *actorly* and 'staged' performances associated with middle-class theatre, which may have
been less familiar to a mass audience. Instead, the newer filmed
drama series might have seemed more accessible to a newer,
wider audience already familiar with cinematic tropes of staging, editing and performance. This wider viewing audience,
increasingly domesticated by the demographic changes I discuss
in Chapter 4, especially the postwar baby boom, would have
constituted a substantial part of the audience in the cinema-
going boom in the immediate postwar period.

I do not want to be technologically determinist here. As I have
suggested, such developments in the use of film in action-
adventure series constitute only one of many different styles
and aesthetics in television drama. Most television drama in
Britain, when it was recorded, tended to be shot on video, still
in the studio. In other instances where film was used the inten-
tion and effects appeared more experimental. This ranged from
the more documentary aesthetics of dramas by Watkins, Loach
and Garnett, or the potentially more avant-gardist sensibilities
of *The Prisoner*, which at times played with conventional narrative structures and challenged the reliability of what the viewer
was seeing. By contrast, explicitly performative styles from political theatre were still found in television dramas in the 1970s,
such as John McGrath's *The Cheviot, the Stag and the Black, Black
Oil* (BBC, 1974).

These developments in recording technology and the impacts
they had on drama presentation over this time importantly coincided with other developments. Changes in drama styles in the
1950s and 1960s coincided with new preoccupations in drama
themes. Since the mid-1950s there had been an increased fascination with working-class life in theatre, literature and cinema. In
theatre this was marked in 1956 with the staging, at the Royal
Court Theatre, of John Osborne's play *Look Back in Anger*. In
literature there was also John Braine's novel *Room at the Top*,
which was about the ruthless self-determination needed to
achieve any degree of success in life. Such works were
characterized by their provincial settings, and the writers came
to be known in the press as 'the angry young men'. Other

novels, including Shelagh Delaney's *Taste of Honey*, were later turned into films that came to be known as 'kitchen sink dramas' or the British new wave.

This was reflected on television in dramas ranging from *Armchair Theatre* to *Cathy Come Home*.[88] It was these developments in British television drama that made working-class life more visible. While middle-class audiences could now watch the drama of working-class life, working-class audiences – who constituted a new audience for television in the 1950s – could now witness their experiences represented dramatically on the television screen. As the range of styles and themes in television drama expanded over the 1950s and 1960s, this made a wider range of programmes possible and available, and it made television accessible to larger and more diverse audiences.

In summary, the increasing use of film and video recording technologies had a profound impact on programme forms and programme aesthetics. It meant the advent of new programme forms, ranging from advertisements to action-adventure series. The new technologies meant that there was an increase in the range of styles that producers could choose from to cover an expanded range of narratives and themes. In particular, it meant that programmes could move away from more theatrical tropes of presentation towards styles of programming, such as the action-adventure series, which potentially had a visual grammar accessible to a wide audience familiar with mainstream cinematic presentation. In a wide range of programming, recording technologies allowed increased flexibility in programme production, facilitating the development of the programme factory.

The deployment of recording technologies was not just, or necessarily, conceived in aesthetic terms, but a means of rationalizing production and making economic savings, and this was part of the shift towards increased professionalism and industrialization in television discussed in Chapter 1. The increased use of recording technologies also benefited the economics of television by providing commodities for export and import. Programme sales abroad generated money for British broadcasters, and buying in programmes from abroad was also a cost-effective way of filling in airtime. Furthermore, as will be discussed in the next chapter, film technology also meant that the emerging television news could now cover filmed reports in a wide range of locations, and there was also the development of other programme forms such as television documentaries and current affairs series. The use of recording technologies in drama and in news and documentary allowed television to represent better the changes that were taking place in Britain and around the world. This will be the focus of the next chapter.

Chapter 4
SPACES

As we have seen so far, television underwent radical expansion in the 1950s and 1960s, and this had consequences for the professionalization of the nascent industry, for the articulation of local and national cultures, and for the use of recording technologies. As I have argued, these developments coincided with social and cultural changes taking place in Britain during the same period. In this chapter I more explicitly examine the *social* change that was affecting a large part of the British population, and explore television's relationship to that change. In a very straightforward sense, television's programming outputs made some of those changes more visible.

Television dramas explored some of the themes and tensions that were preoccupying television writers, producers and their drama audiences. Yet, television emerged as a mass medium precisely because of some of these social changes, in particular the demographic shifts that were affecting Britain. Home-building, urbanization and suburbanization were to have major impacts on how people lived their lives and spent their time. It was as a result of some of these changes that television was taken up by a national audience and why it was to become such a potent cultural force. As I shall argue, television opened up new public space just as its audience became increasingly domesticated and housebound. At the same time, television offered the possibility of transcending domestic and local space to become, in the words of the *Panorama* catchphrase, 'a window on the world'.

I shall therefore start this chapter by looking at the urban and suburban change that affected so many people before going on to examine some of the reasons why people adopted the new medium. I shall then explore the representation of the changes in the British social landscape and their consequences in a range of television dramas. Finally, I shall go on to look at how television negotiated the domestic, the global and the political.

Urban and suburban change

One of the most important developments taking place in Britain in the 1950s and 1960s was a wave of housing construction. The ground had been paved by the 1946 New Towns Act and 1947 Town and Country Planning Act, which led to slum clearances (the evacuation and destruction of older, substandard properties), and legislated for the development of new towns and the rebuilding of city centres, some of which had been severely affected by the war. This legislation was particularly important because it addressed the issue of the long-term expansion of the urban population, fed by a migratory drift from the countryside and already characterized by increasing urban sprawl and an expansion in suburbs, estates and satellite communities. The conscious policy of targeting development was facilitated by industrial change. Making use of the sites of wartime industry, which were often placed as far out of reach as possible of German bombers, government policy deliberately promoted the construction of factory units outside town centres. As the historian Arthur Marwick notes, 'A new urban pattern emerged very clearly. Whereas older industries had been located along the rivers with copious provision of railway sidings, the new industrial estates developed on the outskirts of towns, and depended upon the roads.'[1]

These new industrial estates articulated a shift in modern industry, from heavy industry to new hi-tech, super-modern plants, refineries and factories. This also entailed a shift in labour patterns and working-class culture. It meant that workers moved from heavy physical and manual labour towards factory production-line processes that were cleaner, lighter and more likely to involve the supervision and maintenance of technology. It meant the establishment of new communities and new towns to provide workers, and homes for the workers, for these new industries. For example, the Royal Ordnance factory at Aycliffe became the new town of Newton Aycliffe in the northeast of England, and in South Wales a combination of traditional industries and new industries led to the development of the new town of Cwmbran.[2]

Other new towns, suburbs and estates emerged from the growing urban sprawl. This particularly affected the London area and the southeast of England, with movement out to suburban estates in places like Basildon, Bracknell, Hemel Hemstead and Hatfield. By 1956 these towns were growing by 9000 houses a year.[3] While low-rise housing characterized the new towns and suburbs (the accommodation often included gardens and green spaces), high-rise estates replaced the slums demolished in the inner cities, one notable example being the award-winning Alton East Estate set in parkland in Roehampton, southwest London. The slum clearances and expansion of homebuilding led to radically improved living standards for many people in the working classes.

At the beginning of the 1950s, 70 per cent of dwellings dated back to the late nineteenth or early twentieth centuries, or even earlier.[4] Dilapidated tenements, crowded 'two-up and two-downs', densely packed terraces, and back-to-back houses characterized many urban centres. The shortage of housing at the beginning of the decade meant that conditions were cramped and crowded. For many their living environment was squalid, and at the beginning of this period a third of houses did not have a bath, and many had shared or outside toilet facilities. Located within industrial districts, there was often soot, pollution and grime. In 1956, in the huddled terraced houses along urban hillsides, by canals or the centres of Victorian industry, the three daily battles were against darkness, cold and filth.[5] As Richard Hoggart was to note in his seminal study of working-class life, *The uses of literacy*, life for the inhabitants of these spaces was a matter of coping, of trying not to slip down or succumb to the dirt or squalor.[6] In the new homes of the 1950s and 1960s, therefore, many experienced the luxury of baths and indoor toilets for the first time. In some cases even electricity was a novelty.[7]

These developments across Britian were uneven. Where these new urban and suburban landscapes emerged there was a profound impact on working-class culture and it was not necessarily a happy one. In the first instance, developments may have lacked aesthetic appeal. Part of the issue was that economic growth and geographical redistribution of industry and housing had led to a radical overhaul of Britain's roads. In the 1950s and 1960s the ownership of motor vehicles exploded from just under two and a half million cars and vans in 1950, five and a half million in 1960 to more than nine million in 1965.[8] The expansion of road networks led to the construction of Britain's first motorway, the M1, in the second half of the 1950s.

In 1963 the government's Buchanan Report, acknowledging traffic congestion in towns and cities, recommended building more motorways and roads. In the mid-1950s, however, car congestion and upgrading the road network had been viewed ambivalently. In 1955 the *Architectural Review* predicted, 'By the end of the century, Great Britain will consist of isolated oases of preserved monuments in a desert of wire, concrete roads, cosy plots and bungalows.'[9] Yet, it was not necessarily cosy plots and bungalows, or even leafy suburbs that occupied the spaces between the tarmac roads, but often large concrete developments. In this period, many new housing estates and public buildings were constructed in the new 'brutalist' style, a form of concrete architecture that combined Corbusian modernism with nineteenth-century industrial architecture.[10] This style, of which the Alton East Estate in Roehampton was a model example, came to define the architecture of the welfare state.

While those responsible for social housing in the period perceived the new architecture as innovative, modish and utilitarian, the people who actually had to live there may not have received it so well, as an extract from one of the dramas we shall discuss later in this chapter suggests.[11] Combined with road building and slum clearances, the construction of new estates created radically new urban (and suburban) landscapes. For Marwick, these changes represented a bleak architectural vision descending on Britain as the 'guts were torn out of cities such as Newcastle, Glasgow, and Birmingham and replaced with an ugly jungle of urban motorways and high-rise buildings.'[12]

These changes did not just have aesthetic impacts; they also had psychological, emotional and geographical ones. In the late 1940s and early 1950s, with the exception of the wartime disruption and national service for men, people rarely ventured far from home. Local employment and a lack of adequate public transport tended to keep people within small communities. Working-class social life was also split along gender and age lines, with men spending their time in the pub, club or on the football terraces, women visiting neighbours or relatives, and younger people going to the cinema.[13] For Richard Hoggart, however, the housing policies, developments and redistribution of working-class communities in the 1950s had negative consequences:

> We all know of working class people's difficulties in settling into the new council-house estates. Most react instinctively against consciously planned group activities; they are used to group life, but one which has started from the home and worked outwards in response to the common needs and amusements of a densely packed neighbourhood. In these brick and concrete wastes they feel exposed and cold at first, they suffer from agoraphobia; they do not feel 'It's homely or neighbourly'. Feel 'too far from everything', from their relatives and from the shops.[14]

The shift to these new places in the 1950s and 1960s moved people away from the communities they knew. With new estates, the rebuilding of city centres and the redistribution of

111

sites of industrial labour, working-class communities were often broken up and shifted miles away from friends, family and their traditional leisure pursuits. Cinema-going was one of the victims of this change. Whereas people used to go to the cinema regularly because it was close by and a warm place for being with friends (or for courting), the cinemas were now further away and attendances started to dwindle.[15]

The new houses on the council estates were often more expensive than the slums, where the rents had been capped by legislation. In fact the rents for the new local authority properties were sometimes as much as three times as high.[16] This meant that people had less disposable income. In particular, men who had traditionally given their wives 'housekeeping' money found they had less money for their normal leisure pursuits of beer and cigarettes, so they could afford to go out to the pub less frequently. As a consequence of these changes, public houses were another victim, and between 1939 and 1962 around 30,000 pubs closed down.[17] At the same time, there had been a baby boom in the immediate postwar years, and by the middle of the 1950s children at home were another reason that many more husbands and wives stayed in. Children would also have been a financial burden. Yet, despite having less disposable income, more relaxed hire-purchase arrangements meant that people could obtain commodity items such as television sets and other household appliances on credit (this point is discussed further in the next chapter). It was within this wider demographic context that television emerged as a major domestic leisure activity.

Television and the home

It seems clear that the advent of better housing and the loss of local community created a new space for the television medium to occupy. There are two points I want to explore here in relation to the emergence of television in working-class homes – the expansion of the television service and arrival of commercial competition; and the domestic life of working-class families and their relationship to home and the new medium.

Since the 1950s, it has popularly been assumed that the arrival of ITV promoted the uptake of television receivers. The standard view is that ITV appealed to a working-class audience because of its mode of address and because it contrasted with stuffy BBC values. The implication is that the incentive to acquire television was derived from competition. It is often popularly held that competition between television services leads to a lowering of standards and an appeal to the 'lowest common denominator'. This notion has recently been challenged, with studies showing that the expansion of television competition and services in the 1980s and 1990s has had the effect of allowing 'quality' programmes and niche programme markets and audiences to evolve.[18]

In the 1950s, however, commercialization raised anxieties about low-quality television, brash consumerism and the Americanization of British culture. These fears were present in debates on the 1954 Television Act and had, since the end of the Second World War, had wider currency in other British cultural institutions such as the Arts Council.[19] Thus, the arrival of commercial, popular television seemed to undermine the arts promotion and educational policies of an elitist cadre in the establishment, and it was feared it did this by direct appeal to the working-class masses. Such anxiety had caused some press controversy in 1956 and 1957 when struggling ITV companies appeared to abandon more high-brow programming in favour of popular game shows.[20]

Programmes like *Double Your Money* (A-R) and *Take Your Pick* (A-R) were known as 'the give-aways' because they awarded members of the public cash prizes or commodities. These quiz and game shows, as we shall see in Chapter 5, caused particular concern among cultural critics and commentators because they appeared to promote a crass consumer culture in which people could expect to be rewarded for doing nothing. Programmes like these also worried people like Richard Hoggart who believed that they threatened traditional forms of working-class life.[21] Hoggart strongly articulated these concerns as a member of the Pilkington Committee, which went on to be heavily critical of the new commercial broadcaster.

The arrival of commercial television, with an apparently populist ideology, and the expansion of the television audience in this period has often left the impression that ITV drove up the demand for television sets among a working-class audience. Yet, this idea is unproven. The economist Chris Hand has argued that the idea came about because of two mistaken assumptions.[22] The first is that the ITV institution drove the demand for television rather than the establishment of choice through the advent of a (any) new television service, and the second is that without the arrival of ITV television sets would not have been found in working-class homes. For Hand, the first assumption raises questions about the specific economic nature of television. This is because the decision to acquire a television set is a 'derived demand', meaning that a television is purchased or rented not for the intrinsic value of the set itself, but for the ability to watch television programmes.

Hand describes television in economic terms as an 'experience' good, so that if certain audiences wanted to purchase television sets (or modify their existing aerials) *specifically* to watch ITV, they would have had to have had some prior knowledge or experience of the ITV service. During the 1950s most people would have seen television in locations outside their home, in department stores, television or rental shops, or (though decreasingly if we recall that many working-class people had been isolated from their traditional communities, friends and family) at the homes of friends or relatives. Drawing on the National Readership Survey from 1957, Hand shows that people without television sets were likely (unsurprisingly) to watch television less than once a week.[23] This meant that potential viewers who had not yet acquired a television set were perhaps unlikely to have developed a preference for a particular service or, more significantly, were unlikely to have made the decision to acquire a set on the basis of liking one channel. To have made a decision on the basis of channel preference they would, one assumes, have had to have watched more hours of television. As Hand points out, 'In order to increase their viewing, non-owners would have to acquire a television set (or find exceptionally accommodating neighbours!).'[24] The other possibility, of course, is that the marketing of the new ITV service in the press might have made television seem more attractive, and more research needs to be conducted in this area.

As for the second assumption, that without the arrival of ITV, television sets would not have appeared in low-income households, Hand can find no evidence to suggest this would have been the case. Instead, drawing on research by Bain,[25] Hand argues that ITV expanded the television market by only 7 per cent, which is not a significant increase. As a result, the effect of ITV on the acquisition of television may instead have been related to the expansion of choice itself. As Hand argues, 'One can view the introduction of ITV as effectively a price cut. In return for purchasing or renting a multi-channel television set and a TV licence, the household gained access to two television channels where previously only one was available for the same price.'[26]

The acquisition of television in the late 1950s may also have been related to continuities in working-class life. As we have seen, the redistribution of new industries and housing seemed to have broken down the patterns of traditional working-class life. Yet some sociologists[27] and commentators such as Hoggart argued that many patterns of working-class life persisted. As Hoggart suggests, 'The working-classes have a strong ability to survive change by adapting or assuming what they want in the new and ignoring the rest.'[28] One of these was the way in which the home remained a private sphere, as it had in the working-class terraces and tenements. While men and women often spent time at the pub or visiting relatives, the rest of the time was spent 'staying in'. As Hoggart states, 'The hearth is reserved for the family, whether living at home or nearby, and those who are "something to us", and look in for a talk or just to sit. Much of the free time of a man and his wife will be passed at the hearth, "just staying in" is still one of the most common leisure-time occupations.'[29]

While it was a common middle-class leisure activity to invite friends round to visit for an evening, the working-class domestic 'hearth' was a more intimate, familial space. Now, with new housing developments, family were often further away and came to visit less. Therefore, an increasingly privatized lifestyle also reflected an adaptation of longstanding working-class norms of social activity to new economic social conditions created by mobility and separation from kin.[30] The home space remained a private space, but one where the occupants were removed from other family and friends, and from other leisure pursuits. There would therefore have been an increased psychological and emotional commitment to the home space.[31]

Given that there was a baby boom, more income would have been spent on child rearing and the purchase of domestic household items like refrigerators, cookers and televisions. Indeed, as the cost of television sets gradually came down over the decade (and the size of television screens increased in proportion to the size of the receivers), it seems that in some households the presence of children was an incentive to acquire a television set. For some families the television set was seen as educational and 'improving'.[32] In interviews conducted by Tim O'Sullivan about early memories of television, one respondent noted:

> We did buy it for ourselves, but I remember thinking that it would help the children get on at school, that they would know more about the world and what was going on, they'd be more 'in touch' and be able to see and understand things better – I'm not sure if it did, mind, but we certainly felt that at the time.[33]

Other audience research conducted in the 1950s also indicated that children could be a significant consideration in the decision to acquire a television set. Drawing on such research Hand found that the presence of children in the household made the acquisition of a television set more likely. He goes on to suggest that this might also be related to class, and the expansion of the audience, since working-class families have traditionally tended to have more children than middle-class families. Hand points out, however, that 'It should be noted that the presence of children may not directly influence the demand for television, but rather may be the effect of having children on the parents' leisure time and lifestyle. As opportunities for going out were restricted by having children, this could have increased the demand for in-home entertainment such as television.'[34]

As well as the demographic changes taking place in the 1950s and 1960s, issues of class and status may also have had consequences for the uptake of television. In the historical research conducted by Tim O'Sullivan, the acquisition of television in the 1950s was a mark of status and progress: 'The act of getting a television generally seems to be remembered above all as a sign of progress, a visible sign of joining, or at least of not being left out of, "the new".'[35]

It does also seem that there was a certain amount of 'keeping up with the Joneses'. In a handful of instances, it seems, households without television sets put up aerials to impress their neighbours. Television licensing staff on patrol in detector vans recorded several occasions when they found householders had put up aerials without owning a set or a licence.[36]

Dramatic change: television as a *translocational* medium

As we have seen, Britain in the 1950s and 1960s experienced a major shift in terms of housing. This involved the establishment of new towns, suburbs and estates. At the same time, television expanded to reach a national audience. It is this 'coincidence of the architectural and the televisual',[37] the development of suburbia and the growth of the British television service, that has led Roger Silverstone to argue that television is essentially a suburban medium.[38] Television, according to Silverstone, is also a suburban medium because it dwells on suburban themes.[39] These are themes of community, family, morality and sexuality. Silverstone concedes that these are neither exclusively suburban issues nor that television is watched exclusively in the suburbs, but that the articulation of these themes is grounded in suburban bourgeois experience.

However, I want to qualify Silverstone's suggestion that television explores suburban themes by examining how television, at least in the 1950s and 1960s, often articulated anxieties about suburban *and urban* changes taking place in Britain. Further-more, as we shall see in the next section, television mediated between the domestic and the global. As a result, rather than describing it as a suburban medium, I would prefer to describe television in the 1950s and 1960s as a *translocational* medium. It is translocational because it took the viewer from one place (the place of viewership) to another (the place of the television event). It is also translocational during this period because dramatic themes often concerned the effects of social movement and demographic shifts, the movement – and displacement – of people from one location to another. It is this latter point that I will look at first.

The changes in housing and rise of new urban areas discussed above provided the visible backdrop to some of the television dramas of this period. In some instances, that change provided the premise for some of those dramas. In an obvious and evi-dent sense, the backdrop of physical urban change was to provide some dramas with a sense of 'realism'. 'Realism' is a hotly contested term, but I use it loosely here to denote authen-ticity of setting. The London landscape in *Fabian of the Yard*, which was filmed on location, is as much a character in the drama as the eponymous Scotland Yard detective, his sidekicks and the criminals he pursues. As we saw in Chapter 3, a chase sequence through the wreckage of a house in the 1955 episode 'Bombs in Piccadilly' is accompanied by a voice-over explaining that parts of London were still scarred by the blitz. Not only did this visible bomb damage signify a devastation of the landscape, but it also signalled an urban trauma that needed both physical and emotional repair.

Another television programme from the mid-1950s was *The Grove Family*, which was transmitted on television in 15- and 20-minute episodes between 1954 and 1957. Arguably Britain's first television soap aimed at adults,[40] the series featured a lower-middle-class family of seven living in a house in a suburb in northwest London. The family included a 90 year-old grand-mother, two grown-up children, two younger children and husband and wife, Bob and Gladys Grove. The family were

named after the Lime Grove Studios in west London, which had
been a film studio before the BBC took it over in 1950. The Bob
Grove character was a builder and had his own yard nearby.
One of the creators, Michael Pertwee, explained in an interview
in the *TV Mirror* in 1954: 'Being in business for himself the man
would be subject to all the fluctuations of fortune caused by
economic conditions. He would have many more problems
being in the open market.'[41]

The series was heavily characterized by a 'public service
ethos', with storylines dealing with social and consumer issues,
and these included how to buy a television licence and how to
prevent burglary. Although little of the series survives, a spin-
off film was made in 1955 called *It's a Great Day*, featuring the
television cast and made by the series producer John Warring-
ton. One of the main storylines for the film features Bob Grove
trying to complete a building project on a housing estate in time
for the opening ceremony to be attended by the Queen. Filmed
sequences take place around the building site for the new estate
and Grove, who has to battle against local government bureaucracy, becomes implicated in corruption and a black market
supply of building materials. The film ends happily with the
construction project completed on time and Bob Grove cleared
of any wrongdoing. The film (and by dint also the television
series) hints at a preoccupation with social issues at the time, at
genuine changes in the urban and suburban landscape and at
the practical problems that attended them.

The building construction programme of the period also
provided a backdrop to two other famous series from the 1950s
– *Quatermass II* and *Quatermass and the Pit*. Although these series
dealt with the 'fantastic', with the eponymous professor battling
against alien invasion or alien influences, the landscape and the
series' premises provided what has been described, after
Todorov, as socio-cultural verisimilitude.[42] In this sense, the
backdrop lent a degree of authenticity to the dramatic action,
and the circumstances that initiated the drama were drawn from
plausible events. Although much of the space technology in the
Quatermass series was further advanced than in actuality in the
1950s, the setting was visibly of that decade, and the audience

was invited to believe that it was contemporaneous. No matter that a programme is 'fantastic', aspects of the drama and action relate in some way to most people's experience and understanding of the world.

The premise of the third *Quatermass* serial, *Quatermass and the Pit*, transmitted in six parts between 22 December 1958 and 26 January 1959, grew out of urban regeneration. In this series the writer Nigel Kneale based his idea on the real-life rebuilding on London's bomb sites. During this period, building and excavation work had unearthed archaeological remains, so Kneale took the further step of wondering what would happen if the remains were more sinister. In the first episode of *Quatermass and the Pit*, Professor Quatermass is called to a building site in Knightsbridge, where engineers building an extension to the London underground have found what looks like a bomb left over from the blitz. In the end, the object turns out to be a Martian spacecraft that had crash-landed five million years previously, but the telefantasy premise is based on socio-cultural verisimilitude, and an understanding of what audiences knew to be real.

The *Quatermass* series articulated other anxieties. During the period, as well as the new towns and suburbs, many greenfield sites were developed as part of a new wave of modernization in industry. Many saw this modernization as progressive and beneficial, and in the build-up to the 1964 general election Labour leader Harold Wilson described it as 'the white heat of technological revolution'. It included building Britain's first nuclear power station, Windscale in Cumbria, later known as Sellafield, which started producing electricity in 1956. But there were anxieties about such developments. Concern over nuclear weaponry, for example, led to the establishment of the Campaign for Nuclear Disarmament in 1958.

In *Quatermass II* (a six-part series transmitted on BBC television from 22 October to 26 November 1955) the professor investigates a secretive new chemical plant that has been built over a village at the fictional Winnerden Flats. In the third episode, 'The Food', a working-class married couple and their young son on holiday stop for a picnic by the sea near the secret government refinery. In the drama, the medium shots and close-ups of the plant were filmed on location at the Shell Haven refinery. The wife complains to her husband that it is a pity that the village they visit each year has disappeared, a result of the development of the refinery. In the next episode, 'The Coming', Professor Quatermass visits a local pub to speak to workers who have relocated to the nearby 'prefab' town to help construct the new plant. A worker enthusiastically refers to his 'terrific pay', but an older woman, the wife of one of the workers, regrets moving there, complaining that they are 'right away from the world'.

The disappointment of the picnicking woman and the displacement of the worker's wife articulate an anxiety about social and geographical change. The new town and the chemical plant have spoilt the countryside and the workers, albeit voluntarily, have been displaced from their traditional homes and communities. As the episode develops it transpires that the chemical plant, surrounded by murderous armed guards, is a breeding ground for aliens planning to take over the world. As the fictional articulation of a cultural anxiety about the rash of new, hi-tech and sometimes secret installations sprouting up around the country, *Quatermass II* is perhaps peerless.

At the beginning of the 1960s there emerged two social realist dramas that offered two very different accounts of the urban landscape, *Z Cars* and *Coronation Street*. Running from 1962 to 1978, *Z Cars* grew to become one of the BBC's flagship programmes.[43] It was based on rigorous documentary research and one of the series creators, writer Troy Kennedy Martin, argued that by focusing on policemen the drama would be 'a key way of getting into a whole society'.[44] The series was located in northwest England and set in a fictionalized version of Liverpool, with Seaforth becoming Seaport, and Kirkby New Town simply Newtown. Almost self-evidently, Newtown represented the new kind of urban development we have explored here, yet the representation is a bleak one. As the *Radio Times* highlighted on 28 December 1961, 'Life is fraught with danger for policemen in the North of England overspill estate called Newtown. Here a mixed community, displaced from larger towns by slum clearance has been brought together and housed on an estate without amenities and without community feeling.'[45]

In *Z Cars* the inhabitants of Newtown are portrayed as rootless, displaced and dispossessed. The first episode, 'Four of a Kind', transmitted on 2 January 1962, laid out the premise for the series. A policeman on the beat has been murdered in a robbery and, in response to an increase in crime in the area, the local force wants to establish crime cars that can respond to trouble quickly, the eponymous 'Z cars'. As a detective explains in the episode, 'If we'd had crime patrols like other divisions Reggie Farrow [the murdered policeman] would be alive today'.[46] The incidence of crime in the series reflected a growing tide of violent crime in real life, which had begun to increase from the mid-1950s onwards. In 1955 the number of violent crimes stood at 5869 for the year, rising to 11,592 in 1960, and 15,976 in 1964.[47]

Driving through Newtown in the first episode, two of the detective characters lament the area's lack of community, with new buildings springing up and providing 'just good hiding places for tearaways and villains'.[48] The emphasis on documentary research (rigorous attention to policing methods, fallible characters who smoke on duty, argue, beat their wives, and are not too distant from the some of the people they policed),[49] and narratives grounded in believable situations afforded the series a 'realist' label.

There was a lot of debate about the nature of realism in television in this period,[50] but *Z Cars'* director John McGrath said in a daily newspaper, in capital letters, 'IT IS A SIGHT MORE TRUE TO LIFE THAN ANYTHING ELSE SO FAR.'[51] In one sense, McGrath was claiming that *Z Cars* was more realistic than previous television police series, particularly the then popular *Dixon of Dock Green* (BBC 1955–76). *Dixon* offered a more comfortable version of both urban life and urban policing. Set in a fictitious part of London's East End (the original theme tune was a whistled rendition of 'Maybe it's because I'm a Londoner'), *Dixon's* representation of London life resembles that of the Ealing films, and Dock Green almost has the feel of a village community.[52] This cosy depiction perhaps veered between caricature and myth. As Tise Vahimagi says, 'the series' early mixture of everyday suburban station life, petty larceny, and homely moralizing rarely strayed from its reassuring, never-never world of hearts-of-gold coppers and "cor blimey!" crooks.'[53]

Yet McGrath's claim that *Z Cars* was more realistic than any other previous police television programme 'so far' *could* also be an implicit (if not necessarily intentional) critique of the other new social realist television drama from this period. This was the soap *Coronation Street* that had started in December 1960. Made by Granada, the programme was originally designed as a 12-week series, but has run continuously to the present day. The soap centres on the lives of ordinary people living in the eponymously titled street, a row of terraced houses, set in an industrial working-class district in northwest England. As Lez Cooke argues, 'In its iconography, character types and story-lines, *Coronation Street* tapped into the new mode of social realism, or "kitchen sink" drama, that had been popularized in the theatre, and in literature, since the mid-1950s.'[54]

For Cooke, the series provided a shock of recognition for working-class people living in the north of England, with its depiction of the way people lived their daily lives. There is a problem here and Cooke alludes to it when he describes the series' title music as 'a melancholy signature tune, itself redolent with nostalgia'.[55] In a sense, the vision of working-class life in *Coronation Street* might have been nostalgic. While the period was characterized by working-class themes in literature, theatre and film, Richard Dyer, in his analysis of *Coronation Street* (1981), argues that this moment in British cultural history was 'decisively marked' by Richard Hoggart's *The uses of literacy* discussed above.[56]

In many ways, *Coronation Street* follows closely some aspects of Hoggart's romantic vision of working-class life, the gregariousness of spirit, neighbourliness and the significance of the local shop and pub to community life. One of the main (and longest lasting) characters was Ken Barlow, a 'scholarship boy' who had benefited from a middle-class education that led him into conflict with his working-class family. This too was a sub-

123

ject of Hoggart's writings, and Hoggart too had been a 'scholarship boy'. So *Coronation Street* can perhaps be seen as a romanticized account of working-class life, a way of life that in many ways seemed to be passing. It appeared to contradict the experience of demographic change felt by certain sectors of the working class. At the very least, it appeared to contradict the depictions of those changes in other television dramas.

In the mid-1960s two further seminal single-play television dramas, *Up the Junction* (1965) and *Cathy Come Home* (1966), caught the mood of radical change in the urban landscape, and equally reflected a cultural anxiety about this change. Both were shot on film and exemplify aspects of recording technology discussed in the previous chapter. *Up the Junction* was based on the novel by Nell Dunn about the lives of young working-class people around Clapham Junction in southwest London.[57]

The drama was mainly filmed on location using 16mm film, which gives it a documentary feel. Introductory scenes and establishing shots at the beginning of the programme situate the drama around the huge railway junction area in Clapham, with shots of the lines, platforms and steam trains. The camera then draws back to show shots of modern office blocks next to huddled and smoky terraces. Several sequences focus on houses being demolished in the area, with images of derelict buildings, men swinging pickaxes and walls collapsing, clearly reflecting the slum clearance programme of the 1950s and 1960s.

The cramped and squalid circumstances in which people live are articulated in character dialogues and asynchronous voice-overs. In one sequence, one of the male characters, Dave, picks up one of the female characters in a pub and shows her where he used to live. Filmed footage shows them climbing through the carcass of a building, amid rubble and broken walls, and Dave's voice-over is heard explaining to the young woman, 'This is where we lived, 'till it got demolished. Slum Clearance.' As we saw earlier, the people from these slums were relocated to new housing estates and schemes. However, even the award winning estates like the one in Roehampton may have been negatively experienced by the people who lived there.

Scrambling through the Clapham rubble, Dave tells the young woman, 'They moved us out to lousy Roehampton.'

Like the depiction of rootlessness in *Z Cars*, this is no Hoggartesque romantic depiction of working-class life. Conversations between characters reveal a bleak future, for women and men. For the women, the future holds an early marriage, and one girl who is already working, tells her workmates that she is going to get married when she's sixteen. In one plotline, an unwanted pregnancy is resolved controversially by an illegal, backstreet abortion. In another depressing plotline, a 'Tally man', a door-to-door salesman cum debt collector who sells goods on hire-purchase, explains to camera that the women with whom he deals are stupid for getting themselves into debt. The depiction of the men is equally depressing, with the recurring male characters dabbling in petty criminality or 'on the make'. Unlike Hoggart's working-class sense of community, the representation of working-class life here marks a degree of continuity with the pessimistic vision of *Z Cars*. The fictitious characters of *Up the Junction* are just like those rootless and dispossessed inhabitants of *Z Cars'* fictional Newtown.

The other seminal drama from the period was *Cathy Come Home* (1966), shown in the BBC's 'Wednesday Play' strand. Held up as an example of the so-called 'Golden Age' of British television drama, it draws together documentary and drama conventions to tell the story of a young woman who runs away from small town life to London. She marries and sets up home with Reg in modern, rented accommodation. Cathy's dream of a new life and comfortable living is shattered when Reg has an accident at work and cannot continue to earn a living. They cannot afford their rent and are forced to move into Reg's mother's home, but overcrowding and arguments ensue and they have to move on again. The couple's situation deteriorates as they find themselves in a series of increasingly squalid homes, and finally they are separated and their young children taken away from them. The drama ends with Cathy returning to her home town by herself.

The story is told in an episodic structure and held together by a voice-over commentary by Cathy. Cathy's story was not based on any one individual's recorded experiences, but an amalgamation of a number of different documented experiences of housing difficulties. The filmed footage, shot on location, is on one occasion augmented by a documentary style voice-over, reading government statistics about housing conditions and homelessness. The drama shows the loneliness and alienation of modern, city living, with Cathy dispossessed, separated as she is from home and community. Rather than demonstrating the developments and benefits of modern housing and planning policy, *Cathy Come Home* shows up the failure of the welfare state to replace a loss of community and to look after people who experience housing difficulties.

As I have suggested, these depictions of new urban landscapes represented a cultural anxiety about the social and cultural changes taking place in Britain in the 1950s and 1960s. As we have seen, this preoccupation coincided with technological changes that allowed the television camera to escape the studio walls to explore outside social spaces, while at the same time the television set became an increasingly significant component of domestic, private space. The extension of the camera into the outside world opened up new diegetic spaces in drama for the exploration of different classes and regions. By showing the demographic and geographical mobility of much social change and by bringing it into the home television at this time could be described, as I have suggested, as a translocational medium. Not just a dramatic representation of the lived space literally outside the front door, television was also increasingly bringing representations from further afield, across a range of non-fiction genres. As the domestic sphere became the site of domestic consumption, television increasingly opened up an outside, global sphere and brought it into the home.

Mediating the home and the global

Television in the 1950s and 1960s, then, was a translocational medium in that it depicted demographic and social changes taking place in Britain, as well as the consequences of people moving from one place to another. Television also took (and takes) the viewer from one location to another, from the site of viewing to the site of the television event. The site of viewing was the home. As Roger Silverstone suggests, 'television, above all, offers that route to the global, to an infinity of reach, metronomically playing tunes of alternate threat and reassurance as we watch from the more or less comfortable surroundings of suburban lounge or parlour.'[58]

The global reach from domestic space opened up to the British television audience for the first time during this period. It was this development that allowed for what the geographer David Harvey has called 'time–space compression', where information can travel great distances at great speed.[59] For John Ellis, this has consolidated the twentieth century as the century of 'witness', in that television allows the viewers to see political faces, historical events and faraway places.[60] In the 1950s and 1960s this was a new experience. Technical and geographical reach made places newly visible in live transmissions and recorded footage. At the same time, television documentaries exposed hidden social and institutional worlds, and news and current affairs programming made a political and public sphere highly visible for the first time.

To begin with, we have already looked at two ways in which the use of film in television dramas made social space visible in a new way. First, the increased use of film in British television drama meant that 16mm and 35mm cameras could escape the confines of the studio walls and venture into the outside world. The dramatic experiences being represented may have been taking place down the road, or in the next street, town or city. As we also saw, this could provide dramas (and drama-documentaries) with added 'realism' and socio-cultural verisimilitude by being shot on location.

The use of film (and video) also meant that television programmes could be both exported and imported as commodities. In this way, the importation of American filmed programming in the mid-1950s discussed in Chapter 3, with comedies such as *I Love Lucy*, Westerns such as *Rawhide*, and cop and detective shows such as *Dragnet* and *77 Sunset Strip*, all brought a slice of

US culture into British homes. Encroaching Americanization had been a cultural anxiety for many years, and could be witnessed, for example, in George Orwell's 1946 essay 'The decline of the English murder'.[61] It was something that was feared and reviled at the beginning of the 1950s and, as we have seen, it was something against which cultural institutions like the Foreign Office, Arts Council and BBC had sought to fight.[62] As we have also seen, fears of Americanization had also emerged during the acrimonious public debates for and against breaking the BBC's television monopoly and the advent of ITV.

Yet technological developments took the viewer to a wider range of new spaces (and space). In a very simple sense, the expansion of telecommunications technologies helped extend the reach of live transmission on a global scale. On the evening of 27 August 1950, for example, the first cross-Channel live television pictures between Calais and London were transmitted, an event Asa Briggs described as 'the first real landmark in postwar European television history'.[63] In a 60-minute special programme, BBC viewers saw the iconic clock tower of the Hôtel de Ville in Calais, a torchlight procession, dancing and a fireworks display, accompanied by a commentary from Richard Dimbleby and Alan Adair.

Four years later, in June 1954 it was announced that a television link would connect eight different countries in Europe in a system a journalist had nicknamed 'Eurovision'.[64] The advent of the satellite age was also to expand the possibility of live transmission and image relay. As early as 1956 Richard Dimbleby showed a model of the communications satellite Telstar on an edition of *Panorama* on 10 July of that year – a year even before the first satellite, Sputnik I had been successfully launched into space. At the start of the manned space race, BBC television broadcast the first ever live transmission from Moscow to London of the new Soviet cosmonaut Yuri Gagarin after his successful mission.[65] A year later, in July 1962, Telstar transmitted the first pictures across the Atlantic from the USA to Britain.

Perhaps the biggest technological feat of all was when the BBC and ITV broadcast live coverage of the Apollo II moon landing on 21 July 1969, symbolizing the farthest reaches of what television could make visible. Transmitted in black and white on BBC and ITV, the moonshot was shown in colour on BBC2, where a full colour television service had started in December 1967.[66] An occasion of global proportions and significance, what Dayan and Katz referred to as a media event,[67] it is estimated that the landing was watched by 723 million people in 47 countries.[68]

As well as televising live events from different spaces, the increased use of film recording in television non-fiction programming also took the British viewer to new parts of the world. At the start of the 1960s, for example, Asa Briggs argues, 'There was not one week in 1961 when BBC cameramen were not filming in a foreign country.'[69] A very early type of non-fiction programming filmed abroad was later to become known as the natural history film. In the early 1950s the form on television was non-existent, and matters of a scientific or natural history bent came out of the BBC's Talks Department. A popular panel quiz of the decade, for example, was *Animal, Vegetable, Mineral?* (BBC TV 1952–59). In each studio-bound edition a panel of eminent archaeologists, art historians and scientists had to identify artefacts, which were on occasion natural objects. A popular 'regular' on the programme was the archaeologist Sir Mortimer Wheeler who both knew his subject and knew how to give good television. As the researcher on the programme at the time, David Attenborough, recalls, 'Whatever archaeological object we chose, it seemed to turn out that Sir Mortimer himself had personally dug it up. He played outrageously to the gallery, twirling his moustaches, pretending initially to be baffled then discovering a clue and finally bringing his identification to a triumphant conclusion.'[70]

Attenborough, who went on to carve out an illustrious career in television,[71] had started as a researcher on *Animal, Vegetable, Mineral?* He went on to initiate a programme idea in 1954 to accompany an expedition to Sierra Leone in West Africa to collect different species for London Zoo. Attenborough took a cameraman armed with a 16mm clockwork film camera, and the expedition collected numerous species, including chameleons, weaverbirds and pythons. Produced by the Talks Department, the creatures were presented in the studio show, *Zoo Quest*, over a number of weeks and intercut with the filmed footage taken in Sierra Leone. One of the 'nominal' reasons to go to Sierra Leone was to catch the rare bird Picathartes gymnocephalus, and the quest for this bird became the narrative drive throughout the first series. The effective impact of this, Attenborough recalls, was felt when he was driving in London's Regent Street in an open topped sports car and a bus driver leaned out of his window and asked, "ere Dave ... are you going to catch that *Picafartees gymno-bloody-cephalus* or aren't you?'[72] Six more *Zoo Quests* followed between 1954 and 1961, and they included trips to Guyana, Indonesia, New Guinea, Paraguay and Madagascar.

At the same time the BBC was also showing wildlife documentary films by the Belgian film maker Armand Denis and his wife Michaela Denis. The couple lived in Kenya, and their work centred on African wild animals, and included *Filming Wild Animals* (BBC TV 1954–55) and *Filming in Africa* (BBC TV 1955). They also had documentary films shown on ITV (ATV) between 1955 and 1958 entitled *Michaela and Armand Denis*. As Tise Vahimagi suggests, 'Their on-camera treks across Uganda, Kenya, etc., with Michaela's shapely form constantly darting in front of the lens and Armand's relaxed, almost domestic manner when soft-shoeing after dangerous creatures established the couple as TV favourites during the 1950s.'[73]

As the transmission of the Denis's eponymous films on ITV suggests, the BBC did not have the monopoly on depicting the exotic through the lens of the educational. Globetrotting ITV series included *Survival*, a series of natural history programmes from Anglia Television from 1961, and a documentary series from ATV, *Great Temples of the World*, 1964–66. ITV also boasted a travel series with Orson Welles, *Round the World with Orson Welles*, which started on the second night of the new commercial service on 23 September 1955. As the *TV Times* billed it, 'In this series of films Orson Welles, who is a great cosmopolitan, visits some of the famous places of the world.'[74] The BBC's own urbane and smooth cosmopolitan was Alan Whicker, who started reporting features on the BBC's *Tonight* programme, and

Whicker's World began in 1959 as a look back at some of the *Tonight* films.[75] Subsequent programmes in the 1960s included *Whicker Down Under* (BBC TV 1961), *Whicker on Top of the World* (BBC TV 1962) and *Whicker Down Mexico Way* (BBC TV 1963).

Not just an examination of the distant, foreign or exotic, other programming also started to explore spaces and experiences previously kept hidden, spaces that the social psychologist Erving Goffman calls 'back regions'. For Goffman, everyday life is a matter of performing certain roles. This can be ascertained by the way people behave differently with other groups, whether they be friends, family, colleagues, clients, bosses, subordinates, teachers, students or strangers. The settings for these performances are carefully circumscribed and are kept separate, with specific occupational locations demanding specific behaviour, actions, words and language, and these might be particularly associated with the kind of 'team behaviour' we discussed in Chapter 1.

So, for Goffman, 'A region may be defined as any place that is bounded to some degree by barriers to perception.'[76] Significantly, what Goffman calls a 'back region' is a space where the performer can be 'off duty' – often from other teams (often client or customer groups). As we have seen, television drama can explore such spaces. In *Z Cars*, for example, police officers are seen in the spaces to which the public has no access, such as the police station canteen or in their homes. It was the depiction of fictional policemen as smokers, gamblers, people who complained about authority or who beat their wives that was to provoke the anger of senior police officers in real life.[77] In *Z Cars* the characters are seen as behaving in ways that contradict their institutional roles and public performance of order and control.

During this period, non-fiction documentary television also started to examine the back regions of institutions or particular social groups. Between 1958 and 1964, for example, the BBC ran a controversial series of programmes called *Your Life in Their Hands* that took viewers behind the scenes of hospitals, and inside operating theatres to give a close-up view of the work of doctors and nurses.[78] A single documentary, on the other hand,

The Deliverers (ATV, transmitted on 22 January 1964) was a look at the lives of the RAF crew of a Victor bomber that carried a nuclear payload. Shown 15 months after the Cuban missile crisis of 1962, the documentary painted a picture of a group of ordinary people who had, in effect, an extraordinary job. Though uncontroversial in its depiction of the routine and mundane lives of the aircrew at work and at leisure, the documentary's ideological intent is even handed (or unclear). Either the programme ideologically underpins the principle of nuclear deterrent by demonstrating Britain's military capability, and by reassuring the viewers that their safety is in good hands, or it suggests with pathos that the power to kill millions is held by a small group of ordinary people. The title of the programme itself is clearly euphemistic.

Sometimes the exploration of institutional and public back regions was more controversial. The Granada documentary *The Entertainers*, for example, was initially banned from transmission by the ITA in 1964. Made by producer Denis Mitchell, and the first documentary shot on videotape, the programme follows the everyday lives of a group of real strippers, wrestlers and pub and cabaret singers living together in a single house. Taking a behind the scenes look at show business and the entertainment industries, *The Entertainers* depicts a grubby, squalid and seedy world. A striptease sequence in particular caused some anxiety at the ITA, and it took a year of negotiation before transmission was allowed on 13 January 1965.

During this period, television's own back regions were also the subject of programming. Broadcasting is a matter of staged behaviour because, although events and performances take place in front of the camera, most of the work of television production takes place off-camera. Goffman briefly refers to this kind of staging in relation to broadcasting, 'In these situations, back region tends to be defined as all places where the camera is not focused at the moment or all places out of range of "live" microphones.'[79]

Many programmes took cameras into television's own back regions to show its workings to the viewing public. An early example from the 1950s included a BBC *Children's Newsreel* of the new children's television studio opening at Lime Grove, transmitted on 13 February 1952. Editions of *Panorama* were also given over to the behind the scenes technical work of BBC television, such as Richard Dimbleby giving a tour of the Alexandra Palace Studios on 4 June 1956, and a demonstration of the BBC's VERA videotape system in 1958.

Other examples included news coverage of a press visit to the new BBC Television Centre, broadcast on 15 June 1960, and news coverage of the start of transmissions from the centre on 29 June. A filmed documentary made by the BBC and directed by Richard Cawston was deliberately designed to promote the BBC in anticipation of a government inquiry (by the Pilkington Committee) into television broadcasting. The documentary, *This is the BBC*, followed the work of the BBC (both television and radio) over a 24-hour period. Quite radically, the black and white film ended with a short colour film sequence of a television studio experimenting with new colour television technology, implying that only a publicly funded broadcaster could invest in research and development. The film was projected at meetings around the country, to the great and the good, and transmitted on television on 27 November 1959 (although, of course, the colour sequence would have been seen in black and white on television at the time).

Such depictions of the BBC at work were both a promotion of television technology and the work of the BBC *per se*. As we saw in Chapter 3, *The Dream Machine*, transmitted on 11 November 1964, was an ITV documentary that explored the back regions of television. Produced by Francis Essex, it shows the preparation and production of a light entertainment show, *Six Wonderful Girls*. The documentary demonstrates the studio recording process and it also shows the wiping of videotapes. Sequences take place in the office, in rehearsal rooms, in the staff bar, and in the studio gallery. The opening up of these backstage areas humanized and personalized their institutional protagonists. Significantly, the relationship between the protagonist and the viewer at home is characterized by informality and a new kind of intimacy. While the back regions of broadcasting are opened up on television, the viewer is situated in the private sphere of the home. This too can be constituted as a back region where people can be off duty from the work of public performance (in the street, at school or at work). The apparently open handed way in which television offered its workings, a communication from back region to back region, could be said to offer a new sense of immediacy and connection.

There were other ways in which television could link the home to the global while at the same time offering immediacy and connection. These were news and current affairs pro-grammes. Developments in these programme forms over the 1950s, in a similar manner to the broadcasting of global live events and exotic films and documentaries described above, helped bring images into the home from far-flung places. Not only did television use satellite relay and film recording, but also developments in civilian air travel meant that reporters could traverse the globe quickly. At a time of global change and conflict, and with former European colonies in Africa and Asia uneasily making transitions to independence, there was much to report from abroad. On ITV this was also characterized by a sense of 'internationalism' in its current affairs programmes *This Week* and *World in Action*.[80]

As well as technological advances, four other key develop-ments affected the growth of television news provision and current affairs. The first was the end of what was known as the 'fourteen day rule'. This had been established between the government and the BBC towards the end of the Second World War to constrain controversial coverage of political issues. It meant that news or talk programmes could not report on events that were being discussed in parliament, or were about to be discussed, within the next 14-day period. This caused much editorial chaffing, and the rule was finally suspended at the end of 1956 after the political debacle of the Suez crisis.

The second development was the presentation of in-vision newsreaders. Traditionally, BBC radio sought to depersonalize its presenters as much as possible to represent a unitary BBC identity and to add an air of impartiality and authority. Until 1954, news on BBC television was provided by newsreels of the 'topical' kind seen at the cinema. After 1954, however, filmed footage was accompanied by voice-overs from BBC journalists for the first time. As the first British television newsreader Richard Baker announced on the first BBC news broadcast, 'Here is an illustrated summary of the news. It will be followed by the latest film of happenings at home and abroad.' It was more than a year later, just before the arrival of ITV and ITN, that the BBC allowed newsreaders to appear on screen.[81]

The arrival of the commercial service marked the third and fourth developments in television news – competition and professionalism.[82] It is commonly and popularly held that the advent of ITN news bulletins forced the BBC to revamp its television news service. As Andrew Crisell argues in his book *An Introductory History of British Broadcasting*, the ITN news was of higher quality than the BBC's. It had been set up in May 1955 under the editorship of Aidan Crawley, who had been both a journalist and an MP, and it recruited a team of people to present the news, including Robin Day and Christopher Chataway. They were charged with the duty of being authoritative and journalistic, and were encouraged to emphasize their individual personalities. ITN also used 'an unprecedented quantity of film in its bulletins and incorporated as much informed comment as possible to give viewers a better perspective on events'.[83]

At the same time, however, the BBC was also becoming more comfortable with in-vision presenters alongside filmed reports. As a result, the journalist Hugh Greene, who was to go on to become BBC director general, was reluctant to agree that changes then underway at BBC News had been a result of competition with ITN. In a BBC internal report in 1958 he instead argued that 'one cannot be sure that they [BBC News] would not have attained today's standard even without competition'.[84] Furthermore, as I discussed in Chapter 1, a Gallup poll from December 1957 found that 31 per cent of people found BBC news better than ITN, compared with 15 per cent who favoured ITN. Yet, as we also saw in Chapter 1, the expansion of broadcasting in the 1950s and 1960s certainly facilitated the development of a *professional* ethos. By the end of the 1950s, television news was presented and run by professional journalists, while current affairs was increasingly being characterized by a pro-fessional cadre of journalists and presenters.[85]

What news and current affairs shared with some of the other programmes described above was the face-to-camera address of the presenter. This replicates a fundamental social encounter between people – face-to-face interaction. Writing in the *Journal of Psychiatry* in 1956, Donald Horton and R. Richard Wohl argued that the to-camera presentation of light entertainment hosts such as Johnny Carson, in the *Johnny Carson Show* on US television, constituted a form of 'para-social relationship'. This is a seeming face-to-face encounter between the presenter and the viewer. This relationship between the on-screen performer and the viewer at home is characterized by 'intimacy at a distance', a form of ersatz intimacy separated by physical space.[86] In certain circumstances, this form of representation can *promote* the television experience as a sociable encounter.

Paddy Scannell,[87] drawing on the work of the sociologist Georg Simmel,[88] argues that people like to watch television or listen to radio because it is sociable – it is an activity that is not instrumental or functional, it is a charming way of spending time. I shall critically evaluate Scannell's understanding and deployment of the concept of 'sociability' in more depth in Chapter 6. I shall do this to explore the relationship between on-screen presenters and members of the public in certain television programmes and to examine the way that media power is constructed. For the moment, however, it is worth hanging on to the term sociability here because it alludes to an easygoing charm and social-ness in certain of television's programming.

In the 1950s, one programme that transcended generic boundaries associated with talk and light entertainment programmes to produce this kind of charm was *Tonight*, which ran on BBC television between 1957 and 1965. *Tonight*, a current affairs magazine programme, was scheduled in the tea-time slot that had previously been kept clear of programming, a gap in the schedules in which television traditionally 'closed down' to allow parents to put their children to bed, a slot known as the 'toddler's truce'.[89] For John Corner, the most significant aspect of *Tonight* was that 'the programme developed a modality of easy, familiar address which seemed to resonate perfectly with emerging ideas about social conventions and public values across a wide spectrum.'[90]

Tonight was a 40-minute, topical magazine programme that combined studio items with filmed reports, a programme that looked at big stories and how they affected individuals. As Briggs notes, 'Through its magazine mix, which included music, *Tonight* deliberately blurred traditional distinctions between entertainment, information, and even education; while through its informal styles of presentation, it broke sharply with old BBC traditions of "correctness" and "dignity". It also showed the viewing public that the BBC could be just as sprightly and irreverent as ITV.'[91]

The programme's magazine format was a recognition that at this time of day people would be coming home from work, doing homework, having dinner or getting ready to go out. The fragmented magazine format could accommodate a distracted audience for short bursts of viewing. The chief presenter was Cliff Michelmore, described in parts of the press as 'avuncular, pink-faced, middle brow'.[92] The programme mixed serious items with comic items and music, and many of the team that worked on the programme in the BBC Talks Department went on to work on the satirical *That Was the Week That Was*. For Corner, 'the success of *Tonight* indicates how powerfully television could employ its immediacy and intimacy to construct the terms of a new sociability.'[93] *Tonight* proved very popular with a viewing audience, and in 1957 the programme was attracting an audience of nine million viewers.

The development of new forms of broadcasting, with an emphasis on para-social interaction, intimacy at a distance and sociability (here) may, however, have had negative implications. The emergence of news and current affairs programming in the 1950s increasingly put politicians and others in authority on the screen on a daily basis. Placed within the television flow of the mixed-programme schedule discussed in Chapter 2, politicians, world leaders, civil servants, doctors, scientists, policemen, teachers, artists and writers were as much a part of the television schedule as cabaret singers, dancers, rock stars, films stars, quiz show hosts and comedians. In one sense, placing these people within the television schedule might have been democratizing, bringing them down to earth, making them newly visible and accountable to the viewer and voter. Television brought 'them' into the home.

Richard Hoggart, in *The uses of literacy*, suggests that for the working classes, 'them' were the bosses and public officials, the people who 'got us into this mess', people such as politicians. These people, 'them', were not the 'us' of the working classes.[94] For Silverstone, this quotidian display of politicians, leaders and people in authority on television has resulted, long term, in the suburbanization of the public sphere.[95] The (political) world is viewed through the prism of the home. Yet the breakdown of the barrier between the home (private sphere) and the public sphere for the first time in the 1950s and 1960s might have seemed invasive. As part of a society in which the welfare state and government bureaucracy was an increasing part of every-day life, the intrusion of the public sphere into domestic space via the television set might have made the political process appear oppressively pervasive.

It was for this reason that Stephen Wagg argues that a 'satire boom' emerged in the early 1960s. This was a moment when satire was in vogue across a range of media and arts, and included satirical revues in the theatre, the launch of the satirical magazine *Private Eye*, and the BBC's television show *That Was the Week That Was*. This 'boom' signified a disenchant-ment with the world of politics, and marked a retreat from engagement in the political sphere. For Wagg, 'The principal thrust of the comedy [the satirical depiction of politics, the establishment and social institutions] has, I believe, been toward an elevation of the *private* sphere of individual activities and decision-making at the expense of the *public* realm of parlia-mentary and "party-political" deliberation.'[96]

Satire was a way a distancing oneself from the issues of the day, by pricking the pomposity of politicians and leaders, by not taking them seriously. By viewing public life from the comfort of the home, and by witnessing politicians and leaders as part of the television flow, as part of the ready supply of entertainment, it was possible to take them less seriously. As a consequence, 'they' and 'them' may have been more visible, but in being brought into the home they may also have been less powerful.

To sum up, demographic changes in British society created space for the new cultural form of television. Jobs in new modern industries and homes in new estates, suburbs and towns meant that people moved away from family, friends and community. At the same time, the postwar baby boom meant that young couples were more likely to be at home looking after their children. Also, changes in credit arrangements meant that people could obtain a range of domestic items, like television sets, on hire-purchase.

For many people, slum clearances and new homes were the cause of anxiety and unhappiness and this was explored in television drama forms ranging from telefantasy to police series and single dramas. The emergence of television in the home, and a combination of the development of recording and relay (cable and satellite) technologies meant that the viewer was connected to other people, places and events locally, regionally, nationally and globally. Television not only connected the domestic audience to far-flung places, but also behind the scenes of institutions such as hospitals, the Royal Air Force, the entertainment industry and even television itself.

It is for these reasons that I have described television in this period as a *translocational* medium. It both depicted the demographic movement and displacement of people around the country from their traditional homes, and it connected audiences from the place of viewing to the spaces being occupied and captured by the television camera. New programme forms such as television news, current affairs and documentaries facilitated this increasing sense of connectivity.

With some of the programmes characterized by intimate forms of presentation, there appeared to be an erosion of the boundaries between the public and private spheres. In a society characterized by welfarism and state bureaucracy, the daily presentation of the world of politics and international events in news and current affairs programming may have made the sphere of government seem omnipresent and oppressive.

Within the flow of the mixed-programme schedule, which combined politics and serious drama with comedy and entertainment, this would have constructed and perpetuated the sense that television connected its viewers to the central institutions and concerns of society that I discussed in Chapter 2. In the next chapter I shall explore how television circulated discourses on consumer culture and how this promoted economic and cultural difference and class conflict.

Chapter 5
CONSUMER CULTURE

We shall now explore how television endorsed consumer culture and promoted a sense of social fragmentation and class conflict. In Britain in the 1950s and 1960s the economy boomed. There was full employment, which meant that there was competition for labour and wages were higher. In 1954 rationing came to an end and there was a relaxation of hire-purchase (HP) controls. This meant there were fewer restrictions on what consumer goods people bought. With increased affluence people could spend more on commodities and services or, where money was tighter, they could acquire goods on HP and make regular payments over a period of time. In the year following the end of rationing consumer spending in Britain rose by 8 per cent; on durable goods such as televisions and refrigerators it rose by 10 per cent. In 1957 British shoppers spent £1004 million on durable goods and by 1960 this had risen to £1465 million.[1]

According to the historian Dominic Sandbrook, the consumer boom in the 1950s was an extension of long-term consumer developments that had begun in the Victorian era and that had, despite widespread poverty and economic depression, continued in wealthy pockets in the 1920s and 1930s. This had been disrupted by the war and its immediate aftermath, years that were characterized by restrictions and austerity. From the mid-1950s the combination of full employment, relative affluence and better housing meant that there was increased spending on household items on a much wider scale. A survey conducted by the *Financial Times* found that in the two-year period from 1957 to 1959 the number of households owning a television increased by 32 per cent, washing machines by 54 per cent, and refrigerators by 58 per cent. Electrification before the war and more reliable wiring in the new housing had, of course, made this expansion in the demand for electrical goods possible.

With the rise in supermarkets, shopping was also undergoing radical changes. In 1956, for example, there were around 3000 supermarkets and self-service stores in Britain, but by 1962 there were 12,000. Consumption was restricted not just to household goods, but also to cars, holidays and, for young people, fashion and pop music.

This is not to say, however, that the development of consumer culture was evenly or fairly felt. As the television dramas mentioned in the previous chapter depicted, the demographic changes taking place in Britain did have negative social consequences. Despite the advent of the welfare state, and despite an economy characterized by full employment, many people experienced hardship and low standards of living. For those struggling to make ends meet, hire-purchase and debt exacerbated an already difficult situation. In the drama *Up the Junction*, the 'tally man' who went around collecting HP payments was critical of the young women who got into debt.

It was not just the worst-off who were depending increasingly on credit and HP, but a wider range of people wanting to enjoy the good life. In 1962 a British civil servant, John Vassall, was found to be a spy in the pay of the Soviet Union. When questions were asked in parliament about why no one had noticed Vassall's lavish lifestyle, sponsored by his espionage, the minister responsible replied 'How many of us are living beyond our incomes?'[2] Despite the uneven spread of affluence and continuing deprivation in some quarters, rapid technological advances, brisk economic growth and the overall improvement of living conditions in Britain marked out the period as what Eric Hobsbawm described in his history of the twentieth century as a 'Golden Age'.[3]

The role of television in the emergence of a strong consumer capitalism in the 1950s is a complex one. The expansion and development of television broadcasting and the extension and expansion of the television audience discussed so far were both symptoms and agents of this change. In this chapter I shall look at the way in which the content and forms of television circulated discourses of consumerism and made practices of consumption visible. I shall also examine the ways in which such visible practices were related to social affiliation. Consumer culture is directly related to issues of lifestyle and class membership. Cutting across this are also issues of age and gender. So the representation of social and cultural activity, in television's newly expanding range of outputs in the mixed-programme schedule, from drama to comedy, light entertainment and factual programming, makes lifestyle and class tastes visible to a wider range of social and cultural groups. It includes the kinds of visible markers people display on television, the clothes they wear or the way they clean or decorate their homes. The programmes themselves, drawing on different heritages such as middle-class theatre or working-class variety shows, also constitute and represent cultural and class values. The broadcasting of these different programmes and forms on television in the mixed-programme schedule makes it easier for a range of audiences to be judgemental about the tastes and activities of different groups and classes. As this chapter will demonstrate, the promotion of consumer culture engenders a sense of cultural fragmentation and promotes class conflict.

Advertising consumer culture

One way in which television explicitly made consumerism visible was, with the arrival of ITV in 1955, by placing advertising on screen. As we saw in Chapter 3, the arrival of commercial television in 1955 brought to television a new form of filmed programming, the adverts. The expansion of advertising through television had given the campaign for commercial television a major impetus in the early 1950s, with agencies and companies with goods to sell looking for additional promotional outlets at the dawn of the decade's economic boom.[4] The institution of 'spot advertisements' was a particularly British way of negotiating the demands of market and public-service values in commercial television. In 1951, the Beveridge Committee recommended against the adoption of commercial broadcasting in Britain, partly because it had been unhappy about the way radio and television programmes in the USA were sponsored by advertisers.

The fear was that programme sponsorship by advertisers could influence editorial decision-making in the production process. If an advertiser were unhappy with a particular programme – be it the characters, the personalities or the narrative – then they could exert influence over the production and the programme's content. The ultimate sanction was that the advertiser could withdraw sponsorship money, leaving the programme's financing and future in a perilous condition. As a consequence, during the debates about the breaking of the BBC's monopoly, it was envisaged that 'spot advertisements' would be an important means of keeping finance and editorial decision-making separate in commercial television. A programme would be made by one of the ITV programme companies, but advertising air space would be sold separately to agencies. Obviously, an advertiser might not want their promotions aired alongside a programme that might reflect negatively on their product. In such an instance they could move the advert, but they could not impel the alteration or cancellation of that programme.[5]

The ITA handled the rules on what could be advertised, but under supervision from a statutory advertising committee, which could face close scrutiny from government. On the whole though, the rules were mainly liberal, with no bar on alcohol or tobacco. On the other hand, money-lenders and fortune-tellers were banned from advertising, and no adverts were allowed to be associated with specific religions or the royal family. There had been questions of whether gambling could be advertised, but this was deferred at the time when the Pools Promoters Association indicated that it would not be seeking advertising airtime in the early days of the new service. When commercial television began in 1955 there were strict rules about how much advertising could be shown. The ITA established from the outset that the commercial programme companies could not place advertisements of more than an average of six minutes in an hour, with a maximum of seven minutes on any specific occasion.[6]

As well as spot advertising, there was another kind of promotional programme on ITV. This was a hybrid called the advertising magazine, or more popularly the 'admag', and this caused a problem for the ITA because there was confusion over whether it constituted programme sponsorship or whether it exceeded advertising's six-minute rule. The admag form had been discussed in the Television Act of 1954 as 'shoppers' guides', and they were an early type of consumer programme featuring spots in which specific products were promoted. The difficulty, however, was that advertising had to be clearly distinguishable from other television programming and the admag blurred this distinction. The principles governing the admag turned it into a curious animal. One of these was that all the goods or services being advertised in these magazines had to be related in some way, and this relationship was to be made clear by the presentational links.

The advertisers in effect paid for product promotion in a programme made by one of the ITV programme companies rather than by an advertising agency in-house production department. At first it was suggested that the advertisers should also pay for the presentational links, but this was soon relaxed. When well-known television personalities made the links, it gave the item being promoted an additional fillip. Often the presentation of the programme appeared to be fictional or semi-documentary.[7] Perhaps the most famous admag from the period was *Jim's Inn*, which Associated-Rediffusion made and ran between 1957 and 1963. This particular admag focused on a married couple who ran a pub in the fictional village of Wembleham, and they would discuss the price and quality of various real consumer products with their customers.

The programme's arch premise and delivery provoked some uncomplimentary criticism, and was satirized in a sketch in *Beyond the Fringe*, a stage revue at the Edinburgh Festival in

August 1960, featuring the line-up of Alan Bennett, Peter Cook, Jonathan Miller and Dudley Moore. In Ronald Bergan's book about *Beyond the Fringe*, he describes *Jim's Inn* as a 'puerile advertising playlet in which people in a pub, quite straight-faced, introduced products for praise in conversation.'[8] In the sketch, the barman Jim was played by Dudley Moore, with customers Basil and Nigel played by Jonathan Miller and Peter Cook.

> Basil: Good gracious me – out of the corner of my eye I thought you were wearing a good cashmere.
> Nigel: I'm glad you thought it was cashmere but it's not.
> Basil: I'd put money on it being cashmere.
> Nigel: You'd lose your money, Bas. It's a Niblock Histamine Non-Iron Oven-Dry Visco-Static Dyna-flo, all designed to make a nice sweater with peak purchasing power.[9]

Hundreds of admags were broadcast between 1955 and 1963; they included *Homes and Gardens* (ATV), *What's in Store* (ABC) and two holiday programmes, *Where Shall We Go?* (ABC) and *Over the Hills* (Associated-Rediffusion). Yet there was still an anxiety about whether these admags constituted ordinary programming or specifically a form of advertising. For Sendall, 'There can be little doubt that, however carefully they were labelled, the more successful advertising magazines were seen (even enjoyed) as *programmes* by at least some viewers.'[10] The problem was that it looked as if these programmes had been sponsored through the back door. As Sendall goes on to explain:

> The more plausible and 'intrinsically interesting' the linking theme of an advertising magazine was, the more readily it would resemble a programme and incur, however unjustifiably, the charge of programme sponsorship. The less plausible the theme and the less effective the linking, the more the magazine would seem to be no more than a bunch of unrelated spot advertisements which should rightly be counted against the daily allowance for such.[11]

During the submissions to the Pilkington Committee at the beginning of the 1960s, the first ITA chairman recommended abolishing the admag form on the grounds that they had become a form of programme sponsorship. The committee was unhappy with admags and 'concluded that even if the magazines were within the letter of the Act, they offended against its spirit.'[12] As a result of the Pilkington recommendation, the Postmaster General issued a directive in 1963 that no more admags be made.

Visibility and material display

Advertising and admags were not the only ways in which consumer culture was promoted. In a fairly obvious way, the new visibility provided by television promoted a variety of cultural forms and activities through the relay and, ultimately, 'witness' of cultural events, performances and representations. As we saw in Chapter 1, the impetus for broadcasting had been the promotion of buying and consuming culture. With the advent of first radio, then television, broadcasting effectively promoted cultural consumption to a wider audience, that is consumption of musical performances, plays, light entertainment, talk programmes and sport. As we saw in Chapter 2, the work of the Arts Council in the late 1940s and early 1950s was predicated on the idea that the BBC had already created a national audience for artistic activity. Alongside print media, entertainment outlets and public institutions, broadcasting effectively served to cross-promote a variety of cultural activities within the mixed-programme schedule.

In the 1950s and 1960s, the newly expanded television institution promoted new forms of art and culture to a newly established national audience in new and wide ranging forms of programming, which were linked to class and consumerism in a number of ways. It was not just the cultural consumption of a range of arts that was promoted, but a newly visible range of commodities and lifestyles. As the French sociologist Pierre Bourdieu has shown, art, culture and commodities constitute forms of class communication directly related to lifestyle – both

147

desired and actual. Taste and lifestyle thus become both constituents and definitions of class.[13] As a result, commodities can signify lifestyle while at the same time lifestyle can be bought via commodities. This suggests that social or class definitions and positions are not necessarily static.

As an earlier sociologist, Thorstein Veblen, has shown us, material consumption is one way of expressing a form of class mobility. In his analysis of the French *nouveaux riches* at the end of the nineteenth century (originally published in 1899), Veblen demonstrated that status could be bought by particular social groups through 'conspicuous consumption'.[14] In Veblen's example, an emerging social group built on new money sought to dress up its social pretensions by emulating established wealth. Of course, such an attempt at cultural incorporation into a higher social group was not necessarily successful, and the term *nouveaux riches* has negative connotations. I shall explore this issue later in relation to class conflict, yet what this reveals is that consumerism and the purchase of new commodities and services has class implications.

So, in this period, television showed its audience new commodities through advertising, but also in a range of other programme forms. It presented a range of lifestyles and new forms of behaviour including, but not necessarily restricted to, social mobility, individual and personal freedom, material comfort and convenience. This new behaviour often involved the conspicuous display of (and in some cases relied on) material goods and commodities. In a range of programmes material goods and lifestyle were linked and potentially made desirable. The wide range of programme forms within the mixed-programme schedule, with often different and contradictory ideologies, makes it difficult to draw any easy conclusions about how television promoted consumer culture in its programming. Some examples should illustrate the contradictory ways that television explored consumerism and lifestyle.

In an explicit sense, the ability of television cameras to film and broadcast from around the world in the 1950s and 1960s promoted travel as a particular aspect of cultural activity. As we saw in the last chapter, television was able to report from abroad, and this potentially offered an image of the exotic, of charming and desirable foreignness. The expansion of air travel and the advent of the so-called 'jet age' certainly made it possible for camera crews, and people like Orson Welles and Alan Whicker, to travel round the world more quickly and conveniently.

Foreignness, in natural history programmes and travelogues, became a staple of television output and it was teasingly and tantalizingly promoted under the educational and informative veil of public service broadcasting. It certainly seemed to place Britain at the centre of a world map and imply, in a neo-colonial manner, that Britons (even working-class ones) had the right, if not a duty in the interest of education, to travel and consume the wildlife and culture of foreign places.

Yet, of course, it was cheap air travel, package holidays, relative affluence, hire-purchase arrangements and the 'keeping up with the Jones' that were key factors in the increasing numbers of people travelling abroad on holiday. In 1951, for example, two million foreign holidays were taken by Britons, rising to four million in 1961 and seven million in 1971.[15] In the first ever episode of the popular and enduring sitcom about two young working-class men in the north of England, *The Likely Lads*, shown on BBC2 in 1964, the characters Bob and Terry are seen arriving home from a holiday in Spain. The image suggests that even two working-class lads from the North can aspire to, and achieve, travel to exotic locations.

Holiday-making was not an isolated aspect of consumer culture, but vied with other goods and services for consumer spending. In the same year as *The Likely Lads* above, an episode of the BBC1 sitcom *Meet the Wife*, starring Freddie Frinton and Thora Hird, clearly demonstrates how consumerism impacted on working-class couples and families, and the kinds of financial anxieties it caused. In the episode titled 'Getting Away', transmitted on 21 April 1964, the comedy centres on Thora and Freddie, a northern middle-aged, working-class couple planning to go on holiday. At the beginning of the episode Thora and Freddie are seen arguing over whether they can afford to go abroad, and their argument demonstrates the competing financial claims that the new consumer boom has on their money, as well as the need to be seen to be 'keeping up' socially. Part of what inspires Thora to want to go abroad is a sense of competition with her friends and neighbours.

Reading a holiday brochure in bed, Thora announces, 'The Hotel Splendide, Majorca. Now that's where Mrs Jackson from the sweetshop stayed.' Freddie counters that they cannot afford a foreign holiday because of the money they have spent on household items. 'You've spent too much money around the house, only last month this new bed cost 50 quid.' Thora claims that she only wants what everyone else seems to be doing, 'Why, even the milkman's just come back from Bulgaria. How can he afford to go?' To which Freddie's crisp reply is, 'It was a free gift with his washing machine.' In the end Freddie relents, and books a two-week holiday at the Hotel Splendide with air tickets on British Airways. When Thora asks how they could afford it after all, Freddie tells her that he won the money betting on the dogs. It turns out, however, that he booked the holiday secretly on HP.

In a twist to the story, Thora tells him that she would never obtain anything on credit because of people they know crippled by debt. In the end, Thora finds out Freddie's secret, but they still manage to go on holiday to Spain with the post office savings she has. The episode pokes gentle fun at Thora's aspirations of planning to show off her suntan at the launderette, even though she now has a washing machine, and at her anxieties about flying and foreign food. Some of the comedy comes from Thora packing too much in her suitcase, including her new pair of slacks, a travel iron, a hot-water bottle, and all her various medicines in case of tummy upsets. What the episode articulately demonstrates, however, is the preoccupation with consumer culture and the financial and social anxieties this culture entails.

The way television positioned part of its female audience in the period also demonstrates the complex and contradictory ways in which programming promoted consumer culture. From the late 1940s the BBC had identified women as a distinct audience that was available to view programming during the daytime.[16] As Janet Thumim argues, targeting women as a specialist category was part of a broader strategy to expand the television audience and to establish a wider culture of television viewing.[17] At the same time, as Joy Leman suggests, it was also a way in which television producers could make daytime use of studios and broadcasting personnel.

By situating women in the home during the day, as housewives, they were considered to be both consumers and workers in the home – they kept house, shopped, cleaned, cooked and raised children. As Leman indicates, 'The ideological operation of the programmes arose from society's hegemonic definitions of the family, children and domestic labour, and the desirable attributes and behaviour of men and women.'[18] It was therefore seen as desirable that women in the home conform to idealized visions of womanhood, as being both attractive and efficient domestic workers. It also negated women's wider experiences outside the home, in the workplace. So, from the late 1940s the BBC broadcast numerous daytime programmes in a magazine format, segmented into short, discrete sections tackling different topics such as children, house and home, shopping, cooking and personal appearance. Programme titles included *Designed for Women* (1947), *About the Home* (1952) and *Family Affairs* (1955).

The segmented format of these programmes had been inspired by the fragmented style of print magazines, which had already transferred to radio. Furthermore, by dealing with a wide range of topics it also appealed to a wider audience.[19] As we saw in Chapter 2, Thumim argues that the magazine format is paradigmatic of the mixed-programme schedule in this period. This is because a range of different programmes (in a range of styles and formats, on varying themes and subjects) appeals broadly to a much wider audience. This was particularly important for television broadcasters trying to build a culture of viewing. The magazine format was also seen as desirable, in the USA at least, because segmented programmes allowed women to conduct their housework while watching discrete items of interest or value to them.[20]

When ITV arrived it too adopted a similar model of providing daytime magazine programmes for women who were perceived to be at home, and these tended to be transmitted in the morning. These programmes included *Morning Magazine* (1955–56), *Sunday Afternoon* (1955–56), *Home with Joy Shelton* (1955–56) and *Television Beauty Salon* (1957). However, commercial pressure meant that morning programmes for women were wound up, and by 1957 women's concerns were increasingly seen to be catered to by admags.[21] On the BBC, women's magazine programmes during the daytime tended to evaporate in the early 1960s. The scheduling slot for women's programmes in the afternoon started to be moved around, and then it became increasingly replaced by outside broadcasting of sport. By 1964, there were no longer any programmes on BBC television that specifically addressed women. As Thumim argues, this was because competition for programming resources squeezed out 'women's' programmes as a special category, and because television broadcasting no longer needed to enlist specialist categories of audience to develop viewing cultures.[22]

There is also a class issue here. The tone of the early programmes in the late 1940s and early 1950s was clearly aimed at upper- and middle-class women. This was because in this period only parts of an affluent set in the southeast of England could afford television. Joy Leman refers to an edition of *About the Home* in 1952, for example, which clearly demonstrated class prejudice in an item on food hygiene. The item used a drama documentary technique to depict a stereotypical working-class family living in unhygienic conditions to illustrate the wrong way to prepare food. As Leman explains, 'References to flies, dirty washing-up cloths, meat warmed up in the oven, cats and "grubby boy's dirty fingers" all pointed to the conclusion that "their" dirty habits were the reason for outbreaks in food poisoning.'[23]

As a result, there emerged a 'separation between the "innocent" viewer (assumed to be middle-class) and the "guilty" subject (presented as working-class)'.[24] As Leman argues, *About the Home* sustained this tone, even in the face of the expanding television audience, which was perceived as being increasingly working class, and the arrival of commercial television.[25] These kinds of programmes, and the admags, would also have complemented women's magazines of the day, and in this they would have offered contradictory models of cultural capital, especially for middle-class women.

Janet Winship has argued that women's weekly magazines in the 1950s promoted consumption as a way for women to gain success in their careers as mothers and wives.[26] Knowing the right price of goods, knowing how best to cook and how to clean with the electronic goods and detergents that were becoming available, was increasingly important for women in household management. In this sense, women became 'professionalized' (albeit unpaid) managers of their households.

On the other hand, Winship also suggests that, despite such professionalized status, middle-class women were effectively 'proletarianized' in a material sense after the Second World War because they had to take over the domestic chores that would previously have been done by a maid or hired help. It could therefore be argued that programmes oriented towards women on shopping, cooking and cleaning, may have sought to elevate the housewife's status as a household manager while at the same time condemning her to being a *de facto* domestic drudge.

Nonetheless, Thumim argues that the demise of programmes aimed specifically at women meant that by the early 1960s women's issues had become subsumed into those of a larger, general audience. Within the newly expanded television institution, across the later 1950s and 1960s, women were made visible in a range of television outputs, both factual and fictional, across the mixed-programme schedules. A younger generation of women grew up in the 1960s with these representations of women's role in patriarchal society, and it was from this constituency that a new wave of feminists emerged in the 1970s.[27]

Television (among other media like radio, vinyl records, jukeboxes and magazines) also provided for and gave high profile to a newly emerging social group in this period, teenagers and youth culture. There were several reasons why youth culture came to prominence in the 1950s.

Younger people did not need to support the extended family as they had previously done. Combined with full employment and higher wages for a mobile workforce, this meant that young people who had left school had significantly more disposable income. Young women working in shops and offices, unfettered by the usual male expenditure on beer and cigarettes, were now better able to spend money on commodities such as records, clothes and make-up.[28] It was not just women who were affected, however, because in the 1950s a shift in male culture was underway.

With national service finally abolished in 1956, a new generation of younger males had more free time, more money and more freedom to choose how they dressed. Until the 1950s, the 'suit' had been the predominant mode of male dress – characterized by the issuing of a 'demob suit' to all servicemen at the end of the war. From the end of the 1940s it became increasingly possible for young men to dress in ways that signified their class or group affiliation. In the 1950s the 'teddy boy' emerged, which was a working-class fashion self-styled (and short for) 'the new Edwardians', derived from their Edwardian form of clothing with long jackets, velvet collars and waistcoats. The 'teddy boy' style had been appropriated from upper-class young males at the end of the 1940s, and young working-class men could pay up to £100 for their outfits.[29] Although teddy boys have in some ways become synonymous with the 1950s, and at the time they were associated with youth crime and deviance, it was effectively a fleeting fashion. The term 'teddy boys' was first used in 1954, yet the movement had already passed by 1957 when rock and roll became a music phenomenon.

Importantly here, the emergence of rock and roll in Britain is bound up with the development of new forms of television programming at the end of the 1950s.[30] Programmes such as *Cool for Cats* (A-R 1956–59), *Six-Five Special* (BBC 1957–58), *Oh Boy!* (ABC 1958–59) and *Juke Box Jury* (BBC 1959–67) helped support and fuel interest in the nascent rock and roll movement.[31] These programmes promoted the consumption of music and performances (much as BBC radio had in the 1920s and 1930s) and the purchasing of records. At the same time, these programmes also promoted complementary trends in youth fashion. This was not just the dress and demeanour of popular performers, but also members of the studio audiences in some shows. As John Hill has observed, members of the studio audience in *Six-Five Special* became 'unofficial guides' to fashions in haircuts, clothing and dancing.[32] This was equally the case in *Ready, Steady, Go!* (A-R 1963–66) where 'the audience were as much the stars as the musicians'.[33]

As the passing phase of the 'teddy boy' demonstrates, the conceptualization of youth culture cannot be a stable one because cohorts of teenagers grow older, as do the performers who appeal to them. The rock and roll stars on British television at the end of the 1950s, such as Cliff Richard, Tommy Steel and Adam Faith, had by the start of the 1960s increasingly become associated with more mainstream show business. This partly reflected the ageing of their fan base, as teenagers grew up, married and started to raise families.[34] Furthermore, teenagers of a given period do not necessarily constitute a homogenous group.

In the early 1960s there were the Italian-influenced mods, sharply attired in suits, and the more motorbike-oriented rockers dressed in denim and leather. These groups gained public notoriety in the early 1960s with a series of clashes at seaside towns during bank holidays.[35] The rock and roll teenager was not a classless phenomenon. At the end of the 1950s and early 1960s, many middle-class youngsters, especially those associated with the Campaign for Nuclear Disarmament (CND), tended to be more interested in jazz (and later folk music). Over this period there was intense snobbery about music, and jazz fans were particularly contemptuous of working-class teenagers and 'pop' music.[36]

These different kinds of music were all promoted to varying degrees within the mixed-programme schedule of television, and therefore vulnerable to critical distaste. Pop music shows like *Six-Five Special* were also characterized by the magazine format because they were scheduled in primetime early evening and had to appeal to a wider audience than just teenagers. As a result, *Six-Five Special* combined elements of variety in a magazine format, with music, comedy and feature items.[37] At the same time, however, elements of rock, pop and jazz featured in other mixed bill variety programming. A 'trad jazz' performance, for example, appeared in almost every edition of *Sunday Night at the London Palladium* in 1962.[38] The inclusion of different kinds of music across the schedule meant it was possible for different audience groups to be exposed to the musical tastes and cultures of other parts of the audience. This became the cause of taste conflict.

A particularly compelling example of this is the BBC programme *Juke Box Jury*, which began in 1959. Based on an American idea, the show was hosted by David Jacobs who sat next to a fake jukebox, and played the week's latest pop releases to a panel of four judges who tended to be show business personalities known to the audience. The panellists would then have to decide whether or not the single was going to be a 'hit' or a 'miss'. The programme was scheduled initially on Mondays, but then moved to a slot on Saturdays in the early evening, and so was particularly aimed at capturing a family audience.

The show proved immensely popular and regularly attracted 12 million viewers. For younger people the attraction was the opportunity to hear the latest record releases, whereas for older viewers the interest lay in the show business panellists. The show became, in its way, a generational battleground. As John Hill argues, the guests often articulated the same barbed and disdainful comments that the parents might make. At the same time, younger viewers did not necessarily want the older personalities, or their parents, to understand the appeal of the music. For Hill, 'The art of *Juke Box Jury*, in this respect, was to have it both ways, both confirming adult and youthful prejudices at the same time.'[39] As a result, the show's popularity was based on a form of cultural conflict between different age groupings, and also, it is likely, the taste cultures of different sections of the youth audience itself.

Another programme form that visibly celebrated material display, but in a different way, is the action-adventure genre, especially those involving spies, secret agents and crime solving adventurers, including *The Saint* and *The Avengers*. It has been argued that the adventure series can be seen as a by-product of Americanization. This was very much a case of British television remaking and remarketing genres that had originally been imported from the USA.[40] Jeffrey Miller has argued that these genres were appropriated, reinterpreted and synthesized with cultural elements drawn from Britain and continental Europe. The end product was something that looked very British,[41] yet there is an explicit connection with consumer culture here. Osgerby and Gough-Yates argue that there is a connection between the aesthetics of these adventures and pop culture, with 'the spy's talent for masquerade and mobility representing an ideal vehicle for the exploration of style, surface and "look".'[42]

The heroes and heroines of these action adventure series were socially mobile and sexually liberated characters, whose mobility and liberation were articulated by a masquerade comprised of dressing up and conspicuous consumption. In these series characters wear sharp, expensive clothes, drive fast cars, visit exotic locations and appear at ease in a number of social milieux. In this sense, Osgerby and Gough-Yates argue, 'Action series can be seen as a kind of "lifestyle" television in the way they combine fantasies of thrilling adventure with mythologies of affluence and consumption.'[43]

The Saint, for example, achieved cultural purchase by connecting with important changes taking place in consumption, lifestyle and masculine identities in Britain and the USA, painting hedonistic role models.[44] Of course, as Osgerby and Gough-Yates point out, the situation is far from clear cut. Rather than a straightforward representation of young men living the 'high life', the series effectively serves, they argue, as 'a mythologized fantasy, a vehicle for aspirational fantasies and desires.'[45]

On the other hand, these series, such as *The Saint* and *The Avengers*, could perhaps be read as parodies of those male, 'mythologized fantasies'. In being playful and tongue-in-cheek, the series might be seen to be sending up adolescent daydreams of sexual freedom and masculine omnipotence.

A different series in the action-adventure mould, however, *The Prisoner*, had very serious intellectual pretensions, and this contradicts with the visual celebration of style and material display. *The Prisoner* (1967–68) was about a secret agent being kept captive in a strange village by the sea. He is given the title 'Number Six', and the series follows his attempts to escape or resist the seemingly absurd rules and restrictions of 'The Village', where life is characterized by surreal goings-on and overwhelming surveillance. As a result, one way of reading the series is as 'an existentialist disquisition on the nature of individual freedom in an age of ever-increasing bureaucracy and social control'.[46] This is succinctly articulated in the first episode, and repeated in the title sequence for the rest of the series, when the main character shouts in frustration at his captors, 'I am not a number. I am a free man!' Furthermore, it has been argued that *The Prisoner* is rooted in conservative assumptions – anxieties about growing media manipulation and cultural conformity.[47] The series could therefore be read as offering a critique of mass society, the potentially oppressive conformity of fashion and increasing consumerism.

As we have seen then, the different range of programme outputs in the mixed-programme schedule promoted often contradictory ideologies surrounding consumer culture. In many respects, it could be argued that television showed audiences *what* to consume and *how* to consume it (and in many cases how to *get* it). Programmes may have promoted consumerism in ways that were seen to transcend class, appealing instead to gender and age and, in doing so, offering the possibility of social mobility. Some programmes provided potential role models for the first time in the 1950s and 1960s. They could offer and suggest models for appropriate types of behaviour in particular situations.

Identifications reinforce patterns of consumption by suggesting that by dressing a certain way or acquiring certain commodities, you too can become like the person on screen. Such models do not necessarily work purely at the level of social class or grouping, but also operate at the level of sexual desire. This might be crudely formulated as 'if you wear the smart suit, you too could get the girl.' Yet, as we have seen, social mobility through consumption, in Veblen's sense, implicitly points to elements of class negotiation or conflict.

The depiction of consumer culture in the programmes I looked at above that focused on youth or that were specifically aimed at women, contained within them, or represented, problematic positions, such as intragenerational conflict among teenage cohorts, or the potential 'proletarianization' of middle-class women in the home. Programmes that also appeared to celebrate images of classless masculinity and sexuality through highly conspicuous displays of material affluence may also have been playful with, and even critical of, those very same images. What is clear here is that television made different forms of material display more visible, and in doing so promoted competing discourses about consumer culture. These displays were bound up with issues of taste, lifestyle and cultural capital. As Bourdieu has shown, taste, lifestyle and cultural capital are not only markers of class distinction, but they are also the weapons of class conflict.[48]

Conflict

Class conflict was depicted in a range of dramas in film, theatre, literature and on television during the period. It was well exemplified in 'classic' sitcoms like *Hancock's Half Hour* and *Steptoe and Son*. As Peter Goddard has argued, the sitcom was a new form of television programming in the 1950s, and the comedian Tony Hancock was one of the first to develop the form in Britain from simple slapstick, stand-up or sketches, towards action and humour that were narratively driven.[49]

Hancock's Half Hour had started on radio in 1954 (running until 1959) before being shown on BBC television from 1956 to 1960, with two series of *The Tony Hancock Show* on ITV (A-R) in 1956 and 1957. As well as other appearances on ITV and BBC, Tony Hancock's eponymously titled sitcom, *Hancock*, ran on BBC television in 1961 and included the famous episodes 'The Bedsitter' and 'The Blood Donor'.[50] Throughout the radio series and subsequent television sitcoms the *character* Hancock, rather than the performer Hancock, comes across as a man on the edge: on the edge of the middle class, on the edge of suburbia, and on the edge of respectability.

Hancock was a man with pretensions towards culture and respectability, even though he hailed from the lower middle class. Given the increasing overlap in material existence between the working classes and the lower middle classes in the 1950s, the lower middle classes were often more conscious of their precarious cultural status. This material existence was frequently geographical, with working-class and lower-middle-class households often living in close proximity. The fictitious address for Hancock is a case in point: 23 Railway Cuttings, East Cheam.

The place Cheam was a very comfortable middle-class suburb of south London in the period, but the appendage 'East' had connotations of the East End of London, which was known for being home to working-class communities.[51] The Railway Cuttings address also established the location as being next to the railway lines (perhaps on the 'wrong' side of the tracks) and as being a terrace, rather than the more comfortable semi-detached houses of what Andy Medhurst calls 'high suburbia'.[52]

Hancock's countenance displays a mix of ill-directed guile, pomposity and laziness. As Goddard argues, Hancock is 'the seedy misfit with intellectual pretensions, sure he was missing out while those around him had never had it so good'.[53] His companion Sid (Sid James), while not deliberately holding him back, is intransigent to Hancock's class manoeuvring. While James's obvious working-class demeanour acts as a foil to Hancock's pretensions, his dodgy geezer 'on the make' appeals to Hancock's laziness. In this sense they make the archetypal buddy pairing of opportunist chancers. Yet, despite being a comedy, Medhurst argues that the Hancock series 'added a little grit to the suburban blancmange, which interrogated suburban values rather than taking them for granted'.[54] While Medhurst cautions that the circular nature of sitcom, which returns characters back to where they started, tends to militate against an agenda of radical change, Hancock 'raised the possibility that suburban lives might be restricted lives, petty lives, lives that prompt thoughts of escape'.[55]

While *Hancock's Half Hour* is concerned with class struggle on the fringes of respectable suburbia, *Steptoe and Son* more explicitly demonstrates the conflictual nature of capitalist and consumer relationships. Running on and off between 1962 and 1974, *Steptoe and Son* are father and son rag-and-bone merchants who live in a rundown, decrepit junkyard in west London. The son, Harold Steptoe, played by Harry H. Corbett, takes the horse and cart out every day to pick up old objects and scrap, which they then try to sell on. The objects that are collected often provide the furniture and fittings for the Steptoes' rundown home.

The collection of junk and scrap means the programme can be read in two ways, as a celebration of consumer culture, or as a critique of consumer culture. In one sense the programme is a celebration of objects. It is what the two men (mainly Harold) salvage, and they are often seen arguing over the merits of a particular artefact. These artefacts may have functional or aesthetic value, but never far away is the spectre of class and the cultural capital of the objects they claim.

As a celebration of commodities, it demonstrates that each object has a biography, that it can represent something new to whoever finds it.[56] Objects are part of a constant circulation of meaning. A more pessimistic reading might be that, in many ways, the objects they retrieve are worthless. When they find a functional object it has clearly been discarded not because of its lack of use value (in Marxist terms) but because of its lack of cultural and economic value.

The series demonstrated the poverty of an endless consumption in which objects that were once new will eventually be discarded. Buying one object is not enough, it has to be discarded, replaced or superseded by something that works better or *looks* better, or has more modish, class-based cultural capital. There is also a darker edge here, as described in the *Radio Times Guide to Comedy*, 'It [*Steptoe and Son*] dealt with an underclass previously seen on television only in realistic dramas like *Armchair Theatre*'.[57]

As part of an underclass the duo have to live in very squalid conditions. There is perhaps an implicit moral here in that what defines an underclass is an inability to consume material objects in an appropriate manner. The objects and furnishings that adorn the Steptoe home are not the desirable consumer objects bought new from department stores for the homes that were being built around Britain. As members of an underclass, Alfred and Harold are aberrant because they are not part of the cycle of consumption of mainstream society.

The relationships in *Steptoe and Son* are very complex. Part of the drama is premised on the love–hate relationship between father and son Alfred and Harold. The series started out as a one half-hour 'playlet' transmitted on 5 January 1962 as part of an anthology season of comedies written for the BBC by Alan Simpson and Ray Galton. The original programme was called 'The Offer', and centred on Harold preparing to leave his father because he has an 'offer' of work elsewhere.

Despite being a comedy, the dramatic tension perhaps has more in common with Beckett's *Waiting for Godot*, as Harold opines on why he must go and how he must make his life better. In the end, however, he is thwarted by his own inability to leave. As Beckett's protagonists are frustrated by Godot's very non-appearance, Harold is denied his escape because his father does not offer him the use of the horse to pull the cart with his belongings. In a sense, despite Harold's desperation to leave, part of what holds him back is his own fear and anxiety. In the subsequent series, the ongoing tension comes from Harold trying to escape the grimness and squalor of life where both home and work constitute a 'prison'.[58] Harold's attempts to better himself and find a romantic partner in life are counter-poised against Alfred, a lazy, selfish old man who wants Harold to stay at home to look after him in his old age.

As well as being a generational conflict (a newer generation, restless against the constraints of an older one), the comedy is infused with class conflict. Harold's attempt at self-betterment and refinement, amid the jumble and the junk, comes across as pretentious and pathetic. Instead, Harold seeks cultural capital through the commodities he acquires. As Pierre Bourdieu has demonstrated, consumption and taste define class interests and groupings.[59] Class grouping is not just predicated on economic capital, in Marx's sense, but also on cultural capital, knowledge and learnt behaviour that ascribe to the social rules, conventions, attitudes and moralities of a specific class. Part of that capital involves the cultural display of artefacts and commodities in a manner appropriate to a particular class.

Harold Steptoe's attempts to acquire the status of middle-class refinement and respectability, through ownership of objects and artefacts, are laughable because he lacks the necessary cultural capital to display middle-class status. In collecting junk,

Harold particularly prizes the objects and artefacts that bring with it middle-class cultural capital, even if he does not fully understand their significance. In the episode 'Sixty-Five Today', for example, Harold has been collecting books for his bookcase. Sorting through his new finds, he picks up a book by the existentialist French philosopher Jean-Paul Sartre and utters in astonishment, 'Here, there's a girl here with a bloke's middle name! It's like me being called Harold Gladys.' The pathos is that Harold is denied the very cultural capital (education) that the book represents.

As Bourdieu asserts, it is the display of cultural knowledge that provides the grounds for class conflict. In this conflict, Harold Steptoe's awkward and cringing cultural displays can be funny for a middle-class audience – they are likely to get the joke because they have the relevant cultural capital. On the other hand, a working-class audience might equally find Harold's actions laughable because he is trying to get 'above himself', that he is trying to adopt 'airs and graces'.

In this sense, as Stephen Wagg has suggested, the message of *Steptoe and Son* is essentially conservative because the comedy has the effect of 'telling members of lower social and cultural groups that they should know their place'.[60] As Wagg further suggests, this relates to the depictions of working-class life in *The uses of literacy*, in which Hoggart describes a fatalistic and pragmatic attitude towards life which was necessary for survival.[61]

Among the working class that Hoggart described, there was no sense of aspiration and, in work terms, there was little chance of career advancement, promotion or trying to get ahead. There was also no attempt at competition with others because one's sense of community dictated that you should not put the other man out of a job.

For Hoggart, working-class struggle was a struggle against the environment, against dropping further down the scale rather than a struggle to move upwards. According to Hoggart, the people the working classes did not particularly like were 'stuck up folk', so Harold's attempts at self-betterment and his snobbery were ill conceived, and his embarrassing failure an appropriate comeuppance.

Distaste

As well as being depicted in television dramas and sitcoms, cultural conflict was also waged over particular genres of programming on television in the 1950s and 1960s. Due to the way in which a wider world was newly visible, the activities and interests of other groups were now on display on a regular basis in television programmes, and this could become the focus of *distaste* and cultural antagonism.

For Bourdieu distaste, as a prejudice against other forms of taste, is a key weapon in class conflict.[62] In the late 1950s, one form of programming that was subject to criticism was also notable because it both explicitly and implicitly celebrated consumer culture. This was the quiz and game show. Part of the problem was that the more spectacular versions of these shows appeared on ITV and were couched in discourses of popular appeal, and seemed a long way away from the sober Reithian values of the BBC.

Criticisms of the new quiz and game shows were grounded in class discourses. In particular, the distaste felt among the middle class for game shows of the ITV variety were grounded in a disregard for the working-class vulgarity of show business kitsch, the fairground knockabout, conspicuous consumption, and the idea that people might be winning something for nothing. Such programmes did not necessarily promote specific, branded commodities, but they did promote generic commodity items such as refrigerators, washing machines and televisions. Not only did they promote the desirability of such commodity items, but they also celebrated a culture of desirability for such items.

More complexly, and more implicitly, the formal articulation of the quiz and game show genre *as entertainment* de-emphasized the relationship between programme-maker and audience as a relationship of production and consumption. This meant that audience members enjoyed these programmes as entertainment without realizing that they were consuming the work and labour of television performers and other production personnel. As will be explored in the next chapter, quiz and game shows not only facilitated the promotion of consumer culture with desirable commodity items or sums of cash as prizes, but they also metaphorically instilled wider practices of consumption and ideologically, routinely and ritually celebrated them in spaces of television performance.

Although particularly associated with the arrival of commercial television, the quiz and game show's genesis was an evolution out of existing cultural forms, including magazine and newspaper competitions, holiday camp and village fête contests and, in broadcasting, BBC TV panel game shows, pre-existing radio shows and US television programmes. The new ITV shows, however, which came to occupy a significant amount of airtime, were to cause some anxiety to the ITA and the members of the Pilkington Committee.

In the first instance, ITV companies adopted the new shows as a cheap and successful way of building and keeping the necessary audience numbers that were attractive to advertisers. In the very early days of the ITV service, companies struggled to attract advertising revenue and there was genuine concern that the commercial enterprise would prove a failure. According to the ITA Annual Report for 1955/56, the programme companies were so worried that they reduced the number of more serious programmes such as news, serious talk programmes and classical music by a third.[63] As Roland Gillett, programme controller of Associated-Rediffusion pronounced, 'Let's face it once and for all. The public likes girls, wrestling, bright musicals, quiz shows and real-life drama. We gave them the Hallé Orchestra, Foreign Press Club, floodlit football and visits to the local fire station. Well we've learned. From now on, what the public wants, it's going to get.'[64]

Quiz and game shows were part of this drive for audience numbers.[65] During the first week of the ITV service in September 1955, the *TV Times* listed two, *Double Your Money* (A-R) and *Take Your Pick* (A-R). *Double Your Money*, hosted by Hughie Greene, was a filmed programme that ran for 13 years. Based on the US television show *The $64,000 Question*, the premise of the show was that contestants answered a series of questions, with the cash prize doubling on each question. The climax of the show was the contestant being locked in a soundproof booth for the last question, with a cash prize of up to £1000.

Take Your Pick was also a filmed show, hosted by Michael Miles, with each contestant overcoming minor challenges to have the chance to 'take his or her pick' among 13 boxes that contained ten expensive prizes and three booby prizes.[66] Contestants had to make the agonizing choice of whether to take the cash prize offered by the show's host, or chance a dud box to win a much bigger prize. By January 1957, however, there were eight game show programmes each week, with two more game show segments embedded in other programmes, such as 'Beat the Clock' in *Sunday Night at the London Palladium*. As well as *Double Your Money* and *Take Your Pick*, other quiz and game shows included *Make Up Your Mind* (Granada), *Two for the Money* (A-R), *Do You Trust Your Wife?* (ATV) and *Spot the Tune* (Granada).

For Sendall, this profusion of quiz and game shows, described by the press as give-away shows because of their relatively lavish prizes, was damaging to the reputation of ITV. The reduction of more serious programming and the favouring of quiz and game shows raised questions about the proper balance of programming, and was described in the press as a 'retreat from culture'.[67] Such a view saw quiz and game shows as a low form of culture or, as the phrase 'retreat from culture' suggests, barely recognizable as culture at all. The genre gave ITV a bad name, and fuel to critics who saw this as evidence of crass commercialism and broadcasting to the 'lowest common denominator'.[68]

Although such shows helped the ITV programme companies stave off financial collapse in the earliest stages of the new service, Sendall notes that the quiz show 'strikingly illustrates how ITV found easy success and lingered too long with it for its own eventual well-being'.[69] Despite an ITA intervention early in 1957 limiting the programme companies to one quiz or game show a day, the genre was exemplary of the kinds of trivial programmes for which the Pilkington Report criticized ITV.[70]

These brash shows, with their big prizes, were a far cry from the small, quieter and more intimate panel shows of the BBC from the 1950s, which had more in keeping with Edwardian parlour games. One of the first panel games from the period, discussed in the last chapter, was *Animal, Vegetable, Mineral?*, on which eminent scholars had to identify curious objects placed before them. Produced by the Talks Department of the BBC, and dwelling on archaeological or natural history artefacts from British museums, the programme ostensibly fulfilled a more Reithian purpose of informing, educating and entertaining.

The most popular of the panel shows of the period, or at least the best known, was *What's My Line?* (1951–62). Although it was very much in the format of a parlour game, the programme was in fact derived from a show in the United States. Unlike *Animal, Vegetable, Mineral?*, *What's My Line?* included general members of the public in the game. The simple premise for the show, hosted by Eamonn Andrews, was that a panel of four television personalities had to guess the secret of each contestant. In most cases the contestant was a member of the public, and the panel had to deduce his or her occupation or, in some cases, hobby. The panel had to ask questions to which the contestant could only answer 'yes' or 'no'. The contestant won the competition if the panel had still not guessed their secret after ten 'no's. The successful contestant's prize was simply a certificate to say they had beaten the panel. In each edition, the panel would also be blindfolded while they had to guess the identity of a celebrity.

Another BBC panel game from the period was *The Name's the Same* hosted by Bernard Braden. In a similar style to *What's My Line?*, a panel of four television personalities had to quiz a contestant with 'yes' or 'no' style questions to find out the name they shared with a famous person. In one clip, shown in the programme *What's My Quiz?* (transmitted on 22 July 1991 as part of a day's programming on BBC2, *The Lime Grove Story*, to mark the closing of the BBC's Lime Grove Studios), panellists had to guess the name of a schoolteacher by the name of William Shakespeare and, in another clip, the panellist Frank Muir had to guess the name of a contestant by the name of Frank Muir.[71]

At first glance, what marks out the ITV quiz and game shows from the BBC panel games are the prizes. On BBC shows the prize was ostensibly a certificate of some form (although Jane Root suggests that the real prize was meeting the television personalities and appearing on television).[72] On ITV shows contestants could win actual commodity prizes such as refrigerators, washing machines and television sets. The prizes reflected items that working-class families in particular might have found desirable, and in some cases difficult to afford. Although the prizes were less lavish than in the USA, where in one competition it was possible to win a house, the top British cash prize of £1000 in *Double Your Money* was a significant sum in the 1950s. Many cultural commentators, however, saw the awarding of commodity items and large cash prizes in negative terms.

In *The uses of literacy*, Hoggart derided the competitions that appeared in popular newspapers and magazines. Such competitions, he argued, not only nurtured a materialistic outlook among the working classes with their prizes but also, in terms reminiscent of the Frankfurt School writers, induced a sense of 'shared passivity'.[73] For Hoggart, the competitions in the popular press could only be won by 'pure luck'. This reinforced the prevailing culture among the working classes that no one was better than anyone else, that no one should strive to get ahead, and that one should accept one's fate with a certain sense of humour. The winning of a prize in a competition by good fortune was a happy occurrence, but it did not mean that you were in any way superior to your family, friends, neighbours or colleagues.

As a member of the Pilkington Committee of Inquiry, Hoggart was well able to express his unhappiness with competitions in newspapers and magazines, and this was iterated in the Pilkington Report's disdain for television quiz and game shows. For Whannel, the Pilkington Report's contempt for the form reflected a middle-class disapproval of gambling and the idea of people winning something for nothing.[74] Part of the problem was the relative ease of the questions, the element of chance, and the disproportionate prizes for the skill or knowledge required. As a result, Pilkington recommended that the value of prizes be reduced and that they should be more closely linked to the skill or knowledge required.[75] Yet, as Jane Root suggests, it seems ungenerous to suppose that the contestants of these programmes were motivated by greed, or that viewers enjoyed purely the vicarious delight of material gain.[76]

In many respects the attractiveness of these shows to

audiences was the enjoyment of the games being played. In this, the BBC panel games had much in common with the ITV give-away shows. In shows involving knowledge or deduction, the audience at home was actively invited to participate. In BBC programmes such as *What's My Line?* or even *Animal, Vegetable or Mineral?*, the audience watching on television had the choice of trying to deduce the contestant's secret, or the artefact's identity, from the questions being asked. If they wanted to play the game at home, the compere advised them to look away from their television sets as the contestant's secret or the object's identity was revealed on screen. Alternatively, the viewer could see the secret, and enjoy the progress of the game as panellists drew nearer to guessing the correct answer, or wandered off on unrelated tangents. In ITV quiz shows, the viewer at home could simply try and answer the question before the contestant did.

The supposed ease of the questions of some of the shows (as anxiously commented upon by Hoggart and Pilkington) reflected a wider set of values concerning shared knowledge. As Tulloch has argued, quiz shows celebrate knowledge as possession of certain facts, divorced from context and excluding reasoned argument or interpretation.[77] As a result, the kind of knowledge required has more in keeping with a Victorian style school education premised on rote learning.[78]

It should also be considered to what extent these shows increasingly relied on questions relating to the medium of television itself. As we saw in Chapter 1, in an edition of *What's My Line?*, the celebrity contestant was Victor Sylvester who had had a long-running music television show in the late 1940s and early 1950s. Without being a regular viewer of television, the audience member would not have had access to the cultural information that would have allowed him or her to participate in or enjoy this part of the game. As a result, the organization of television knowledge may be articulated by Scannell's formulation that television should address the *anyone* of the audience as *someone*.[79] Though addressed in a general way, the audience member recognizes that the television host or presenter is addressing him or her. As a result, I would argue here, the knowledge of quiz and panel shows, especially in respect of television knowledge *per se*, is socially validated as *knowledge that is available to anyone and everyone*. Television therefore, in some instances, validates its own knowledge provision. It is perhaps easy to see why critics like Hoggart might have been anxious about the kinds of knowledge increasingly being displayed in the quiz shows as they decreasingly relied on discourses of learning from 'high culture' and the arts.

To summarize, in this chapter I have demonstrated how television promoted consumer culture in the 1950s and 1960s and, on the ITV service, this was done through advertisements and admags. Both ITV *and* BBC television promoted consumer activity to its audiences through developments in programming that provided viewers with a range of identificatory resources. Through the *widest* range of television output, from dramas and sitcoms to women's programmes, pop shows and quizzes, lifestyle and cultural activities were presented in a range of guises.

These developments in television broadcasting made particular groups visible to each other. Visibility, organized around the mixed-programme schedule and by increasing programme diversity, became a marker of cultural fragmentation as groups and classes were exposed, explicitly and continuously, to the culture and entertainments of other classes. In the sense of Pierre Bourdieu's *Distinction*,[80] where taste and consumer choice can become the grounds for class conflict, the new visibility now made it possible to voice disdain for the 'debased' or 'pretentious' cultures of other groups being regularly exposed on television for the first time. As a result, differences in consumer, lifestyle and cultural tastes on television became the matter of class conflict. In the next chapter I shall explore how television's ability to promote consumer culture and class conflict became embedded and naturalized over time, and I shall examine the implications this has for the construction and operation of media power.

Chapter 6
CONSUMING TELEVISION CULTURE

As we saw in the last chapter, television promoted consumer culture and a sense of class difference and conflict in the 1950s and 1960s. In this chapter I shall explore how the developments I have discussed promoted not just consumer culture but a culture of consuming television. To examine this I want to concentrate on a particular form of television output: the quiz and game show. Focusing on a specific genre can illuminate wider elements of television culture. As we have already seen, Janet Thumim has argued that the magazine programme is paradigmatic of television more widely in the 1950s and 1960s.[1] This is because the segmentation of programmes into short, discrete items of varied interest was designed to appeal to broad audiences. This segmentation also characterized the mixed-programme schedule designed to appeal to a wide audience and to develop a television viewing culture in Britain. I shall argue here that the quiz and game show also tells us something important about the wider development of consumer and television culture in the period.

In the first instance, these programmes are significant because they were popular and they helped ITV, in particular, build an audience in its early years of operation. Quiz and game shows are also interesting because, as we saw in the last chapter, they

were the subject of class based criticism. They explicitly promoted a consumer culture by displaying desirable commodities
and consumer items as prizes. Quiz and game shows are significant because they contain 'television personalities' – professional presenters and performers. I shall therefore also focus
this chapter on the early 'celebrity' in television. I shall argue
that appearing on television as a professional necessarily constitutes a form of work that is consumed by the television
audience. The appearance of professional television performers
in quiz and game shows is juxtaposed against the inclusion of
ordinary members of the public in these programmes. Quiz and
game shows in the 1950s and 1960s therefore highlight the
emerging hierarchical relationship between professional television people and ordinary people.

I shall then go on to look at the development of 'fixed-point
scheduling' on British television. I shall examine the phenomenological properties of television and the relationship between
scheduling, programme serialization and the increasingly
routine consumption of television in the home. I shall argue that
watching television is analogous to other forms of consumption,
and therefore legitimizes other consumption practices more
widely. I then return to look at issues of celebrity and the hierarchical relationship between the professional presenter and lay
person who appears on television. By combining an analysis of
fixed-point scheduling with the emerging relationship between
presenter and ordinary member of the public, the chapter will go
on to show how unequal relations of power became increasingly
naturalized and legitimized on television in the 1950s and 1960s.
The development of quiz and game shows on television in this
period therefore tells us something important about the
development of media power.

Fun as ideological work

Quiz and game shows on television (and radio) were a
development from a combination of parlour games and holiday
competitions. What separates the quiz and game shows from
parlour games at home and other public entertainments is the

glitz, glamour and fun of the television event. As Richard Dyer has discussed in regard to television variety shows, there is a celebration of gaiety and abundance, a vision of a utopian world where work, drudgery, need and want are dispelled.[2] Whannel has argued that the same is true of quiz and game shows.[3] The fun of the games, the glamour of the television world, and the lavish prizes go towards dispelling the drudgery of the everyday. It is under the guise of fun that the ideological work of promoting consumer and television culture here is conducted.

A significant part of the quiz or game show, and part of the fun, as Whannel suggests, is the presence of celebrities.[4] Celebrity, however, might be a problematic term when thinking about television in the 1950s and 1960s. This is because television was still in the process of defining and establishing its own well-known personalities. As Frank Muir has dryly observed about television panellists in the 1950s, for example, 'There was no established pool of telepersons, so an extraordinary cross-section of people were invited to take part, most of whom did something quite different for a living.'[5]

In early editions of *This is Your Life*, for example, the subjects of the show were often members of the public who had been notable for heroic deeds during the war or who had done good works for the community.[6] In many ways the panellists on BBC shows in the early 1950s, and the subjects of *This is Your Life*, might conform to what Chris Rojek has described as 'achieved celebrity', where persons earn a degree of fame through success in their fields.[7] 'Achieved celebrity' would include sportsmen or women, actors, musician or artists. It could also be stretched here to include television panellists such as Lady Isobel Barnett, a JP (Justice of the Peace) and doctor, on *What's My Line?*, or Sir Mortimer Wheeler, the regular archeaologist on the panel of *Animal, Vegetable, Mineral?*

The difficulty comes when thinking about Rojek's term 'attributed celebrity', where people achieve fame through intensive and compressed media attention. Such a category is certainly useful when considering the almost paradigmatic hold 'celebrity' has had over the media landscape in the 1990s and early 2000s. During this latter period, as television moves into

an 'era of plenty',[8] multi-channel television has not only promoted 'celebrity' through the routine exhibition of well-known
actors and presenters, it has even elevated ordinary members of
the public to celebrity status in reality television programming.
Such celebrity has been promoted across a range of media
platforms such as tabloids and glossy magazines like *Hello*, *OK*
and *Heat*, which circulate images, news and gossip about
celebrities, and numerous fan and celebrity sites have grown on
the internet.

What characterizes celebrity culture of the 1990s and 2000s is
the expanding range of media outlets and platforms that circulate an ever-increasing volume of celebrity traffic at an ever-
increasing velocity. By contrast, the extent and speed of media
circulation of celebrity discourses in the 1950s was more limited
and much slower. Drawing on John Ellis's suggestion that television creates personalities,[9] and Andy Medhurst's discussion of
Gilbert Harding,[10] whose case I shall explore below, it seems
particularly useful here to use the term 'television personality'.
This allows us to differentiate the condition of television-
generated fame in television's era of scarcity (using Ellis's
historical periodization of the development of the medium)
from the notion of 'celebrity' in the emerging era of plenty.[11]

In the 1950s the television personality was an emerging phenomenon.[12] It was a phenomenon that reflexively and tauto-
logically television itself recognized, with programmes valorizing
performers from other shows, such as big band leader Victor
Sylvester appearing in an edition of *What's My Line?* and Eamonn
Andrews – also the presenter of *What's My Line?* – being the
victim of the 'sting' in the first ever British edition of *This is Your
Life*. Indeed, one of the biggest names in television (and radio) in
the 1950s, and the 'first paradigmatic television personality',[13]
was the *What's My Line?* panellist Gilbert Harding.

An unlikely candidate for television fame, Harding was a
middle-aged man who had studied at Cambridge University
before a succession of jobs, including working as a teacher, a
policeman and journalist in the 1930s. With aspirations to work
in the more serious and intellectual side of broadcasting, he
unhappily found himself in the field of light entertainment after

the war. Although he had first appeared as a panellist on *What's My Line?* in 1951, Harding found notoriety in the following year when he took a dislike to a contestant and told him live, on-screen, 'I am tired of looking at you.' As Medhurst suggests in his study of Harding, 'Now it was, perhaps, not one of the great savage put-downs of all time, but this was 1952 ... when the world of BBC television was a world of almost inconceivable niceness.'[14]

For Medhurst, the explosiveness of Harding's simple statement had as much power as when the critic Kenneth Tynan first used the word 'fuck' on television in the following decade. Harding's uncivil comment was reported in the national press long before television reached a national audience, and the incident ensured that Harding was thereafter known for his rudeness and irascibility. He was constantly in the news and, over the decade, turned in a number of appearances across a range of media.

These included working with television cook Fanny Craddock, appearing in films including the 1959 *Expresso Bongo* alongside the young pop star Cliff Richard; he wrote newspaper articles and a number of books appeared under his name – but they were in fact ghostwritten.[15] Harding's forthrightness and rudeness were underpinned by his deep rooted unhappiness and dissatisfaction, and on occasion fuelled by alcohol, but his irritable outbursts were what the public came to enjoy and expect. Medhurst suggests that the public perceived Harding's demeanour as an 'act', while in fact it was an *aspect* of *who* he was. Harding had himself claimed, 'I just behave as I am and talk as I think, which for some reason appears to be remarkably novel.'[16]

There is, however, another interpretation for Harding's popularity. Rather than enjoying his performances as an act, perhaps the audience, or at least parts of it, appreciated Harding's honesty or *authenticity*. Since the 1960s, writers such as Goffman,[17] and later post-structuralist and postmodernist theorists, have come to see individual lives and biographies as fragmented, performative and constructed by social discourses. Goffman, for example, describes an individual's everyday life as a set of performances displayed before different audiences (family, friends, teachers, clients, colleagues and bosses).[18]

In such views, there is no centralized self, but a number of different selves that experience the world, and speak and behave differently at different times and places, and among different social groups. This fragmentation of self in the contemporary world may be a significant reason why media coverage of 'celebrity' holds such fascination. The sociologist Jeremy Tunstall has argued that celebrity in Britain is characterized by 'integrated personality'. So in Britain, a celebrity is 'A real person with real teeth, a real accent, and amusing prejudices – who can be presented in such varied settings as a talk show, an awards ceremony, a record request session, a quiz game, a newspaper interview.'[19]

This can be interpreted to mean that a celebrity (in Britain at least) can be constituted as someone who maintains a unity and coherence of persona across a range of media platforms. Such unity and coherence, if the persona is perceived as real or authentic, and especially if accompanied by charisma and good looks, can prove powerfully attractive and reassuring in a world otherwise characterized by fragmentation. In the 1950s, Harding could hardly have been described as good looking, but his irascibility and forthright rudeness transcended a number of media platforms, and his outbursts were certainly honest.[20] As a result, his audience appeal may have derived from his *apparent* honesty and, therefore, his authenticity.

Authenticity here relates to the concept of sincerity in broadcasting. For Paddy Scannell, performance implies insincerity, whereas sincerity presupposes a lack of performance. For people to be perceived as 'real' or the 'genuine article', they must be seen to eschew performance. Sincerity is important because it is the basis for trust and intimate relations.[21] For the television encounter between the presenter and audience to constitute 'intimacy at a distance',[22] there has to be trust that the presenter is speaking sincerely. This is particularly important in forms of factual programming such as the news and certain kinds of expositional documentaries, yet it is common in other forms of broadcasting where presenters speak to camera. It is even common in light entertainment formats where the presenters are well-known personalities and where talk is characterized by joking and humour.

As we discussed in Chapter 4, drawing on the work of Georg Simmel[23] and Paddy Scannell,[24] the television studio becomes a sociable space, where conversation, chat and joking (sociability) appear to take place for their own sake, for the sheer enjoyability of the social encounter. For the sociable encounter to work the audience members must feel as if they are being treated equally, and must feel, in effect, that they are being treated fairly, honestly and sincerely. There is a problem here, however, since authenticity or sincerity can be staged. While Gilbert Harding was apparently behaving authentically and honestly in the 1950s, it was a painful irony that he kept his homosexuality hidden.[25]

The *appearance* of sincerity here is significant for the promotion of consumer culture and consumption, since most people who were seen on television in the 1950s and 1960s were paid. The whole range of television personalities in the 1950s and 1960s made a living from appearing on television, whether newsreaders like Kenneth Kendall or Robin Day, presenters like Eamonn Andrews or Bruce Forsyth, or comedians like Tony Hancock or Benny Hill. Television for these people was work, and in these positions they had to perform numerous roles. Television requires performance in some way.

As Paddy Scannell has observed, however, sincerity involves a 'performative paradox'.[26] If a presenter or television personality effectively invokes sincerity, then they are also crucially proposing a lack of performance. If performance is work, then sincerity proposes work's absence. When 'integrated personalities' appear across a range of media platforms displaying unified and coherent personae, then they are effectively appearing as themselves, and the lack of apparent performance means it looks as if they are not working.

This does not just occur in talk programmes or other shows in which television personalities address a presenter or the audience directly, but in the widest range of programmes. As we saw in Chapter 4, much of the work of broadcasting takes place behind the scenes, in the space Goffman describes as a 'back region'.[27] This work is usually hidden. As we saw in Chapter 3, for example, Tony Hancock insisted the BBC let him use Ampex Video to record his shows because the strain of live performance was too stressful. This demonstrates that live performance *is* work, but the work is even more effectively hidden by the use of new recording equipment. What was therefore happening on television for the first time in the 1950s and 1960s was that the work of the 'television personality' comedian or performer was becoming increasingly hidden from the viewer. Yet the viewer was consuming and appropriating this work under the guise of fun and entertainment.

In quiz and game shows, it was not just the work of the host or presenter that was being consumed, but also the work of the contestants. While middle-class commentators may have complained that contestants and participants in these shows were effectively getting something for nothing, they were in fact having to work for their prizes. In one sense there is the strain and nervousness that accompanies an appearance before cameras, either live or recorded. There is also the potential humiliation that one might answer a question wrongly, or make a fool of oneself in one of the games. Significantly here, in the context of fun as work, members of the public have to, as Goffman would argue, 'swap teams'.[28] As Goffman has suggested, in any social encounter individuals play a performative role, especially where the individual performance is associated with a particular team. Teams are social groups that demand a coherence and unity of performance, and are often visibly found in the work place.[29]

In Goffman's analysis, embarrassment and humour are often occasioned when an individual changes team. They are derided (with good humour or ill) by their former team mates for leaving them behind, and they are teased and belittled by their new team members because they have not yet been fully initiated or assimilated into the new group. This is exactly a description of the television experience for a member of the public appearing on a quiz or game show, since the audience constitutes one team, and the producers of television another. The member of the public who stands in front of the camera is effectively changing teams. Humour can be derived from this situation, and the audience may support, cheer or jeer at the on-screen competencies of the lay performer. At the same time codes of sportsmanship compel the participant, who is often the subject of gentle ribbing, jokes and asides, to accept his or her subsidiary role to the central performance of the presenter.[30] Although the member of the public is on television, a potentially privileged position, he or she is certainly not in command of the situation.

As Whannel has observed,[31] the appearance of a member of the public on television in a quiz or game show often illuminates the professionalism of the television presenter. The presenter, often an experienced broadcaster, is paid to appear on television, whereas the member of the public is an unpaid television amateur. On Tyne Tees opening night programme *The Big Show* on 15 January 1959, for example, Bill Maynard presented a short segment to highlight a forthcoming show to appear on the new service. In this new programme members of the public have the chance to tell their own jokes and anecdotes.

In the promotional segment Maynard is dressed casually in slacks, with a shirt and tie topped by a cardigan. This contrasts markedly with the two members of the public, clearly drawn from the audience, who come in front of the camera to tell a joke. They are dressed smartly in what appears to be their Sunday best. The man is dressed in a suit with a shirt and tie, whereas the middle-aged woman is dressed in a hat and coat. In particular the hat and coat appear at odds with the seeming informality in which the more casually dressed Maynard presents the segment, joshing with the audience and making gentle jibes at the man and woman's expense.

A segment featuring the audience later in the show captures men and women sitting formally in hats and coats. This direct contrast clearly signals Maynard's status as separate and distinct from the audience. While he displays a slight nervousness in the live segment, and while the piece perhaps works less successfully or wittily than intended, Maynard is clearly the person in charge. This is further emphasized when Maynard rewards the man with a television set and the woman with a washing machine. Importantly, Maynard's performance constitutes work. Yet, in the context of the segment here, with the glamour and lights of showbusiness, with a sense of abundance, prizes and attendant television personalities, the performances look like fun. This fun disguises the inherently ideological process of consumption, where the labour of another individual (or team of individuals) is consumed and appropriated in the viewership of television.

While Paddy Scannell would describe the above enounter as a 'sociable' occasion, this would not fit Simmel's strict definition which is that 'sociability' is a 'play form of association' that operates between equals and without motivation.[32] The situation here, however, has not emerged between equals (in play), but is a *structured* event, taking place within the formalized setting of the television studio, scheduled in advance and staged by television producers and supporting personnel. The encounter between the host, Maynard, and the non-professional performers is far from equal and, indeed, there is an emerging discourse here based on formalized and unequal relations.

Occupying the newly socialized space of the television screen, this consumption of labour and the hierarchical relationships it involved were publicly and *ritually* celebrated on television. As I shall argue, this kind of encounter in quiz and game shows can be characterized by the term *structured sociability* or, for thinking about how such on-screen relations become naturalized over time, *ritualized sociability*. This latter term in particular will be important for thinking about how television promotes consumer culture, and the consumption of television culture *per se*.

Before returning to this I want to examine how the expansion of the television industry coincided with the production of programme formats and the development of new forms of scheduling. I then explore the impact this had on the relationship between the broadcasting institution and the viewer. I then develop this further to show how scheduling and familiarity legitimizes the inequalities inherent in *ritualized sociability*, and consider the implications this has for the construction of media power.

Scheduling and television's *nearness-over-time*

As Paddy Scannell has succinctly argued, television occupies time, airtime.[33] The expansion of television in the 1950s and 1960s had a direct relationship with the temporal arrangements of broadcasting (production and scheduling) and this facilitated the development of consumer culture during this period. As we saw in Chapter 1, rationalization of the nascent television industry led in part to the routinization of production and the emergence of the 'programme factory', a piecemeal production-line approach to programme making. It made the programme-making process quicker and cheaper. Recording programmes meant that they could be shot scene by scene in a cost-effective and efficient manner. It meant that production could take place when actors and performers, production personnel and studio resources were available.

At the same time, with the development of recording technologies the production process created programmes for sale as commodities on film and video. Yet, as Scannell has observed,[34] the routinization of production had another consequence for the nature of television programming. If production-line processes and recording technology meant that staff, casts and studio resources could be used more cost effectively and efficiently, then cost effectiveness and efficiency could be increased even further by making more editions or episodes of the *same* programme format at the same time. A direct consequence of this was the emergence of serialization.

For Jacobs,[35] this new routinization complemented the television aesthetic of 'intimacy' in the 1950s by repeating television as a familiar pattern. It did this in two ways – *internally* and *externally*. Familiarity and intimacy were achieved internally by the weekly representation of cast and characters in television series. The internal construction of familiarity was significant not just for drama, but also for a range of other television genres. This could be argued for news, for example, which shares, as Ellis has suggested,[36] some of the formal properties of serial dramas such as soap operas in which there is a recurring cast list of players. For Jacobs, familiarity was also constructed externally through the arrangement and timing of programmes amid the wider output – the other programmes in television's mixed-programme schedule. To understand how familiarity is structured externally, we have to pay some attention to the emergence of a new kind of scheduling in the 1950s, fixed-point scheduling – the transmission of a television series at the same time and on the same day each week. This was different to the way that scheduling on BBC television had previously been organized which was less structured and more *ad hoc*. This was partly the result of production practices in live television, and partly the result of a wider philosophy about the relationship of the BBC to its audience.

In the first instance, a change in scheduling came about as a response to the increasing rationalization and professionalism of the expanding television industry. In the late 1940s and early 1950s, for example, there was much dispute at the BBC over the last-minute scheduling of programmes.[37] As a predominantly live medium before the 1950s, a small number of television producers and staff at BBC television ran a small number of programmes on shorter production cycles and were subject to the availability of casts and performers. Television broadcasting was therefore also subject to last-minute change. As staff and technological resources grew, however, programme making became increasingly industrialized.

With a more bureaucratized and efficient management and organizational structure emerging, production had to be carefully matched with available transmission times. Advance management of schedules could mean better rationalization of production resources. Fixed-point scheduling meant that producers could plan series productions more strategically; they knew longer in advance when a particular episode or edition of a programme was required. Even if the programme were a live current affairs programme like *Tonight*, which required a turn-around in production on a daily basis, an effect of more rationalized scheduling was that the production infrastructure, the allocation of resources such as studios and personnel that made daily transmission possible, had been established in advance. At the same time, the development of recording technologies meant that repeat or new programmes could be stockpiled for future transmission.

Scheduling was significant in other ways. In the mid-1950s it became an important strategy in facing television competition. As Jacobs argues,[38] scheduling was impelled by the necessity to differentiate BBC products from ITV ones, and this meant that schedules started to be organized around precise and consistent patterns with which viewers could become familiar. Prior to this, fixed-point scheduling had been deployed by radio, but there was a reluctance at the BBC to schedule television in this way because it was felt that the new medium should not be watched continuously or habitually. In a climate where television was undervalued within the BBC, and perhaps culturally at large, people were not encouraged to become routine or habitual viewers. The aim of the *Radio Times* was to promote careful, reasoned and informed viewing choices, rather than to encourage the viewer to leave the television set on all the time.

This attitude changed with the arrival of ITV, when BBC television felt increasingly pressurized to justify its licence fee in terms of its viewer numbers. Ironically, this has been a perpetual problem for the BBC ever since. If only a small number of viewers watch BBC television, questions are raised about whether it is reasonable for the majority to be paying for a minority service. On the other hand, if the BBC pursues large audiences, which is what commercial television traditionally sought to do before the advent of specialized boutique programming,[39] further questions are raised. The first is whether or not the BBC is fulfilling a public service broadcasting remit, and the second is whether it is fair, in an open marketplace, for the BBC to have the advantage of the licence fee while ITV struggles competitively for audiences numbers and advertising revenue.[40]

Fixed-point scheduling became significant in terms of competition because audiences could become attuned to knowing habitually *when* their favourite programmes were on. Fixed-point scheduling therefore helped build and sustain audiences in the mid-1950s, and in commercial terms this was important because ITV and advertisers could better predict and target audiences for specific programmes.[41] Indeed, it was during this period that market and audience research became an important phenomenon in television broadcasting.

Prior to this, the BBC had conducted audience research among radio listeners in the 1930s when they were facing competition from Radio Normandie and Radio Luxembourg. In the mid-1950s, as Caughie asserts,[42] the BBC now vigorously pursued audiences, and audience research grew in importance. As an example of viewing figures as a commodified form of knowledge, the BBC sold some of its own research to some of the programme companies, but mainly the ITV companies used outside audience research companies such as TAM (Television Audience Measurement) or the US company Nielsen. What is significant in the 1950s is that viewers were increasingly positioned by audience and market researchers as consumers rather than members of the public. Advertisers and market researchers not only needed to know what audiences were viewing, but *when*. As a result, viewers were now placed within the new economy of commercially organized broadcasting.

To return to the earlier point about familiarity, we must recall Jason Jacobs's argument that the establishment of the fixed-point schedule in the 1950s complemented early television's 'intimate address'.[43] This is because intimacy is facilitated by the familiarity of regular, routine and habitual viewing. At the same time, we should also recall that the expansion of broadcasting effectively meant more television programming. By 1964, a national audience could watch television seven days a week. As a result, television had evolved from being a medium for special occasions and for selective, intimate viewing for a minority audience towards being a familiar and everyday form of cultural activity for a national audience.

In this sense we can argue that television's definitional characteristics shifted in nature from the intimate to the *intimate-and-quotidian*. While television dramas tended to expand on-screen diegetic space, which undermined earlier notions of television intimacy, other programmes still negotiated intimacy at distance[44] and characterized the viewing experience by familiarity, informality and structured sociability. At the same time, television receivers still occupied privatized domestic space, so the television apparatus itself was characterized by nearness. This relationship between intimacy and the everyday is a vital clue in understanding how television newly promoted consumer culture in the 1950s and 1960s.

As Roger Silverstone has argued, television schedules are intricately connected to how people live their lives.[45] In a broadcasting environment that seeks to maximize its audiences, schedules are designed to reflect who will be watching and at what time of the day. In the 1950s, as we saw in the previous chapter for example, it was anticipated that housewives would be at home during the day, so television broadcast programmes aimed at women during daytime hours. Peak hours for viewing were considered to be in the evening when men had returned from work and when women had completed their household chores.

In the mid-1950s there were, however, certain viewing restrictions, such as a ban on programming between 6 p.m. and 7 p.m., the 'toddler's truce'. This ban was lifted in February 1957 after ITV companies lobbied the Postmaster General to extend programming hours. One of the programmes that appeared in the new slot on BBC television was the *Tonight* programme, previously discussed. An innovation of *Tonight* was that it took account of the domestic viewing experience, assuming that 6 p.m. was a busy juncture in household activities, with dinner being prepared and husbands and children coming and going.[46] As a result, the segmented structure and magazine style of *Tonight* permitted both fragmented and distracted viewing.

This dovetailing of the routines and activities of everyday life with the daily and repetitive natures of broadcast scheduling can have a reassuring influence. It contributes to a confidence and trust in the routines and taken-for-granted habits of the everyday, what the sociologist Anthony Giddens describes as ontological security.[47] One of those habits, for the first time in the 1950s and 1960s, was the process of everyday consumption that was promoted through the act of viewing television. As Roger Silverstone argues,[48] television provides symbolic resources for the imaginative work of consumption and identity appropriation through a range of programming. It also offers models of group behaviour, whether predicated on class, age or gender. As we have seen, the cultural capital displayed on television – associated with different classes, ages and genders – can be appropriated through television and become the grounds of group conflict.

With the expansion of broadcasting in the 1950s and 1960s, and the mixed-programme schedule, different classes and groups were exposed to the cultural tastes and activities of other groups. This meant that groups were able to voice distaste for the cultural tastes of other groups. The middle-classes voiced disapproval of vulgar and tacky shows derived from explicitly working-class forms of entertainment. It was the increased visibility of working-class entertainment that had caused anxiety among an establishment elite that had sought to promote high culture and the arts.[49] At the same time, working-class audiences could voice disdain for the stuffy and pre-tentious entertainments of the middle classes. It was this new articulation of conflict and distaste that seemed to undermine an establishment view of cultural consensus.

Furthermore, as we have also seen, the act of viewing television involves the act of consuming something, work, that is produced by other people. In some cases, new styles of television 'being', the 'television personality', or new styles of performance, hid the process of work implicit in television production. As a result, the process of consumption, through television itself, became both hidden and routine. There is a further point to be made here.

The process of consuming television programming is analogous with the process of ownership, and the routine way in which television is watched legitimizes and habituates other consumer and consumption activities. Georg Simmel,[50] writing in Germany at the beginning of the last century, has argued that, just in the same way that workers in capitalist societies are alienated from the products of their labour in a Marxian sense, so too do people have the potential to be alienated from the objects they consume.

The objects that people consume are not necessarily inherent or intrinsic to their lives or to their being. The ownership of items such as cars, television sets and fashionable clothing is not a necessary condition of human existence. Many people find them valuable parts of their lives, but that value is culturally constructed. The objects, the material artefacts *per se*, are physically distinct, separate and apart from the individual, so how can one be said to consume them? The answer is that the consumption and subsequent material display of these cultural artefacts is made possible legitimately, in capitalist societies, by purchasing the object (or by hiring it, inheritance or receiving it as a gift). As a result, Simmel argues that ownership of property is the means by which people best try to appropriate alienated products.

The act of purchase may seem self-evidently necessary for the acquisition of a new commodity (other than hiring, receiving gifts or thieving), but the sociological point is that the process of ownership is the means by which it is possible to keep these objects near and available for use. As a result, it can be proposed here that the process of ownership involves the maintenance of an asset, which has use value and/or symbolic value that is *near-over-time*. The characteristic properties of this asset are effectively available, nearby (near), for the duration of the asset's or owner's life (time).

At the same time, as we have seen, the television set is an object that is intimately located in the household and it too is physically *near-over-time*. Yet there is an even more profound relationship between television, ownership and consumption. As I have argued, television in the 1950s and 1960s was a trans-locational medium, and from this period onwards it negotiated intimacy-at-distance, and constructed familiarity, informality and structured sociability.

With the extension of broadcasting hours, the serialization of programming and the rationalization of the fixed-point sched-ule, I have also argued that from the same period television's definitional properties can be increasingly characterized as the *intimate-and-quotidian*. This suggests that television's properties have something in common with the *nearness-over-time* that characterizes the process of ownership. Television is an object that is near-over-time, and television's regular broadcast out-puts bring programme forms (and the places, events, people and objects they display) near-over-time.

This includes the potential for both continual and serial viewing of programmes, and their constitutive performances, their invitations for identifications and resources for imaginative work, and their valorization of commercial and consumer values. Indeed, within the television flow, watching one programme is never enough. Like the perpetual consumption of commodities and artefacts within consumer society, watching television constitutes an ongoing consumption practice. In a sense, therefore, the consumption of television becomes the model of consumption *par excellence*. In the 1950s and 1960s, the newly expanded institution and the newly expanded audience of television allows this to happen for the first time.

Ritualized sociability

As I suggested earlier in this chapter, the kind of performances that take place in programmes such as quiz and game shows constitute a form of *structured sociability*. As the sociologist Georg Simmel has argued,[51] sociability revolves around a sociable encounter that is enjoyable and entertaining for its own sake. This has *something* in common, therefore, with the kinds of joking and banter one encounters in the broadcast experience. As a result, this has led Paddy Scannell to describe sociability as 'the most fundamental characteristic of broadcasting's communicative ethos.'[52]

Yet Simmel also argues that for sociability to work, it must negate the structures and hierarchies that determine ordinary interaction and encounters between people. As a consequence, Scannell overlooks the ways in which sociability in Simmel's sense is undermined by formalized codes and conventions of interaction within certain broadcasting encounters. In light entertainment programmes such as quiz and game shows where presenters interact with ordinary members of the public, there are conventions for how the member of the public should behave.

In these encounters there is an unequal relationship between the professional presenter, who controls or manages the on-screen encounter, and the amateur lay person. These situations can therefore be characterized by inequality and hierarchy. This we saw, for example, in *The Big Show* segment featuring Bill Maynard and two ordinary people telling jokes. This means that the broadcasting experience of this encounter cannot be described as 'sociable' in Simmel's definition. Being structured within the production processes and schedules of broadcasting, and operating under the *appearance* of sociability, the on-screen encounter between a television presenter and a member of the public in light entertainment programming constitutes, I would argue, *structured sociability*.

In television in the 1950s and 1960s, the repetition of structured sociability on a daily basis across a variety of programme forms across the schedule means that the on-screen encounter between the television host and ordinary person has the potential to be *ritualized*. As a result, the iteration of structured sociability in broadcasting over time constitutes what I would describe as *ritualized sociability*. This is partly because of the way television culture, and cultures of television viewing, evolved new patterns of production and consumption over this period. With the development of the fixed-point schedule, which I discussed above, the consumption of television, by an audience, could become an increasingly routinized and habituated activity. Viewers could come to know when a particular television series was broadcast on a particular day and at a particular time in the week. This meant that television viewing could become embedded increasingly within everyday practices and routines.

Nick Couldry argues, however, that there are other ways of thinking about the media and ritual, and these are useful for understanding how media power is constructed, legitimized and exercised in everyday life.[53] Couldry is particularly interested in formalized actions, repeated in strictly determined or conventionalized ways that have a transcendent relationship to wider social values. These kinds of formalized action can be found precisely in ritualized sociability.

In television in the 1950s and 1960s, for example, the encounters between the professional host and the amateur member of the public in the quiz and game shows became formalized by the demands of programming *formats*. As we have seen, Paddy Scannell has argued that with industrialized

189

modes of practice a format becomes a template by which other programmes are made on a weekly basis.[54] Performances within specific formats were therefore routinized. The rules of *What's My Line?*, for example, were repeated every week. And although the individual panellists may have varied from week to week, and the members of the public changed constantly, the programme followed the same process and patterns in each edition. It was not just the repetition of the rules of the show that were repeated each week, but also the quirks and characteristics of the panellists came to be repeated. This repetition was what gave members of the television audience the pleasure of anticipating one of Gilbert Harding's regular outbursts.

At the same time, as we have seen, lay participants have to follow codes and conventions for appearing on screen. They have to endure the good natured and gentle ribbing from the professional host who commands the situation and manages the on-screen space. Within this relationship, in quiz and game shows, the guest participant follows the format's rules to win prizes. Not only does this constitute formalized action, but what specifically constitutes these encounters as a form of ritual is that they connect the performers and participants to wider, transcendent values.

The relationship between ritual and transcendence can be demonstrated, for example, in those religious rituals where a participant might feel that they are transcending earthly bounds to experience some kind of spiritual communion. In sociological terms, drawn from Emile Durkheim in his seminal work *The elementary forms of the religious life*,[55] the individual is effectively communing with the rules and values of a wider society. It might be argued, therefore, that viewing a quiz or game show in the 1950s and 1960s (especially on ITV) *might* constitute a transcendental experience for two reasons – first because the programme itself takes the viewer from the space of viewing to the space of production, the *translocation* I discussed in Chapter 4, and second because the viewer is taken from the dreary world of everyday-life, as Dyer argues,[56] towards a utopian fantasy of plenty. These programmes celebrate the wider values of consumer culture through glitz and through the highly visible display of commodities as prized objects.

Couldry argues, however, that the relationship between media, ritual and transcendence does *not* lie in the consumption of media content.[57] What he argues is that media rituals are *actions* that revolve around media related *categories*. These actions validate hierarchical values that relate to categories such as media sites (spaces of media production) and non-media sites, and media people and non-media people. What these categories refer to is the sense that media sites and media people are different and symbolically more important than non-media sites and non-media people.

Therefore, media rituals refer to specific modes of action that are both constituted by and sustain that hierarchical value that the media is more *special* than other aspects of social life. A media ritual might therefore be constituted by a tourist, an ordinary person, visiting (or making a pilgrimage to) a media site such as a television or film studio. It might also be consti- tuted by the same ordinary person meeting a media person, such as a film or rock star, and asking for an autograph. What is significant is that both these encounters may be experienced as special by the ordinary, non-media person.

In certain light entertainment programmes of the 1950s and 1960s, therefore, such as the quiz and game shows discussed here, the act of meeting a media person (a television person- ality) occurs within media space (the television studio) and within the media itself (on screen and on television). The ritual- ized sociability of the on-screen hierarchical encounter, broad- cast repetitively on a daily basis across schedules, constitutes a media ritual revolving around media categories.

These are categories that television has established – the tele- vision personality and the non-television lay participant. In this encounter, the television personality, the host, has more authority than the non-television person. This legitimizes the notion that television people (media people) are somehow more special than non-television people (non-media people). By expressing this hierarchy, television makes visible a mechanism by which it asserts its value and importance over everyday life. It asserts that what is presented on television is significant, and that the television people who appear regularly on it are more important than ordinary people who do not. As a result, the wider, transcendental values to which ritualized sociability connects is the sense that television has more special value than other elements of ordinary everyday life.

This relates directly to the exercise of media power. As Nick Couldry argues, media rituals' validate and naturalize the media's claim to symbolic power. The concept of symbolic power was developed by the sociologist Pierre Bourdieu who defined it as 'the power of constructing reality'.[58] As a result, for the purposes of my argument here, the construction of reality can be regarded as definitions of the world that have real effects – such as creating, sustaining and legitimizing hierarchies and power structures. In the encounter between a television personality (a media person) and a non-television person (a non-media person) discussed above, for example, the event is characterized as special or remarkable precisely because the television has already defined television people (and television space) *as* special. This clearly demonstrates that television has the ability to define specific experiences of social reality.

Couldry questions the *extent* to which the *media* have the power to define (all) social reality, but seeks to make explicit the mechanisms by which the media claim that they do. In any event, what is important is that the broadcast encounter I have described here, structured sociability, replicated and broadcast extensively over time across the television schedules, has the power to create and maintain television categories of television-person and non-television person. These categories make claims that television has the potential to define hierarchical values and social experience. Connecting the formalized actions of structured sociability to wider, transcendent relations of media power, repeated over time, means that this process can be described here as *ritualized sociability*. The longer-term historical effects of this in relation to wider society and culture should be the subject of further important analysis. The point here, however, is that in the 1950s and 1960s, in a television culture that had newly expanded and industrialized, and that now reached a national audience, television was able to establish and maintain its own media categories for the first time.

Conclusions
EXPANSION, DIVERSITY, VISIBILITY AND MEDIA POWER

In this book I have examined the relationship between social and cultural change in Britain in the 1950s and 1960s and the expansion of British television. I began by asking three interrelated questions – on the impact that the expansion of television had on itself as *an institution*, on the impact of the social and cultural context on the development of television, and on the impact that television had on the social and cultural context. In considering these interconnected issues, and thinking about Thumim's feminist analysis of television,[1] it is perhaps useful to reformulate the last question as how did television *produce* social and cultural change in this period? To understand how these questions intersect, and to answer this last question in particular, we need to draw together and review here the developments I have explored over the book as a whole.

To start with, there is the social and cultural context in which television became a mass medium in Britain. With the consumer boom of the 1950s, with full employment, high wages and the loosening of regulations pertaining to borrowing and hire-purchase, television was one of the new, mass-produced consumer items that emerged. This was complemented by demographic changes that altered traditional patterns of cultural and leisure activity of a significant part of the television audience. The postwar baby boom meant that a generation of young couples became more housebound than they had been before. Coupled with workers having to move to new sites of employment, along with suburbanization and the development of new towns and housing estates, many people were being relocated away from their friends and family. This apparent progress, which was part of a programme of change consistent with the development of the welfare state, involved the clearance of slum housing in some areas and this had the painful and negative effect of destroying traditional working-class communities. As a result of these changes, it was into an increasingly affluent, domesticated and isolated society that television emerged as a significant cultural form.

Expansion and diversification

The arrival of first the ITV companies and then BBC2 also expanded the institution of television. As explored in Chapter 1, these new services expanded television by establishing and equipping new television studios and creating new jobs. As the production base of BBC television and ITV expanded so too did the number of programmes being produced. This expansion of the amount of programmes being made had two interrelated consequences. First, the *way* in which programmes were produced and, second, the *range* of programmes that were produced.

In the first instance, there was rationalization, industrialization and professionalization. These three issues are closely related, and the way that industrial practices, on a larger, mass scale could operate came through rationalized administrative and management structures, such as an expanded bureaucracy and more planned use of resources and scheduling. One particular development of industrialization, and this also came about through the increased use of film and video recording technologies that was explored in Chapter 3, was the advent of the 'programme factory'. This was programme production along increasingly industrialized lines, very much like factory production where a specialist worker constructs part of a product before passing it along to the next stage in the production process where another worker completes a specialized task. In this way products, or programmes here, could be produced on an economy of scale. As suggested in Chapter 1, this was facilitated by greater specialization of production roles and more professionalization.

This was evident, for example, in the increased unionization of television that the arrival of ITV brought, with specific technical staff contracted to work in explicit roles. As we saw in Chapter 1, this happened in the development of weekly programming when the producer's and director's roles in television production were separated. A producer increasingly came to have control over running a whole series, whereas directors had responsibility for leading the specific, on-the-ground production of individual episodes or editions.[2] This was facilitated by training courses (at the BBC), increased staff movement between broadcasting organizations and media (such as radio, film and the press) and increased reflexivity among professional peers (through team reviews of recorded programmes, management intervention in programming decisions, the trade press and interpersonal dialogue and discourses). Such professional groupings, with the strong allegiances to immediate professional peers they engender, can take on a tribal quality and this was highly visible, for example, in the area of journalism. Professional practice was not necessarily confined to industrial and individual competence in programme-making, but extended also to the debates and discourses on aesthetics and generic innovation.

This links directly to the second consequence of the expansion of television, namely the increasing diversity of programme outputs. The increasingly industrialized patterns of production that professional specialization, technological developments and more efficient systems of management and administration facilitated, in one sense favoured a move towards series programming and a standardization of programme formats. Yet, in the developing *ecology* of television broadcasting of the 1950s and 1960s this did not mean the simple reproduction of a handful of programme formats and styles, but rather the flowering of diverse programme forms and outputs.

This was partly a function of the public service broadcasting ethos of television in this period favouring a mixed-programme schedule – with its somewhat Reithian imprint to inform, educate and entertain. The new ITV service inherited some of these principles in the 1954 Television Act, and the appropriate balance of outputs in the mixed-programme schedule was to cause much hand-wringing at the ITA. Reaching a broad audience was also one of the key principles of the mixed-programme schedule in this period. As Janet Thumim has argued, different programmes, both factual and fictional, in different styles and tones, on different subjects and themes, were able to appeal to a wide range of people.[3] It is for this reason that Thumim suggests that the magazine programme made up of short discrete segments in different styles on different subjects is paradigmatic of television's endeavour to develop an audience and viewing culture in the 1950s and 1960s.[4]

As we saw, the appeal of the mixed-programme schedule was explicitly articulated by Lew Grade when he argued that television scheduling should be like planning a mixed bill at the variety theatre – in this way most of the audience will be pleased some of the time. This appeal was also particularly evident in the way that BBC2 had to back away from minority and specialist programming to offer a more mixed schedule to try and persuade members of the public to acquire new 625-line television sets.

With the expansion of television, new industry practices, more production personnel, professionalization, new technologies, and more broadcasting hours to be filled within the mixed-programme schedule, it was increasingly likely that there would be an expansion in the number of new programme forms and innovation in existing forms. In metaphorical terms, in the biological sciences (and sociology) it is well understood that as any organism expands it grows more complex. As it grows more complex, the likelihood of mutation, diversity and differentiation increases. As the ecology of television broadcasting expanded in this period, complexification meant a greater likelihood of change and diversification in forms and genres of programming. At the same time, the expanding variety of programme forms became better able to reflect emerging differences and changes in British society. While the expansion of the industry led to new programme forms and styles, changes in British society and culture provided material and a backdrop for television's outputs. The material ranged from the desirable consumer prizes for its quiz and game shows explored in Chapter 6 to the grim new landscapes of Britain that became the subject of, and provided the background for, its realist dramas explored in Chapter 4.

The new visibility and media power

This expansion of television was complexly interwoven with social and cultural change. As television expanded in the 1950s and 1960s, with a wider range of programmes, of different kinds in different styles, with competing and even contradictory representations, and broadcast within the mixed-programme schedule, it brought 'witness'[5] into the home on an increasingly daily basis. With live and recorded broadcasts from around the country and abroad, and with the television camera reaching new spaces, even 'space', the viewer was able to experience the world in new ways.

It is for this reason that I have proposed in this book that the expansion of the television production base, the expansion of programming and the expansion of the television audience can be characterized as creating and constituting a 'new visibility'. By making social and cultural phenomenon visible in a new way, television emerged as a cultural force that had the capability both to promote and to produce change. In this book I have demonstrated how television promoted changes that were already developing within British culture and society in the period. Yet what has also emerged, first in Chapter 2 and more explicitly in Chapter 6, is how institutional expansion increasingly established television itself as a centralized site of 'symbolic power'[6] that has the potential to produce change. First, however, I shall review here the two important ways that television promoted change – through the presentation of difference and through its relationship with consumer culture.

In the first instance, television made visible, in a new way, social and cultural *difference*. In histories of the 1950s the arrival of ITV is often seen as the moment when the consensus culture of postwar Britain was ruptured.[7] For the historian Richard Weight, this is because it signalled the end of a top-down model of cultural provision. Until the arrival of ITV, culture was seen as being brought to the masses by an educated elite through Oxbridge institutions and through the interdependent work of the BBC and the Arts Council. This top-down model dominated elitist views of culture in this period and it was for this reason that Raymond Williams argued that working-class culture was mostly invisible.[8]

The arrival of ITV was considered problematic because it undermined the apparent work of the cultural elite. In one sense, the arrival of ITV, developed along regional lines, could be said to undermine the cultural hegemony of the golden triangle of London, Oxford and Cambridge.[9] On the ground, however, the network carve-up and continuing monopoly London seemed to hold on the entertainment industries may ultimately have undermined the principle of regionality.[10] The cultural elite also saw the arrival of ITV as injecting commercial interests, crass consumerism and American values into British society.

However, as I have argued, commercial television in Britain was subjected to the public service principles that had governed earlier broadcasting, and ITV was established under a publicly appointed regulatory body with public service values. That ITV *was* commercially funded by advertising revenue both reflected and promoted the burgeoning consumer culture of the 1950s. Yet, editorial control over programme-making was kept separate from the hardcore business of attracting advertising revenue. There were quotas on how much American programming could be accepted, and within the mixed-programme schedule ITV broadcasted serious intellectual and cultural programmes ranging from news and current affairs to critically acclaimed and challenging drama in the *Armchair Theatre* strand.

Difference, however, was probably most obviously articulated in the structure of the mixed-programme schedule on BBC *and* ITV, for it was crucial both for building an audience and delivering public service values. As television expanded to a wider audience, it produced and transmitted a wider range of programmes in different forms and styles to appeal to diverse tastes. Different forms of culture were explored and repre-sented, ranging from serious dramas, action-adventure series, soap operas, sitcoms, variety shows, quiz and game shows to magazine programmes, news and current affairs.

As I have argued, the visible articulation of different forms of culture disrupted the sense of top-down cultural consensus. Within the television schedule, programmes drawing on working-class culture, such as variety shows, were shown alongside serious programmes about art or music that drew on middle-class discourses. The presentation of variety shows that drew on working-class traditions of variety theatre and end-of-the-pier entertainments, made working-class culture highly visible and brought it into the home on a regular basis. This made working-class culture visible, for the first time, to educated and middle-class elites, and this seemed to disrupt a sense of cultural consensus (for that middle-class elite). There was particular anxiety in the late 1950s, for example, when there was an apparent 'retreat from culture',[11] as ITV companies scheduled an increasing number of quiz and game shows to try to build audiences to overcome initial anxieties about adver-tising revenue.

These shows were criticized for their brassy celebration of consumer culture, and for offering lavish prizes to ordinary people for winning relatively easy quizzes or games. Richard Hoggart, an influential member of the Pilkington Committee, which heavily criticized the ITV service, was particularly hostile to these kinds of entertainments. Yet, just as Hoggart was able to criticize the ITV quizzes and games, so too was it possible for members of the working-class audience to dismiss or sneer at more serious bourgeois programming.

This demonstrates that the schedule itself, as well as particular forms of programming, could become the focus and articulation of class difference and conflict. In a different context, the sociologist Dean MacCannell has argued that tourism allows individuals in affluent Western societies to engage in a wider social totality, to transcend the social and cultural limitations imposed on them by the division of labour.[12] By going on holiday, a Western worker is able to engage in a wider range of cultural experiences, meet new people and encounter a different range of lifestyles in a way that the daily temporal and spatial structures of working life prohibits. In a similar way, television makes visible a wider range of social and cultural experiences to its viewers at home, experiences that might otherwise be inhibited by age, gender, class or economics.

As this discussion of difference suggests, consensus in the early 1950s was illusory. Britain was deeply divided by class and, as Arthur Marwick has observed,[13] there were also vast regional differences, partly due to the effects of war and partly because of economic and demographic changes. As a result, television was making visible pre-existing social and cultural fault lines. The advent of the new consumer boom was also seen to disrupt the top-down sense of cultural consensus. Until 1954 there had been rationing, so there was a certain degree of homogeneity in what people could purchase or afford. After this, however, there was a major upturn in the economy, with full employment and high wages, with relaxed rules on hire-purchase, and with a range of new desirable consumer goods on which to spend money.

Consumer goods, ranging from clothing to record players and washing machines are markers of style and lifestyle. In Pierre Bourdieu's sense, style and lifestyle are markers of taste, and taste is a marker of class.[14] Although there were middle-class and elitist anxieties about the rise of a homogenous consumer culture in this period, the expansion of affordable commodities meant there was an increasing number of ways in which social groups, defined by class or age, could differentiate themselves.

As a result, the second way in which television promoted change was through its complex relationship to consumer culture. Television's role in the consumer boom was that it was a commodity item in its own right, alongside record players, washing machines and refrigerators. It was also the promise of this boom that motivated advertisers and retailers to agitate in favour of the new commercial service to increase advertising opportunities for the new commodities. Yet, importantly, television also promoted consumer activity in other ways. The expansion of programme forms, and innovations in aesthetics and performances, as we saw in Chapters 2, 3, 4 and 5, provided viewers with a new and wide range of identificatory resources.

Whether it was the image of the efficient and attractive housewife smoothly running her home, the sharply suited, sexually liberated and mobile secret agent, or the leather and denim clad rocker, television's programming offered models of social behaviour to be accepted, applauded, emulated, rejected or sneered at. Just as Thorstein Veblen demonstrated that social groups like the French *nouveaux riches* could seek social status through conspicuous consumption,[15] the conspicuous display of consumption on television provided the models for how people in different groups could display their social allegiances.

Representations of different commodities, of different lifestyles and forms of consumption, even when consumption is absent in documentaries and dramas about poverty or deprivation, are closely bound up with class identities and behaviours. The absence of consumption, or the inability to participate in the new consumer culture, is itself an indicator of social, cultural and economic status. As a result, the representation of different forms of culture on television, and the representation of different lifestyles and forms of consumption are also markers of difference, and therefore grounds for class conflict.

It was not just through the representation of commodities or of different forms of consumption or lifestyles that television promoted consumer culture. There were two other ways in which television promoted consumer culture and these are mutually dependent on the promotion of the consumption of television culture *per se*.

In the first instance, purchasing or hiring a television set is both consistent with and a constituent of consumer activity. Not only is it characterized by the consumer parting with cash in single or several instalments, but by an ongoing relationship in which the viewers consume television programming. This consumption takes place on an everyday basis, which is significant; both Silverstone and Scannell point to 'dailiness' as the key phenomenological characteristics of television and broadcasting respectively,[16] yet for a majority of the television audience 'dailiness' was a new experience in the 1950s and 1960s. With the television set in the home, routine television production practices, fixed-point scheduling, serialization, programming schedules and individual programme forms became familiar and everyday. This promotes consumer culture because it establishes a long-term relationship between television and the viewer at home.

As I argued in Chapter 6, watching familiar programmes on an everyday basis is analogous with the process of ownership. This is because ownership can be characterized as a relationship to an object that is *near-over-time*. Even if television programming for the viewer in this period was ephemeral (the viewer not being able to record or keep the images), the regular patterning of series programming over the schedules meant that television programmes too were near, available to the viewer through the domestic screen, over time. While television promotes the development of a viewing culture in this period through the mixed-programme schedule that appeals to a broad audience,[17] fixed-point scheduling and serialization also promote viewing cultures because they invite *sustained* viewership. This therefore also promotes consumer culture because it suggests that consumption is endless. Watching one programme in the flow of television is never enough.

A further way in which television promotes consumer culture has implications not only for thinking about television's relationship to social and cultural change, but also for thinking about the longer-term significance of media power. Television's relationship to consumer culture could already be said to implicate it within wider power structures in society. This would especially be the Frankfurt School and Marxist perspective where the presentation of popular culture and the advertising and presentation of desirable commodity items promotes capitalist ideology, false consciousness and the alienation of labour.

I want to step back from such assessments here because there is intense debate about whether consumer or consumption practices constitute subservience to capitalist hegemony or whether they constitute individual autonomy and creativity. In recent years this has been the terrain of cultural studies, and it is evident, for example, in the work of Hebdige and Fiske.[18] Instead, I want to focus on a particular kind of media power. To start with, I want to refer to the consumption of another person's labour that is implicit in the television personality or celebrity encounter. As I argued in Chapter 6, much of the work of broadcasting, the production process, goes on behind the scenes, in spaces Goffman would describe as 'backstage'.[19] With the exception of occasional programmes such as *That Was the Week That Was* and *The Dream Machine*, the work that goes on backstage is mostly unseen.

What I want to concentrate on here, however, is the work that goes on front stage, or literally on-stage. This is the work conducted by presenters, panellists, comedians and musicians, and a whole range or people who appear *on* television on a regular basis, the people who can be considered celebrities or, as I have preferred to refer to them here in relation to the 1950s and 1960s, television personalities. In thinking about celebrity, Tunstall has argued that these are people who present a unity and coherence of persona across a range of media.[20] In the 1950s personalities such as Eamonn Andrews and Gilbert Harding appeared across an array of television programmes, and were also presented in different media. As I argued, the attractiveness of these individuals, presenting coherent personas, is that they appeared authentic or sincere. That is to say, they appeared to be themselves.

Yet, as we saw, authenticity and sincerity can be performed and staged. Even though Gilbert Harding might have been perceived as authentic, because of his grumpiness and irascible outbursts, his homosexuality was kept hidden. The point here is that performance constitutes work, and the more successfully the presenter or personality can convince an audience of his or her sincerity, the more they are effectively hiding the process of their work. An immediate effect of this is that the work of the performer is being consumed, but it does not look like work. This argument is inevitably tinged with a Marxist hue, but I want to go further here. To do this I have focused on programmes that involve both television personalities and members of the public, a notable example of which is the quiz and game show.

As we saw in Chapter 6, Gary Whannel has argued that the amateurishness of the member of the public often accentuates the power, authority and professionalism of the presenter in quiz and game shows.[21] There is potentially a tension between the idea of someone appearing as themselves and appearing professional. There are two ways to consider this. First, the television personality's professional demeanour can be read as the way they negotiate their coherent individual persona (their apparent sincerity) and the power they are required to exercise in the broadcasting encounter with an 'ordinary' person. Second, the television personality does not work in any given programme in isolation, but in conjunction with a wider range of performances and appearances across the mixed-programme schedule over any given period of time. Therefore the roles they undertake – such as being a presenter or panellist will be consistent with their coherent persona.

As we also saw in the last chapter, the television personality belongs to what Goffman describes as a 'team'.[22] The audience constitutes one team, and the on-stage television personality belongs to the broadcaster's team. In Goffman's analysis, humour will emerge when an individual changes team, and he or she will often be the focus of teasing from members of the new team. In television light entertainment forms that feature ordinary people there tends to be joking and humour, with the ordinary person having to endure gentle ribbing and mockery from the show's presenter. For Scannell,[23] drawing on the sociologist Georg Simmel,[24] this kind of joking and joshing in broadcasting can be considered 'sociable'. Yet, as I pointed out in the last chapter, Simmel held that the sociable encounter is unstructured and negates hierarchy. Since the hierarchy of the presenter over the ordinary person in the broadcasting setting is an unequal encounter, this cannot be described as 'sociability' in Simmel's sense.

As a result we have what I have described as *structured sociability*, an encounter that has the appearance of sociability but that is hierarchical and unequal. In this period, in the 1950s and 1960s, as television was increasingly becoming a mass medium, with industrialization, serialization and fixed-point scheduling, these kinds of encounters became progressively more visible and repeated. This means, on the one hand, a repetition of the competition rules in quiz and game show formats that feature ordinary members of the public and, on the other hand, the conventionalization of the on-screen power structure between the presenter and lay participant.

I would argue, therefore, that over time the encounter characterized by structured sociability becomes *ritualized sociability*. What I mean by ritualized is not the common-sense notion that ritual is a habitual or routine activity (although television viewing *could* become increasingly habitual and routine within the period). Instead, I have referred to Couldry's understanding of 'media rituals' as formalized actions that connect to transcendental values. For Couldry, ritualized action is not the consumption of media content, but relates to actions that revolve around the creation and maintenance of media related categories.[25]

Most powerfully, media related categories are comprised of the distinction between media people and non-media people, and between media sites and non-media sites. In creating these distinctions, the transcendental value to which these media categories point is the media's ability to define categories that have broader social and cultural resonance. This resonance is a sense that the media experience is more special, and potentially more powerful and important, than ordinary, everyday experience. It is in this way that the media can define and shape social experience. Of course, the processes that Couldry seeks to identify relate to the total media landscape of today. Yet my analysis here shows how television in the 1950s and 1960s made explicit the distinction between a television personality and a non-television personality. With the expansion of the nascent television industry, with the extension of formats and serialization to a new, mass audience, we can see how television started to define its own media related categories for the first time. Ritualized over this period, these categories could point to television's increasing ability potentially to define social experience.

This is complemented by the way the mixed-programme schedule, in which different forms of culture and different cultural forms could be presented and represented within a unified flow of broadcasting, consolidated, embedded and naturalized the television duopoly's ability to define social experience. Television, viewed nationally by a mass audience, provided the cultural references, discourses and talking points that could be shared by all.

As we saw in Chapter 2, it is tempting to see television as the unified cultural form against which cultural fragmentation and difference could be measured. This, however, would be to perpetuate what Couldry has described as the 'myth of the mediated centre'.[26] It would be to assume uncritically that the media, in their entirety, allow access to the central issues and concerns of society. In more contemporary perspectives of the media this would also be to assume that the media constitute that centre. Even to suggest that media provide the arena in which competing ideologies and discourses are played out is to perpetuate this myth. To argue, for example, that television in the 1950s and 1960s was the way in which cultural consensus was disrupted or measured against, or to suggest that television provided a form of 'social cement' in the context of public service broadcasting would, in sociological terms, be highly problematic.

The fact that television can potentially be seen in these terms is, however, important. As Couldry has argued,[27] there *are* beliefs or assumptions that the media somehow connect their audiences to the centre of society, or that they speak on behalf of society. This can perhaps be seen most explicitly in the broadcasting of media events such as coronations, state funerals, sporting events and moon landings, explored by Dayan and Katz.[28]

On these occasions, such as the 1953 coronation covered by the BBC on television and radio, the disruption of everyday schedules, the concentration of media focus and the apparent attention of a national audience powerfully evoke a sense of that connection between the media and the central concerns of society. What this suggests is that the media construct these categories of events as important for their television viewers. Just like the distinction between television personality and non-television person, it promotes the view that if something is *on television*, it must be important.

It is this ability to influence the social categories by which people define and shape their social and cultural activities that allows television, and the media, to exert a powerful force. And it is through media rituals and the 'myth of the mediated centre' that this apparent centralization of media and symbolic power becomes legitimized.[29] As a result, therefore, the social and cultural change that television in Britain *produces* in the 1950s and 1960s is the sense that *television itself* has the cultural legitimacy to define and shape cultural values and social experience. In the history of television and the media in Britain, it is in this period that television confidently asserts cultural and symbolic power for the first time. The impact of this has been profound and long lasting.

NOTES

Introduction

1. The low-definition service ran on a 30-line system. The high-definition service, which started in 1936, alternated on a weekly basis between John Logie Baird's 240 line system and Marconi's 405 line system. From February 1937 the BBC television service ran on the Marconi system.
2. Both the 1954 and 1963 Acts were consolidated into a single Act of Parliament in 1964.
3. Briggs 1995.
4. Sandbrook 2005.
5. Hobsbawm 1995.
6. Marwick 1996.
7. Corner 2003, p. 275.
8. Johnson and Turnock 2005a.
9. Ibid.
10. Creeber 2006.
11. Thumim 2004.
12. Ellis 2000.
13. Ibid., p. 9.
14. Thumim 2004, p. 1. Emphasis in original.
15. Ellis 2000.
16. Hopkins 1963.
17. Corner 2003.
18. Bonner (with Aston) 1998 and 2003; Potter 1989 and 1990; and Sendall 1982 and 1983.
19. Silverstone 1985.
20. Chapman 2002.
21. Johnson 2005.
22. Sydney-Smith 2002.
23. Other programme forms and genres that have received analysis of this kind have included drama, see for example Caughie (2000) and Cooke (2003), and current affairs, see Lindley (2002), Holland (2006) and Goddard, Corner and Richardson (forthcoming).

24. Corner 2003.
25. Jacobs 2000; Holmes 2005.
26. Williams 1974.
27. Winston 1998.
28. Silverstone 1994; Scannell 1996.
29. Corner 2003.
30. Carr 1987.
31. White 1978.
32. Jenkins 1995, p. 20, emphasis in original.
33. Corner 2003, p. 276.
34. Sendall 1982 and 1983.
35. Thumim 2004, p. ix.
36. Hobsbawm 1995; Marwick 1996; Sandbrook 2005.
37. Scannell 1996.
38. Bourdieu 1984.
39. Simmel 1971.
40. Goffman 1990.
41. Couldry 2003a and 2003b.
42. Corner 2003, p. 277.
43. Ibid.
44. Thumim 2004.
45. Sandbrook 2005.

Chapter 1: Rationalization

1. Thumim 2004.
2. See, for example, Jameson 1991.
3. Both services closed down during the Second World War, and Radio Luxembourg commenced broadcasting again after the war ended.
4. There had been some exceptions to this, however, such as during the Second World War. See Briggs 1970.
5. See, for example, Briggs 1995 and Curran and Seaton 1997.
6. Briggs 1995, p. 4. There were numerous prescriptions and proscriptions. For example, ITV was obliged to provide religious programmes, it had to adhere, initially to the 'toddler's truce', and it was not allowed to cause offence or disrespect to anyone still alive – a condition that inhibited the development of satire on the service in the early 1960s. See Sendall (1982) for full details of regulations, and see Carpenter (2002) for satire on ITV.
7. Jameson 1991.
8. Ellis 2000, p. 39.
9. The Baird Television Development Company had begun experimental 30-line broadcasts from a BBC transmitter in the London area as early as 30 September 1929. This was followed in 1932 by the BBC's first public low-definition television service from Broadcasting House in London, using a Baird equipped studio. This was superseded in 1936 with the launch of a new high-definition service on 2 November. For details see, for example, Briggs 1965; Crisell 1997; and MacDonald 1994.
10. Sendall 1982.

11. Sydney-Smith 2002.
12. See, for example Briggs 1995; Crisell 1997; Curran and Seaton 1997; Johnson and Turnock 2005b; and Sendall 1982.
13. Crisell 1997.
14. Briggs 1995.
15. Curran and Seaton 1997; Sendall 1982.
16. Gallup 1976.
17. Crisell 1997, p. 77.
18. See Marwick (1996) and Sandbrook (2005) for full details.
19. Sendall 1982.
20. Crisell 1997. See Tunstall (1983) for details of how advertising expenditure on television (out of all media) increased from 1.1 per cent in 1955 to 24.5 per cent in 1964.
21. Sendall 1982, p. 18.
22. Ibid.
23. Ibid.
24. Sendall 1982.
25. Wilson 1961.
26. Sendall 1982.
27. See also the programme *This Week*, 'The Birth of ITV', Thames Television, transmitted 16 September 1976, producer Lesley Mitchell.
28. Curran and Seaton 1997.
29. Jenkins 1961.
30. Bernard Sendall, although the authorized historian for Independent Television in the two volumes that cover the period 1946–68, was also the former deputy director general of the ITA (and then IBA). This means that his extensive and important account is inevitably, at times, partisan.
31. Sendall 1982.
32. Ibid.
33. PMG statement quoted in Sendall 1982, p. 177.
34. This tale is drawn from Bernard Sendall's account (1982), and it raises the question of why no one else senior at the ITA intervened or responded on the chairman's behalf. This might be partly answered by the fact that there was a culture at the regulatory body (ITA and, later, IBA) of 'Members of the Authority' ignoring the advice or over-turning decisions of members of staff (see Goddard, Corner and Richardson, forthcoming). So this may have led to a climate where important decisions or issues were 'referred up' or, in this instance, deferred.
35. Sendall 1982.
36. Sir Ian Jacob, 'The tasks before the BBC today', *The Listener*, 21 October 1954, vol. 52, no. 1338, pp. 661–2.
37. Baily 1955.
38. Goldie 1977.
39. Sendall 1982.
40. The institution of spot advertising had been a recommendation of the Beveridge committee to keep editorial control away from sponsorship constraints. The ITA could in *theory*, however, exert the ultimate editorial control by withdrawing licences.

41. *Sight and Sound*, vol. 25, no. 4, Spring 1956, p. 200.
42. See, for example, Curran and Seaton 1997.
43. Hand 2003a, p. 20.
44. *The Listener*, 6 October 1955, p. 569.
45. *The Listener*, 27 October 1955, p. 717.
46. See Gallup 1976 for details of polls in this period.
47. Sendall 1982, p. 123.
48. Ibid., p. 93.
49. BBC Handbooks 1955–64.
50. See Sendall for the full details of the company start-ups discussed here.
51. Sendall 1982.
52. Ibid., p. 122.
53. The other companies were Westward Television for the southwest of England starting from 29 April 1961; Border Television for the Scottish borders from 1 September 1961; Grampian Television for northeast Scotland from 30 September 1961; and Channel Television for the Channel Islands starting from 1 September 1962.
54. Briggs 1985.
55. Cited from Briggs 1985, p. 18.
56. Burns 1977.
57. Briggs 1995.
58. Briggs 1979.
59. Cited from Sendall 1982, p. 111.
60. Seglow 1978, p. 30.
61. Jacobs 2000.
62. Ibid.
63. Ibid.
64. Ibid., p. 11.
65. Sydney-Smith 2002.
66. Ibid. Sydney-Smith (p. 20) explains that this is 'a stage-derived term named from striking the set'.
67. ABC 1956–69; Thames Television 1970–74.
68. Shubik 2000, p. 26.
69. Cooke 2003.
70. Caughie 2000.
71. Sydney-Smith 2002, p. 19.
72. Goldie 1977, p. 79.
73. Ibid., p. 90.
74. Briggs 1995.
75. See, for example, Jacobs 2000.
76. Thumim 2004.
77. 'Report on television talks and documentaries', BBC Written Archive Centre document reference WAC T31/164/1 A0 April 1951 (cited from Thumim: 2004, p. 49).
78. Goffman 1990.
79. I shall return to Goffman's analysis of 'teams' in Chapters 4 and 6.
80. Burns 1977.

81. Whannel 1992a. The development of recording technologies will receive extended discussion in Chapter 3.
82. Simmel 1971.
83. Goldie 1977, p. 112.
84. See Goddard et al. forthcoming; Holland 2006; and Lindley 2002.
85. Goddard et al. forthcoming.
86. See ibid. for further details about this incident.
87. Sydney-Smith 2002.
88. Ibid.
89. At this time, recurring programme titles tended to appear on television about once a month at most. See Sydney-Smith 2002.
90. Sydney-Smith 2002, p. 77.
91. Ibid., pp. 77–8.
92. Thumim 2004.
93. Holmes 2005.
94. Scannell and Cardiff 1991.
95. Cultural provision is discussed in relation to regionality in Chapter 2, and specifically in terms of class in Chapter 5.
96. See, for example, Johnson 2005.

Chapter 2: Centralization

1. See Scannell's (1996) discussion of the inclusiveness of wartime radio programmes.
2. Calder 1992.
3. Marwick 1996.
4. Numerous historical accounts have sought to challenge the 'myth' of consensus. See, for example, Brooke 1992; and Pimlott 1988.
5. Marwick 1996, p. 22.
6. Weight 1995.
7. Arnold 1961.
8. Weight 1995, p. 62.
9. Ibid., p. 66.
10. Weight 1995.
11. Williams 1983.
12. Kumar 1981.
13. Briggs 1995.
14. This reinforces the notion, perhaps, that London is equated with 'the national'.
15. Briggs 1995, pp. 623–4.
16. Sendall 1982.
17. Goddard et al. forthcoming.
18. Medhurst 2002a. See also Medhurst 2005.
19. See Holmes (2005, p. 10) for a discussion of how television in the 1950s attempted to 'borrow and capitalize on cinema's glamour'.
20. Sendall 1982.
21. Ibid., p. 303.

22. Ibid.
23. Sendall 1982. It is important to note, however, that other behind the scenes' work on the production would have been conducted in Manchester, such as the construction and striking of the set.
24. Medhurst 2002b.
25. Davies 1994; Medhurst 2002b.
26. Goddard et al. forthcoming.
27. As indicated previously, the main account here is Bernard Sendall's who was deputy director general of the ITA, so his defence of the regulator's position here has to be understood in terms of both his proximity to events and to his potentially partisan position.
28. Sendall 1982, pp. 303–4.
29. Cited from Sendall 1982, p. 63.
30. Cited from ibid.
31. Ibid.
32. The wheeling-dealing Lew Grade, deputy head of ATV, was later to claim in interview that six months of scheduling for the ITV 'network' was worked out over three separate meetings in three days between the four main companies. *The Persuader: The TV Times of Lord Lew Grade*, transmitted 27 August 1994, BBC2.
33. Sendall 1982, p. 308.
34. Dayan and Katz 1992.
35. Ibid., p. 139.
36. Scannell 1990, p. 14.
37. Cited from Scannell 1990, p. 14.
38. Weight 1995.
39. Ibid., p. 190.
40. Briggs 1979.
41. Scannell 1996.
42. Scannell and Cardiff 1991.
43. Ibid., p. 14.
44. Ibid., p. 277.
45. Weight 1995.
46. Shils and Young 1956.
47. The more jaded observer might suggest, however, that the apparently magnanimous neighbour was only showing off his or her new acquisition (television) to make the other jealous.
48. Hoggart 1969, p. 110.
49. Scannell and Cardiff 1991.
50. For more discussion of this issue see Couldry (2003a; 2003b), and for examples of ambivalent or indifferent audiences responses to recent royal related events such as the death and funeral of Diana, Princess of Wales, see Thomas (2002) and Turnock (2000).
51. Dimbleby 1975.
52. Cited from Scannell 1996, p. 83.
53. Ziegler 1978; cited from Weight 1995, p. 195.
54. Hand 2003b.
55. Briggs 1995.

56. Scannell 1990.
57. Scannell and Cardiff 1991, p. 273.
58. Ibid., pp. 254–5.
59. Ibid., p. 254.
60. Scannell 1990, p. 16.
61. Cited from *The Persuader: the TV Times of Lord Lew Grade*, transmitted 27 August 1994, BBC2.
62. Thumim 2004.
63. Scannell and Cardiff 1991, p. 278.
64. Ibid.
65. Hobsbawm 1983.
66. Anderson 1991.
67. Scannell and Cardiff 1991.
68. The subject of celebrity and 'television personalities' will receive more extended discussion in Chapter 6, but for more details about Gilbert Harding and the *Face-to-Face* interview see Medhurst (1991).
69. Scannell and Cardiff 1991.
70. Scannell 1996, pp. 87–8.
71. Ellis 2000.
72. Although ITV companies had experimented with some satirical revues, such as *Melvillainy* on Southern Television, satire was, however, inhibited by a clause in the 1954 Television Act. This prevented programme companies (though excluded the BBC) from 'offensive representation of, or representation to, a living person'. See Carpenter (2002) and also Sendall (1982).
73. Holmes 2005.
74. Cited from Sandbrook 2005, p. 546.
75. Couldry 2003a, 2003b.
76. Dayan and Katz 1992.
77. Shils and Young 1956.
78. See Couldry (2003a and 2003b) for his criticism of the functionalist assumptions which underlie the notion of the 'centre'. There are also academics who argue that the concept of society is no longer helpful. See, for example, Ingold 1996.
79. Thumim 2004.

Chapter 3: Technologies

1. By 'film' here I refer to the technological process of capturing sequences of images on a strip of chemically treated, light sensitive material which, when developed and projected at an appropriate speed, presents on screen the appearance of life-like movement. In the period being explored here, recording of sound and film at the same time in the studio had been well established, but capturing sound on location was still a relative innovation. For a history of film technology see, for example, Winston 1996.
2. Meyrick 1976.
3. Ibid., p. 109.

4. Ibid.
5. Jacobs 2000.
6. Meyrick 1976.
7. Ibid.
8. Ibid.
9. Ibid., p. 110.
10. Ibid.
11. Ibid., p. 110.
12. Ibid.
13. Ibid.
14. Goddard 1991.
15. Landay 2003.
16. Ibid.
17. Ibid.
18. Goddard 1991.
19. For details of some of these programmes see Vahimagi (1996).
20. The calculation was made on the basis of an *average* figure over a three-month period. On any given week, the total number of imported programming could not exceed ten hours (Sendall 1982).
21. See, for example, Bakewell and Garnham (1970) and Crisell (1997).
22. For an erudite discussion about declining audiences and factors inhibiting the British film industry in the 1950s see Docherty et al. 1987.
23. For details of this at the BBC see, for example, Jacobs (2000) and Sydney-Smith (2002), and for details for ITV see Chapman (2002), Osgerby (2001), and Osgerby and Gough-Yates (2001).
24. For details of these programmes see Vahimagi (1996).
25. For a further discussion of the production of *The Adventures of Robin Hood*, see Neale (2005).
26. Chapman 2002.
27. Osgerby and Gough-Yates 2001.
28. Chapman 2002.
29. Ibid.
30. See, for example, Chapman (2002) and Osgerby and Gough-Yates (2001).
31. See Chapman (1999; 2002) for a discussion of the relationship between *Danger Man* and James Bond.
32. Chapman 2002.
33. See *The Persuader: The TV Times of Lord Lew Grade*, transmitted 27 August 1994, BBC2. For a discussion of the iconic status that Lew Grade holds in television historiography see Bignell (2005).
34. Chapman 2002.
35. Chapman 2002, p. 10. See Chapter 5 for discussion of the relationship between these action-adventure series and consumer culture.
36. See Jacobs (2000) for a discussion about the aesthetics of drama in early British television.
37. Jacobs 2000.
38. Barr 1996.
39. Ibid.
40. Jacobs 2000, p. 127.

41. Ibid.
42. Ibid.
43. Sydney-Smith 2002, p. 9.
44. For further discussion of *The Quatermass Experiment* see Johnson (2005), and for *Nineteen-Eighty-Four* see Jacobs (2000).
45. Gorham served as head for 18 months in 1946–47, but had resigned because of the BBC's then apparent lack of commitment to the medium.
46. Jacobs 2000, p. 80.
47. Whannel 1992a.
48. Jacobs 2000.
49. Gorham 1949, p. 39, cited from Jacobs 2000, p. 80. The BBC had been chronically short of studio space through the latter part of the 1940s and 1950s. The Corporation moved into vacant film studios at Lime Grove in 1950, and had to wait for a decade until purpose built studios were constructed near Shepherd's Bush in west London.
50. See Jacobs (2000) for details of some of the wrangles and conditions involved.
51. *Clive of India* had been a successful West End stage play in 1934 by W. P. Lipscomb and R. J. Minney. See Jacobs (2000) for details of discussion with Twentieth Century Fox and case study of the televised version.
52. Jacobs 2000.
53. Ibid., p. 12.
54. The transmission of the coronation footage in the USA, not hindered by the tyranny of being live, was punctuated by advertisement breaks, and this caused a storm of protest among campaigners in Britain who were vehemently opposed to commercial television.
55. Sydney-Smith 2002, p. 101.
56. McLoone 1996.
57. *Up the Junction* and *Cathy Come Home* will be discussed further in Chapter 4 in relation to the representations of social change in Britain.
58. I am grateful to John Ellis for reminding me of the importance of this development. The use of 16mm film was also particularly important in news, current affairs and documentary work.
59. Videotape could not be used on location for programme recording, except for well resourced departments like sport. This is because it needed vast amounts of power; the cameras had to be linked to the recording apparatus by cables, and the recording apparatus was very heavy and could not be moved except when installed in specialized outside broadcast (OB) trucks. I am grateful to John Ellis for emphasizing this point.
60. For detailed discussion of the background details of developments in video, see Abramson (2003), Armes (1988), Axon (1981), Barr (1996), Ginsburg (1981) and Kirk (1981).
61. Abramson 2003.
62. Axon 1981, p. 18.
63. Goddard 1991.
64. For an extended discussion of Tony Hancock and the development of the sitcom form see Goddard (1991).
65. Goddard 1991.

66. Ibid.
67. It is important to note, however, that many programmes were still shot before a live audience in the studio to help with the performer's timing.
68. Goddard 1991.
69. Quoted in Barr 1996, p. 64.
70. Quoted in Barr 1996, p. 65.
71. Briggs 1995, p. 835.
72. Ginsburg 1981.
73. Briggs 1995, p. 835.
74. Fiddy 2001.
75. Auslander 1999 quoting Burger 1940.
76. Auslander 1999.
77. Auslander 1999, p. 21 quoting Burger 1940.
78. Jacobs 2000.
79. Barr 1996; Jacobs 2000.
80. Jacobs 2000, p. 121.
81. Jacobs 2000.
82. Johnson 2005.
83. Jacobs 2000.
84. Barnouw 1990.
85. Ibid., pp. 133–4.
86. Caughie 2000.
87. Bordwell et al. 1985.
88. See Caughie (2000) for detailed discussion of these movements and their relationship to television.

Chapter 4: Spaces

1. Marwick 1996, p. 24.
2. Marwick 1996.
3. Ibid.
4. Ibid.
5. Quoted in Sandbrook 2005.
6. Hoggart 1969.
7. In 1956 14 per cent of homes were still without electricity, and in many of the older houses wiring was often unreliable or dangerous (Akhtar and Humphries 2001; cited in Sandbrook 2005).
8. Marwick 1996.
9. Sandbrook 2005, p. 116.
10. Frampton 1992.
11. The effects of slum clearances are referred to in the drama *Up the Junction* (1965), and the Roehampton estate merits a brief, disparaging mention.
12. Marwick 1996, p. 119.
13. See, for example, Docherty et al. 1987; and Hoggart 1969.
14. Hoggart 1969, p. 68.
15. Docherty et al. 1987.
16. Marwick 1996.

17. Sandbrook 2005.
18. See, for example, Caldwell 1995; and Johnson 2005.
19. Weight 1995.
20. Sendall 1982.
21. Hoggart 1969.
22. Hand 2003b.
23. Ibid.
24. Ibid., p. 12.
25. Bain 1962.
26. Hand 2003a, p. 4.
27. See, for example, Goldthorpe et al. 1969.
28. Hoggart 1969, p. 32.
29. Ibid., p. 35.
30. Goldthorpe et al. 1969.
31. Docherty et al. 1987.
32. O'Sullivan 1991.
33. Ibid., pp. 166-7.
34. Hand 2003b, p. 6.
35. O'Sullivan 1991, p. 166.
36. Reported in an article by Geoff Howard (1954, p. 10) on television detector vans.
37. Silverstone 1997, p. 9.
38. Silverstone 1994 and 1997.
39. Ibid.
40. A domestically set series called *The Appleyards* was transmitted by BBC television 1952–57 but was aimed at children.
41. See the Television Heaven website, www.televisionheaven.co.uk/grove.htm
42. Todorov 1981. See Johnson (2005) for an extended discussion of socio-cultural verisimilitude in relation to the *Quatermass* series and 'telefantasy', and Neale (2000) for a discussion of the theory in relationship to film genre.
43. Sydney-Smith 2002.
44. Quoted in Syndey-Smith 2002, p. 164.
45. Quoted in Laing 1991, p. 129.
46. Quoted in Sydney-Smith 2002, p. 167.
47. Marwick 1996.
48. Quoted in Sydney-Smith 2002, p. 167.
49. See Laing 1991.
50. See, for example, Caughie (2000) and Cooke (2003).
51. Sydney-Smith 2002, p. 153. Originally quoted in 'Why do Z-men shock the police? TV chief answers that "oafs" criticism', *Daily Sketch*, 1 May 1962.
52. Sydney-Smith 2002.
53. Vahimagi 1996, p. 48.
54. Cooke 2003, p. 33.
55. Ibid., p. 34.
56. Dyer 1981.
57. See Cooke (2003) for an extended discusson on the drama.

58. Silverstone 1997, p. 10.
59. Harvey 1990.
60. Ellis 2000.
61. In Orwell's analysis, the 'perfect' English murder in the prewar period was committed cunningly by a professional, such as a solicitor or dentist living a respectable bourgeois life in the suburbs, who had been stirred by strong emotions. Americanization, spurred by both Hollywood films and the effects of the war, instead meant that murder had become sordid and meaningless, with an air of thrill and cheap glamour. See Orwell 2003.
62. Weight 1995.
63. Briggs 1979, p. 484.
64. Ibid.
65. Briggs 1995.
66. See ibid.
67. Dayan and Katz 1992.
68. Vahimagi 1996.
69. Briggs 1995, pp. 141–2.
70. Attenborough 2002, p. 20.
71. Attenborough was to become Controller of BBC2 and presenter of such landmark BBC television series as *Life on Earth* (1979), *The Living Planet* (1984) and *The Trials of Life* (1990).
72. Attenborough 2002, p. 46.
73. Vahimagi 1996, p. 67.
74. *TV Times*, 20 September 1955, p. 21.
75. Vahimagi 1996.
76. Goffman 1990, p. 109.
77. Laing 1991.
78. Vahimagi 1996.
79. Goffman 1990, p. 121.
80. See Goddard et al. forthcoming; and Holland 2006.
81. See *Radio Times: 50 Years of BBC TV News*, p. 2, supplement to *Radio Times*, 3–9 July 2004.
82. For a critical history of ITN between 1955 and 2005, see Harrison (2005).
83. Crisell 1997, pp. 92–3.
84. Quoted in Briggs 1995, pp. 156–7.
85. See, for example, Briggs 1995; Goddard et al. forthcoming; Goldie 1977; and Holland 2006.
86. Horton and Wohl 1956. Such intimacy has also been discussed in terms of non-reciprocity and 'quasi-mediated interaction', see Thompson 1995.
87. Scannell 1996.
88. Simmel 1971.
89. See Corner (1991) and Hill (1991) for a discussion of the demise of the 'toddler's truce', the emergence of *Tonight* during the week and new pop programmes on Saturday evenings.
90. Corner 1991, p. 8.
91. Quoted in Briggs 1995, p. 162.
92. Ibid.
93. Corner 1991, p. 12.

94. Hoggart 1969.
95. Silverstone 1994 and 1997.
96. Wagg 1992, p. 255.

Chapter 5: Consumer culture

1. The statistics in this section have been cited from Sandbrook (2005).
2. Quoted in Sandbrook 2005, p. 597.
3. Hobsbawm 1995.
4. Crisell 1997.
5. This separation of advertising revenue and editorial decision-making can perhaps be seen most evidently, and successfully, in current affairs programmes on ITV such as *This Week* and *World in Action*. Until the arrival of Channel 4 impelled changes in accounting practices at ITV in the 1980s, journalists and production personnel in these programmes had a lot of financial freedom to follow stories and investigate leads. See Goddard et al. forthcoming; and Holland 2006.
6. See Sendall 1982 for further details.
7. Sendall 1982.
8. Cited from Bergan 1989, p. 12.
9. Ibid.
10. Sendall 1983, p. 108. Emphasis in original.
11. Ibid.
12. Ibid., p. 109.
13. Bourdieu 1984.
14. Veblen 1934.
15. Marwick 1996.
16. Thumim 2004.
17. The other special category of audience that the BBC identified was children, see Thumim 2004.
18. Leman 1987, p. 91.
19. Thumim 2004.
20. Spigel 1992.
21. Leman 1987.
22. Thumim 2004.
23. Leman 1987, p. 82.
24. Ibid.
25. Ibid.
26. Winship 1992.
27. Thumim 2004.
28. Hobsbawm 1995.
29. Sandbrook 2005.
30. Hill 1991.
31. Ibid.
32. Hill 1991, p. 95.
33. Ibid., p. 103.
34. Sandbrook 2005.

35. Cohen 1972.
36. Sandbrook 2005.
37. Hill 1991.
38. Sandbrook 2005.
39. Hill 1991, p. 102.
40. Osgerby et al. 2001.
41. Miller 2000.
42. Osgerby and Gough-Yates 2001, p. 24. See also Buxton 1990.
43. Osgerby and Gough-Yates 2001, p. 3.
44. For a discussion of the promotion of fashion in *The Avengers*, see Chapman 2002.
45. Osgerby and Gough-Yates 2001, p. 43.
46. Osgerby et al. 2001, p. 25.
47. Buxton 1990.
48. Bourdieu 1984.
49. Goddard 1991.
50. For further details see Hancock's entry in Lewisohn's (1998) *Radio Times guide to TV comedy*.
51. Wagg 1998.
52. Medhurst 1997.
53. Goddard 1991, p. 78.
54. Medhurst 1997, p. 253.
55. Ibid.
56. See Appadurai (1986) for an examination of how objects have a 'social life'.
57. Lewisohn 1998, p. 637.
58. Lewisohn 1998.
59. Bourdieu 1984.
60. Wagg 1998, p. 13.
61. Hoggart 1969.
62. Bourdieu 1984.
63. Sendall 1982.
64. Quoted in Sendall 1982, p. 328.
65. Sendall 1982.
66. See Sendall (1982) and Vahimagi (1996) for further details.
67. Sendall 1982.
68. Ibid.
69. Ibid., p. 348.
70. See also, for example, Whannel 1992b.
71. The definitional term used to describe people who regularly appeared on television in this period will be discussed in the next chapter, as will an analysis of the on-screen relationship between presenters and ordinary members of the public.
72. Root 1986.
73. Hoggart 1969, p. 189.
74. Whannel 1992b.
75. Ibid.
76. Root 1986.
77. Tulloch 1977.

78. Tulloch 1977; Whannel 1992b.
79. Scannell 2000.
80. Bourdieu 1984.

Chapter 6: Consuming television culture

1. Thumim 2004.
2. Dyer 1973.
3. Whannel 1992b.
4. Ibid.
5. *What's My Quiz?*, BBC2, 22 July 1991.
6. Holmes 2006.
7. Rojek 2001.
8. Ellis 2000.
9. Ellis 1982.
10. Medhurst 1991.
11. Ellis 2000.
12. Medhurst 1991.
13. Ibid., p. 72.
14. Ibid., p. 62.
15. See Medhurst 1991 for further details.
16. Quoted in ibid.
17. Goffman 1990.
18. Ibid.
19. Tunstall 1983, p. 2.
20. Medhurst 1991.
21. Scannell 1996.
22. Horton and Wohl 1956.
23. Simmel 1971.
24. Scannell 1996.
25. Medhurst 1991.
26. Scannell 1996, p. 58.
27. Goffman 1990.
28. Ibid.
29. A simple example is the relationship between a service industry worker in a shop or restaurant and his or her client. Both belong to different teams, and both will often complain about the other to their fellow team members – the worker about rude and obnoxious customers, and the client about impolite and inefficient service.
30. Whannel 1992b.
31. Ibid.
32. Simmel 1971, p. 134.
33. Scannell 1996.
34. Ibid.
35. Jacobs 2000.
36. Ellis 1982.
37. Jacobs 2000.

38. Ibid.
39. See, for example, Caldwell 1995; and also Johnson 2005.
40. See also Curran and Seaton 1997.
41. Curran and Seaton 1997; Sendall 1982.
42. Caughie 2000.
43. Jacobs 2000.
44. Horton and Wohl 1956.
45. Silverstone 1994.
46. Goldie 1977.
47. Giddens 1991. See Silverstone (1994) for an extended discussion of Giddens's theory and its relevance for understanding television.
48. Silverstone 1994.
49. Mandler 2003.
50. Simmel 1971.
51. Ibid.
52. Scannell 1996, p. 23.
53. Couldry 2003b.
54. Scannell 1996.
55. Durkheim 1915.
56. Dyer 1973.
57. Couldry 2003b.
58. Bourdieu 1991, p. 166; quoted in Couldry 2003b, p. 2.

Conclusions: expansion, diversity, visibility and media power

1. Thumim 2004.
2. Sydney-Smith 2002.
3. Thumim 2004.
4. Ibid.
5. Ellis 2000.
6. Bourdieu 1991.
7. Marwick 1996; Weight 1995.
8. Williams 1983.
9. Kumar 1981.
10. Sendall 1982.
11. Ibid.
12. MacCannell 1976.
13. Marwick 1996.
14. Bourdieu 1984.
15. Veblen 1934.
16. Scannell 1996; Silverstone 1994.
17. Thumim 2004.
18. Fiske 1989; Hebdige 1979.
19. Goffman 1990.
20. Tunstall 1983.
21. Whannel 1992b.
22. Goffman 1990.

23. Scannell 1996.
24. Simmel 1971.
25. Couldry 2003b.
26. Couldry 2003a.
27. Couldry 2003a and 2003b.
28. Dayan and Katz 1992.
29. Couldry 2003b.

REFERENCES

Abramson, A. (2003) *The History of Television, 1942 to 2000* (Jefferson, North Carolina: McFarland & Company)

Akhtar, M. and S. Humphries (2001) *The Fifties and Sixties: A Lifestyle Revolution* (London: Macmillan)

Anderson, B. (1991) *Imagined Communities: Reflections on the Origin and Spread of Nationalism* (London: Verso)

Appadurai, A. (ed.) (1986) *The Social Life of Things: Commodities in Cultural Perspective* (Cambridge: Cambridge University Press)

Armes, R. (1988) *On video* (London: Routledge)

Arnold, M. (1961) *Culture and Anarchy*, edited by J. Dover Wilson (Cambridge: Cambridge University Press)

Attenborough, D. (2002) *Life on Air* (London: BBC Books)

Auslander, P. (1999) *Liveness: Performance in Mediatized Culture* (London: Routledge)

Axon, P. E. (1981) 'VERA: an experimental broadcast VTR', in D. Kirk (ed.) *Twenty-five Years of Video Tape Recording* (Bracknell: 3M)

Bain, A. D. (1962) 'The growth of television ownership in the United Kingdom', in *International Economic Review*, vol. 3, no. 2, pp. 145–67.

Baily, K. (ed.) (1955) *The Television Annual for 1956* (London: Odhams)

Bakewell, J. and N. Garnham (1970) *The New Priesthood: British Television Today* (London: Allen Lane)

Barnouw, E. (1990) *The Tube of Plenty: The Evolution of American Television* (New York: Oxford University Press)

Barr, C. (1996) '"They think it's all over": the dramatic legacy of live television', in J. Hill and M. McLoone (eds) *Big Picture, Small Screen: The Relations Between Film and Television* (Luton: University of Luton Press)

Bergan, R. (1989) *Beyond the Fringe ... and Beyond: A Critical Biography of Alan Bennett, Peter Cook, Jonathan Miller and Dudley Moore* (London: Virgin)

Bignell (2005) 'And the rest is history: Lew Grade, creation narratives and television historiography', in C. Johnson and R. Turnock (eds) *ITV Cultures: Independent Television over Fifty Years* (Maidenhead: Open University Press)

Bonner, P. (with L. Aston) (1998) *Independent Television in Britain*, volume 5, *ITV and IBA, 1981–92: The Old Relationship Changes* (London: Macmillan)

(2003) *Independent Television in Britain*, volume 6, *New Developments in Independent Television, 1981–92: Channel 4, TV-am, Cable and Satellite* (London: Palgrave Macmillan)

Bordwell, D., J. Staiger and K. Thompson (1985) *The Classical Hollywood Cinema: Film Style and Mode of Production to 1960* (London: Routledge & Kegan Paul)

Bourdieu, P. (1984) *Distinction: A Social Critique of the Judgement of Taste* (London: Routledge)

(1991) *Language and Symbolic Power* (Cambridge: Polity)

Briggs, A. (1965) *The History of Broadcasting in the United Kingdom*, volume 2, *The Golden Age of Wireless* (Oxford: Oxford University Press)

(1970) *The History of Broadcasting in the United Kingdom*, volume 3, *The Sounds of War* (Oxford: Oxford University Press)

(1979) *The History of Broadcasting in the United Kingdom*, volume 4, *Sound and Vision* (Oxford: Oxford University Press)

(1985) *The BBC: The First Fifty Years* (Oxford: Oxford University Press)

(1995) *The History of Broadcasting in the United Kingdom*, volume 5, *Competition* (Oxford: Oxford University Press)

Brooke, S. (1992) *Labour's War: The Labour Party during World War 2* (Oxford: Clarendon Press)

Burger, H. (1940) 'Through the television camera', *Theatre Arts*, 1 March, pp. 206–9

Burns, T. (1977) *The BBC: Public Institution and Private World* (London: Macmillan)

Buxton, D. (1990) *From The Avengers to Miami Vice: Form and Ideology in Television Series* (Manchester: Manchester University Press)

Calder, A. (1992) *The Myth of the Blitz* (London: Pimlico)

Caldwell, J. T. (1995) *Televisuality: Style, Crisis, and Authority in American Television* (New Brunswick: Rutgers University Press)

Carpenter, H. (2002) *That Was the Satire that Was: The Satire Boom of the 1960s* (London: Phoenix)

Carr, E. H. (1987) *What is History?* (London: Penguin)

Caughie, J. (2000) *Television Drama: Realism, Modernism, and British Culture* (Oxford: Oxford University Press)

Chapman, J. (1999) *Licence to Thrill: A Cultural History of the James Bond Films* (London: I.B.Tauris)

(2002) *Saints and Avengers: British Adventure Series of the 1960s* (London: I.B.Tauris)

Cohen, S. (1972) *Folk Devils and Moral Panics: The Creation of the Mods and Rockers* (London: MacGibbon & Kee)

Cooke, L. (2003) *British Television Drama: A History* (London: British Film Institute)

Corner, J. (1991) 'General introduction: television and British society in the 1950s', in J. Corner (ed.) *Popular Television in Britain: Studies in Cultural History* (London. British Film Institute)

(2003) 'Finding data, reading patterns, telling stories: issues in the historiography of television', *Media, Culture and Society*, vol. 25, pp. 273–80

Couldry, N. (2003a) 'Television and the myth of the mediated centre: time for a paradigm shift in television studies?', paper presented to *Media in Transition 3* conference, MIT, Boston, 2–4 May 2003. Can be downloaded from: http://cms.mit.edu/mit3/papers/couldry.pdf

(2003b) *Media Rituals: A Critical Approach* (London: Routledge)

Creeber, G. (2006) 'Review: Catherine Johnson and Rob Turnock (eds) ITV cultures: independent television over fifty years', *Screen*, vol. 47, no. 2, Summer, pp. 261–5

Crisell, A. (1997) *An Introductory History of British Broadcasting* (London: Routledge)

Curran, J. and J. Seaton (1997) *Power without Responsibility: The Press and Broadcasting in Britain* (London: Routledge)

Davies, J. (1994) *Broadcasting and the BBC in Wales* (Cardiff: University of Wales Press)

Dayan, D. and E. Katz (1992) *Media Events: The Live Broadcasting of History* (Cambridge, MA: Harvard University Press)

Dimbleby, J. (1975) *Richard Dimbleby* (London: Hodder & Stoughton)

Docherty, D., D. Morrison and M. Tracey (1987) *The Last Picture Show? Britain's Changing Film Audience* (London: British Film Institute)

Durkheim, E. (1915) *The Elementary Forms of the Religious Life* (London: Allen & Unwin)

Dyer, R. (1973) *Light Entertainment* (London: British Film Institute)

(1981) 'Introduction', in R. Dyer, C. Geraghty, M. Jordan, T. Lovell, R. Paterson and J. Stewart (eds) *Coronation Street* (London: British Film Institute)

Ellis, J. (1982) *Visible Fictions* (London: Routledge & Kegan Paul)

(2000) *Seeing Things: Television in the Age of Uncertainty* (London: I.B.Tauris)

Fiddy, D. (2001) *Missing Believed Wiped: Searching for the Lost Treasures of British Television* (London: British Film Institute)

Fiske, J. (1989) 'Moments of television: neither the text nor the audience', in E. Seiter, H. Borchers, G. Kreutzner and E.-M. Warth (eds) *Remote Control* (London: Routledge)

Frampton, K. (1992) *Modern Architecture: A Critical History* (London: Thames & Hudson)

Gallup, G. H. (1976) *The Gallup International Public Opinion Polls, Great Britain 1937–1975* (New York: Random House)

Giddens, A. (1991) *Modernity and Self Identity: Self and Society in the Late Modern Age* (Cambridge: Polity Press)

Ginsburg, C. P. (1981) 'The development of Ampex Quadruplex', in D. Kirk (ed.) *Twenty-five Years of Video Tape Recording* (Bracknell :3M)

Goddard, P. (1991) '"Hancock's half hour": a watershed in British television comedy', in J. Corner (ed.) *Popular Television in Britain: Studies in Cultural History* (London: British Film Institute)

Goddard, P., J. Corner and K. Richardson (forthcoming) *Public Issue Television: World in Action 1963–98* (Manchester: Manchester University Press)

Goffman, E. (1990) *The Presentation of Self in Everyday Life* (London: Penguin)

Goldie, G. W. (1977) *Facing the Nation: Television and Politics 1936–76* (London: Bodley Head)

Goldthorpe, J. H., D. Lockwood, F. Bechhofer and J. Platt. (1969) *The Affluent Worker in the Class Structure* (Cambridge: Cambridge University Press)

Gorham, M. (1949) *Television: Medium of the Future* (London: Percival Marshall)

Hand, C. (2003a) 'The advent of ITV and television ownership in low income households', unpublished paper, Department of Media Arts, Royal Holloway, University of London

(2003b) 'Television ownership in Britain and the coming of ITV: what do the statistics show?' unpublished paper, Department of Media Arts, Royal Holloway, University of London.

Harrison, J. (2005) 'From newsreels to a theatre of news: the growth and development of Independent Television News', in C. Johnson and R. Turnock (eds) *ITV Cultures: Independent Television over Fifty Years* (Maidenhead: Open University Press)

Harvey, D. (1990) *The Condition of Postmodernity: An Enquiry into the Origins of Cultural Change* (London: Basil Blackwell)

Hebdige, D. (1979) *Subculture: The Meaning of Style* (London: Methuen)

Hill, J. (1991) 'Television and pop: the case of the 1950s', in J. Corner (ed.) *Popular Television in Britain: Studies in Cultural History* (London: British Film Institute)

Hobsbawm, E. (1983) 'Introduction: inventing traditions', in E. Hobsbawm and T. Ranger (eds) *Invention of Tradition* (Cambridge: Cambridge University Press)

(1995) *The Age of Extremes: The Short Twentieth Century 1914–1991* (London: Abacus)

Hoggart, R. (1969) *The Uses of Literacy* (Harmondsworth: Penguin)

Holland, P. (2006) *The Angry Buzz: This Week and Current Affairs Television* (London: I.B.Tauris)

Holmes, S. (2005) *British TV and Film Culture in the 1950s: 'Coming to a TV Near You!'* (Bristol: Intellect)

(2006) '"Torture, treacle, tears and trickery": celebrities, "ordinary" people and *This is Your Life* (BBC 1955–65)', in S. Holmes and S. Redmond (eds) *A Reader in Stardom and Celebrity* (London: Sage)

Hopkins, H. (1963) *The New Look: A Social History of the Forties and Fifties in Britain* (London: Secker & Warburg)

Horton, D. and R. R. Wohl (1956) 'Mass communication and para-social interaction: observation on intimacy at a distance', *Psychiatry*, vol. 19, no. 3, pp. 215–29

Howard, G. (1954) 'Pirates', *TV Mirror*, 20 February, vol 2, no. 8

Ingold, T. (ed.) (1996) *Key Debates in Anthropology* (London: Routledge)

Jacobs, J. (2000) *The Intimate Screen: Early British Television Drama* (Oxford: Oxford University Press)

Jameson, F. (1991) *Postmodernism, or the Cultural Logic of Late Capitalism* (London: Verso)

Jenkins, C. (1961) *Power Behind the Screen: Ownership, Control and Motivation in British Commercial Television* (London: MacGibbon & Kee)

Jenkins, K. (1995) *On 'What is History?': From Carr and Elton to Rorty and White* (London: Routledge)

Johnson, C. (2005) *Telefantasy* (London: British Film Institute)

Johnson, C. and R. Turnock (2005a) 'Introduction: approaching the histories of ITV', in C. Johnson and R. Turnock (eds) *ITV Cultures:*

Independent Television over Fifty Years (Maidenhead: Open University Press)

(2005b) 'From start-up to consolidation: institutions, regions and regulation over the history of ITV', in C. Johnson and R. Turnock (eds) *ITV Cultures: Independent Television over Fifty Years* (Maidenhead: Open University Press)

Kirk, D. (1981) 'VTR development prior to 1956, an introductory overview', in D. Kirk (ed.) *Twenty-five Years of Video Tape Recording* (Bracknell: 3M)

Kumar, K. (1981) 'The nationalisation of British culture', in S. Hoffman and P. Kitromilides (eds) *Culture and Society in Contemporary Europe* (London: Harper Collins)

Laing, S. (1991) 'Banging in some reality: the original "Z Cars"', in J. Corner (ed.) *Popular Television in Britain: Studies in Cultural History* (London: British Film Institute)

Landay, L. (2003) '"Reality" and the founding discourses of television or, why we "Love Lucy"', paper presented to Media in Transition 3 conference, MIT, Boston, 2–4 May 2003. Can be downloaded from: http://cms.mit.edu/mit3/papers/landay.pdf

Leman, J. (1987) '"Programmes for women" in 1950s British television', in H. Baehr and G. Dyer (eds) *Boxed In: Women and Television* (London: Pandora Press)

Lewisohn, M. (1998) *Radio Times Guide to TV Comedy* (London: BBC)

Lindley, R. (2002) *Panorama: Fifty Years of Pride and Paranoia* (London: Politico's Publishing)

MacCannell, D. (1976) *The Tourist: A New Theory of the Leisure Class* (London: Macmillan)

MacDonald, B. (1994) *Broadcasting in the United Kingdom: A Guide to Information Sources* (London: Mansell)

McLoone, M. (1996) 'Boxed in? The aesthetics of film and television', in J. Hill and M. McLoone (eds) *Big Picture, Small Screen: The Relations between Film and Television* (Luton: University of Luton Press)

Mandler, P. (2003) 'Two cultures – one – or many?', in K. Burk (ed.) *The British Isles since 1945* (Oxford: Oxford University Press)

Marwick, A. (1996) *British Society since 1945* (London: Penguin)

Medhurst, A. (1991) 'Every wart and pustule: Gilbert Harding and television stardom', in John Corner (ed.) *Popular Television in Britain: Studies in Cultural History* (London: British Film Institute)

(1997) 'Negotiating the gnome zone', in R. Silverstone (ed.) *Visions of Suburbia* (London: Routledge)

Medhurst, J. (2002a) 'Messiah or Mammon? Commercial television in Wales in the 1960s', conference paper at Re: Visions: Broadcasting Archaeologies, Histories, Impacts, Futures, University of Central Lancashire, 20–22 June

(2002b) 'Servant of two tongues': the demise of TWW', *Llafur: Welsh Labour History*, October

(2005) 'Mammon's television? ITV in Wales, 1959–63', in C. Johnson and R. Turnock (eds) *ITV Cultures: Independent Television over Fifty Years* (Maidenhead: Open University Press)

Meyrick, D. (1976) 'Twenty one years of television commercials', *Twenty One Years of Commercial Television 1955–1976*, a supplement to postal subscribers of *Broadcast*, 20 September 1976

Miller, J. S. (2000) *Something Completely Different: British Television and American Culture* (Minneapolis: University of Minnesota Press)

Neale, S. (2000) *Genre and Hollywood* (London: Routledge)

(2005) 'Transatlantic ventures and *Robin Hood*', in C. Johnson and R. Turnock (eds) *ITV Cultures: Independent Television over Fifty Years* (Maidenhead: Open University Press)

Orwell, G. (2003) 'Decline of the English murder', in George Orwell, *Shooting an Elephant and Other Essays* (London: Penguin)

Osgerby, B. (2001) 'So *you're* the famous Simon Templar': The Saint, masculinity and consumption in the early 1960s', in B. Osgerby and A. Gough-Yates (eds) *Action TV: Tough Guys, Smooth Operators and Foxy Chicks* (London: Routledge)

Osgerby, B. and A. Gough-Yates (2001) 'Introduction', in B. Osgerby and A. Gough-Yates (eds) *Action TV: Tough Guys, Smooth Operators and Foxy Chicks* (London: Routledge)

Osgerby, B., A. Gough-Yates and M. Wells (2001) 'The business of action: television history and the development of the action TV series', in B. Osgerby and A. Gough-Yates (eds) *Action TV: Tough Guys, Smooth Operators and Foxy Chicks* (London: Routledge)

O'Sullivan, T. (1991) 'Television memories and cultures of viewing, 1950–65', in J. Corner (ed.) *Popular Television in Britain: Studies in Cultural History* (London: British Film Institute)

Pimlott, B. (1988) 'The myth of consensus', in L. Smith (ed.) *The Making of Britain: Echoes of Greatness* (London: Macmillan)

Potter, J. (1989) *Independent Television in Britain*, volume 3, *Politics and Control, 1968–80* (London: Macmillan)

(1990) *Independent Television in Britain*, volume 4, *Companies and Programmes, 1968–80* (London: Macmillan)

Rojek, C. (2001) *Celebrity* (London: Reaktion Books)

Root, J. (1986) *Open the Box: About Television* (London: Comedia)

Sandbrook, D. (2005*) Never Had it So Good: A History of Britain from Suez to the Beatles* (London: Little, Brown)

Scannell, P. (1990) 'Public service broadcasting: the history of a concept', in A. Goodwin and G. Whannel (eds) *Understanding Television* (London: Routledge)

(1996) *Radio, Television and Modern Life: A Phenomenological Approach* (Oxford: Blackwell)

(2000) 'For anyone-as-someone-structures', *Media, Culture and Society*, vol. 22, no. 1, pp. 5–24.

Scannell, P. and D. Cardiff (1991) *A Social History of British Broadcasting: Serving the Nation, 1923–1939* (Oxford: Blackwell)

Seglow, P. (1978) *Trade Unionism in Television* (London: Saxon House)

Sendall, B. (1982) *Independent Television in Britain*, volume 1, *Origin and Foundation, 1946–62* (London: Macmillan)

(1983) *Independent Television in Britain*, volume 2, *Expansion and Change, 1958–68* (London: Macmillan)

Shils, E. and M. Young (1956) 'The meaning of the coronation', *Sociological Review*, vol. 1, no. 2, pp. 63–82

Shubik, I. (2000) *Play for Today: The Evolution of Television Drama* (Manchester: Manchester University Press)

Silverstone, R. (1985) *Framing Science: The Making of a BBC Documentary* (London: British Film Institute)

(1994) *Television and Everyday Life* (London: Routledge)

(1997) 'Introduction', in R. Silverstone (ed.) *Visions of Suburbia* (London: Routledge)

Simmel, G. (1971) *Georg Simmel on Individuality and Social Forms*, edited by D. Levine (Chicago: Chicago University Press)

Spigel, L. (1992) *Make Room for TV: Television and the Family Ideal in Postwar America* (Chicago: University of Chicago Press)

Sydney-Smith, S. (2002) *Beyond Dixon of Dock Green: Early British Police Series* (London: I.B.Tauris)

Thomas, J. (2002) *Diana's Mourning: A People's History* (Cardiff: University of Wales Press)

Thompson, J. B. (1995) *The Media and Modernity: A Social Theory of the Media* (Cambridge: Polity Press)

Thumim, J. (2004) *Inventing Television Culture: Men, Women, and the Box* (Oxford: Oxford University Press)

Todorov, T. (1981) *Introduction to Poetics*, translated by R. Howard (Ithaca: Cornell University Press)

Tulloch, J. (1977) 'Gradgrind's heirs: the quiz and the presentation of "knowledge" by British television', in G. Whitty and M. F. D. Young (eds) *Explorations in the Politics of School Knowledge* (London: Driffield)

Tunstall, J. (1983) *The Media in Britain* (London: Constable)

Turnock, R. (2000) *Interpreting Diana: Television Audiences and the Death of a Princess* (London: British Film Institute)

Vahimagi, T. (1996) *British Television: An Illustrated Guide* (Oxford: Oxford University Press)

Veblen, T. (1934) *The Theory of the Leisure Class* (New York: The Modern Library)

Wagg, S. (1992) '"You've never had it so silly": the politics of British satirical comedy from *Beyond the Fringe* to *Spitting Image*', in D. Strinati and S. Wagg (eds) *Come on Down? Popular Media Culture in Post-war Britain* (London: Routledge)

(1998) '"At ease corporal": social class and the situation comedy in British television, from the 1950s to the 1990s', in S. Wagg (ed.) *Because I Tell a Joke or Two: Comedy, Politics and Social Difference* (London: Routledge)

Weight, R. (1995) 'Pale stood Albion: the formulation of English national identity 1936–56', unpublished Ph.D. thesis, University College, London

Whannel, G. (1992a) *Fields in Vision: Television Sport and Cultural Transformation* (London: Routledge)

(1992b) 'The price is right but the moments are sticky: television, quiz and game shows, and popular culture', in Strinati, D. and S. Wagg (eds) *Come on Down? Popular Media Culture in Post-war Britain* (London: Routledge)

White, H. (1978) *Tropics of Discourse* (Baltimore: Johns Hopkins University Press)

Williams, R. (1974) *Television: Technology and Cultural Form* (London: Fontana)

(1983) *Culture and Society 1780–1950* (New York: Columbia University Press)

Wilson, H. H. (1961) *Pressure Group: The Campaign for Commercial Television* (London: Secker & Warburg)

Winship, J. (1992) 'The impossibility of best: enterprise meets domesticity in the practical women's magazines of the 1980s', in D. Strinati and S. Wagg (eds) *Come on Down? Popular Media Culture in Post-war Britain* (London: Routledge)

Winston, B. (1996) *Technologies of Seeing: Photography, Cinematography and Television* (London: British Film Institute)

(1998) *Media, Technology and Society: A History from the Telegraph to the Internet* (London: Routledge)

Ziegler, P. (1978) *The Crown and People* (London: Collins)

INDEX